Gouverneur Morris
and the
American Revolution

GOUVERNEUR MORRIS, 1779

DRAWN IN OCTOBER, 1779, BY PIERRE EUGÈNE DU SIMITIÈRE AND EN-
GRAVED BY B. L. PREVOST. COURTESY OF EMMET COLLECTION, MANU-
SCRIPT DIVISION, NEW YORK PUBLIC LIBRARY, ASTOR, LENOX, AND TILDEN
FOUNDATIONS.

Gouverneur Morris
and the
American Revolution

by Max M. Mintz

UNIVERSITY OF OKLAHOMA PRESS

NORMAN

International Standard Book Number: 0–8061–0900–9

Library of Congress Catalog Card Number: 70–108792

To my wife, Pat

Preface

Gouverneur Morris was that fortunate amalgam of the aristocrat and the man of talent. Self-assured in manner, tall and distinguished in appearance, rich-voiced and charming in speech, he could write with grace and precision, commit detailed information effortlessly to memory, and solve complicated mathematical problems in his head. And he topped these gifts with zest, wit, and a capacity for hard work.

Uninhibited in his convictions, he had, said James Madison, a "fondness for saying things and advancing doctrines that no one else would."[1] He rejected the eighteenth-century belief in the perfectability of man, preferring to confront him "as he is, without pretending to be wiser than his Maker or supposing my countrymen to be better than those of other people."[2] No less than the idealists, he fervently desired to see human freedom established in America. He wished to open wide her gates "as an Asylum to mankind," to "comfort and cheer the oppressed, the miserable and the poor of every nation and of every clime."[3] He was a champion of freedom of religion and of the press. He attempted to outlaw entailed and sumptuary estates as marks of hereditary privilege. He fought to arrest slavery, "the curse of heaven in the States where it prevailed."[4] But these liberties could triumph only when adequate safeguards were provided to protect them against attack. Those safeguards consisted in firm protection of private property

[1] Quoted in "N. P. Trist: Memorand," September 27, 1834, in Max Farrand (ed.), *Records of the Federal Convention*, III, 534 (hereafter cited as *Records*).
[2] "An American," *Pennsylvania Packet*, April 11, 1780.
[3] Committee of Congress, *Observations on the American Revolution*, 132.
[4] DIFUAS, 497.

and the compartmentalization of government so as to prevent any social class from dominating the others. In a republic this compartmentalization meant the subdivision of the legislature into two branches, one representing men of considerable wealth and the other representing small property owners. Such an arrangement would spur the growth of commerce, fostering individual accumulation of wealth and civilized refinement.

It happened that Morris' opinions and capabilities suited the special enterprise of creating the new American republic. First in the colony and state of New York and then in the Continental Congress, in Robert Morris' Office of Finance, and in the Constitutional Convention, he fought steadily and prophetically for centralized stable government, with a strong executive. He was less attuned to the coming of the era of the common man. Arguing that a government must reflect the tradition and temper of a people but refusing to accept the new direction of that temper, he set himself obdurately against the French Revolution. Afterward, in America, he fought Jeffersonian Republicanism, not only for its freedom-denying slaveholders but also for its leveling frontiersmen. His career, in both of its phases, spanned the great epic of the triumph of American egalitarian nationalism. In this biography I have concentrated on the period of his most constructive contributions. I have also given particular attention to the hitherto untold story of his secret negotiations in the Nootka Sound controversy and his later switch from pro-French to anti-French policies.

In my research I have benefited from access to Morris' personal papers. Large portions of them have been acquired separately by Columbia University and the Library of Congress. A third major collection was split up and auctioned at the Parke-Bernet Galleries in New York City on April 7, 1970. Previously all these documents had been made available only to Jared Sparks in 1831. Combined with dispersed manuscripts in scattered depositories, they help to correct misconceptions, fill in puzzling gaps, and reveal Morris in greater depth and detail than has been possible until now. I wish to express thanks for the permission granted by the late Roland Baughman, head of Special Collections of the Columbia University Libraries, to quote from the Gouverneur Morris Collection and the John Jay Papers. Thanks are also due the American Philosophical Society for permission to quote from the Correspondence of Richard Henry and Arthur Lee; Mr. Hamilton Fish Armstrong for permission to quote from Margaret Armstrong's *Five Generations: Life and Letters of an American Family, 1750–1900*, published by Harper and Brothers in 1930; Mrs. Paul Hammond for permission to publish a print of her painting of Catherine Livingston; the Library Company of Philadelphia for permission to publish the cartoon "Zion Besieg'd and Attack'd"; the Massachusetts Historical Society for permission to quote from the Henry Knox Papers and the Livingston Papers; Mr. Angus J. Menzies, a direct descendant of Gouverneur Morris, for permission to publish a print of his pastel of Mrs. Gouverneur Morris; the New-York Historical Society for permission to quote from the Robert R. Livingston Papers, Manuscripts of Joseph Reed, Duane Papers, and Richard Harison Papers; the New York Public Library for permission to quote from the Robert R. Livingston Papers (Bancroft Transcripts), Emmet Collection, and William Smith Papers and to publish B. L. Prevost's engraving of Pierre Eugène du Simitière's painting of Gouverneur Morris; the Rutgers University Library at New Brunswick for permission to quote from the (Robert) Morris Papers; Miss Ethel Turnbull for permission to publish a print of her pastel of Gouverneur Morris; and the William L. Clements Library of the University of Michigan for permission to quote from the Nathanael Greene Papers. Quotations from the Jared Sparks Manuscripts are by permission of the Harvard College Library.

I wish also to acknowledge the assistance given me by the staffs of the Connecticut Historical Society, the Historical Society of Pennsylvania, the Henry E. Huntington Library, the New York

State Library at Albany, the Parke-Bernet Galleries, the Southern Connecticut State College Library, the University of Pennsylvania Library, and the Yale University Library; and the staffs of the libraries of the Bronx County Courthouse, the New York City Hall of Records—Office of the County Clerk and Surrogate's Office, the New York State Court of Appeals at Albany, and the Philadelphia City Hall Prothonotary's Office, and the West-chester County Office Building Division of Land Records.

My greatest debt of gratitude is to Professor Bayrd Still, head of the Department of History at New York University, who read the first version of the entire manuscript, suggested revisions, and provided genial encouragement. Professor Brooke Hindle read the first six chapters and saved me from a number of pitfalls. Professor Wesley Frank Craven, of Princeton University, gave wise counsel during the book's earliest stage. The late Beverly McAnear permitted me to consult his manuscript on the early history of American colleges and supplied additional information on King's College during Morris' student days. All errors are, of course, my own responsibility.

I owe more than I can say to my wife, who has helped with her keen sense of literary form and her patient understanding.

MAX M. MINTZ

Hamden, Connecticut
May, 1970

Contents

Illustrations

Gouverneur Morris
and the
American Revolution

Abbreviations

DIFUAS — Charles C. Tansill, ed. *Documents Illustrative of the Formation of the Union of the American States.*

GMDFR — Gouverneur Morris. *A Diary of the French Revolution by Gouverneur Morris.* Ed. by Beatrix Cary Davenport.

JCC — Worthington C. Ford and Gaillard Hunt, eds. *Journals of the Continental Congress, 1774–1789.*

JPC — [New York State], *Journals of the Provincial Congress, Provincial Convention, Committee of Safety, and Council of Safety, 1775–1777.*

LMCC — Edmund C. Burnett, ed. *Letters of Members of the Continental Congress.*

PPGC — George Clinton. *Public Papers of George Clinton.* Ed. by Hugh Hastings and J. A. Holden.

Seed-Time

B Y EVERY accepted criterion of the day, the Morrises of Morrisania ranked among the first families of mid-eighteenth-century New York. Their 1,920-acre manor, across the Harlem River from Manhattan Island and ten miles north of the city of New York, was according to one account "the prittiest and best conditioned Farm in America."[1] At a time when it was observed that many of "the most opulent families, in our own memory, have risen from the lowest rank of people,"[2] they traced their lineage to distinguished forbears in both the Old World and the New. A persistent strain of restless intelligence marked them out from the aristocracy itself, and their talents reached across provincial boundaries to place gifted Morrises in high office in New York, New Jersey, and Pennsylvania. Individualists to the point of eccentricity, they enlarged upon their own foibles, until, throughout Westchester County and as far as New York and Long Island, tall tales came to be known as "Morrisanias."[3]

The Morrises were of Welsh descent. Their ancestral home was Tintern, in Monmouthshire. Three Morris brothers served in Cromwell's armies. Because of the exploits of the eldest, Colonel Lewis Morris, in capturing and burning the castle of Chepstow,

[1] Lord Adam Gordon, "Journal of an Officer Who Travelled in America and the West Indies in 1764 and 1765," in Newton D. Mereness (ed.), *Travels in the American Colonies*, 453.

[2] Cadwallader Colden to Earl of Halifax, February 22, 1765, in Edmund B. O'Callaghan (ed.), *Documents Relative to the Colonial History of the State of New York*, VII, 705 (hereafter cited as *Docs. Col. Hist. of N.Y.*), quoted in Paul Hamlin, *Legal Education in Colonial New York*, 37.

[3] Thomas Jones, *History of New York During the Revolutionary War* (ed. by Floyd de Lancey), I, 140 n.

the family assumed a crest of a castle in flames, with the motto *Tandem vincitur* ("At length it is conquered"). The brothers emigrated to Barbados, and then, in 1668, for reasons unknown, Captain Richard (his commission in Lewis' cavalry regiment) sailed to New York, where he purchased jointly for Lewis and himself a 500-acre tract in what was then part of Westchester County for £140 from one Samuel Edsall. Richard had scant opportunity to enjoy his new possessions, for he and his wife died in 1672, leaving Lewis, an only child of six months. The elder Lewis thereupon came from Barbados to take charge of the estate and of his orphaned nephew. He expanded the original 500 acres to 1,920, and he purchased an additional 3,540 acres in East Jersey on the Shrewsbury River, which he named Tintern estate and Monmouth County, after the family seat in England. When he died without leaving any sons in 1691, his nephew succeeded to the entire property.[4]

The younger Lewis entered actively into politics, where he became a center of controversy. He served as the first native-born chief justice of the Supreme Court of New York from 1715 until his dismissal by Governor William Cosby in 1733, as a result of a blunt decision which he had handed down, denying Cosby's suit for arrears in salary. The publication of Morris' attacks on Cosby by John Peter Zenger resulted in the famous trial and acquittal of the printer on the charge of seditious libel, a victory for freedom

[4] Robert Bolton, *The History of the Several Towns, Manors, and Patents of the County of Westchester; with Numerous Genealogies of County Families* (ed. by C. W. Bolton), II, 455–59, citing a genealogy compiled by Valentine Morris in 1790; Jerrold Seymann, *Colonial Charters, Patents, Grants to the Communities Comprising the City of New York*, 35–39; Lewis Morris to John Boon [Bowne], Barbados, August 8, 1665, *Historical Magazine*, Vol. I (February, 1872), 118; Lucy D. Akerly, *The Morris Manor*, 6; Ezra Stiles, *Extracts from the Itineraries and other Miscellanies of Ezra Stiles, D.D., LL.D., 1755–1794, with a Selection from His Correspondence* (ed. by Franklin B. Dexter), 404; East Jersey Records, B. 155, cited by William A. Whitehead, *East Jersey Under the Proprietary Governments*, 172n.; Robert Hunter Morris to Valentine Morris, June 7, 1763 [draft], (Robert) Morris Papers, Box 3, Rutgers University Library; [New York State] *Calendar of N.Y. Colonial Manuscripts Indorsed Land Papers; in the Office of the Secretary of State of New York, 1643–1803*, 35.

of the press of which Morris' grandson, Gouverneur, was always proud. Morris regained official favor with Cosby's successor, and in 1738 was appointed governor of New Jersey. A man of convivial habits and personal oddities, he had had little formal education, but a ranging curiosity drew him to a course of wide reading, and he built up an impressive library of between two and three thousand volumes, containing works of law, politics, history, philosophy, the sciences, and theology. At his death in 1746, while still governor, he left the Westchester estate, for which he had obtained a patent as the manor of Morrisania in 1697, to his eldest son, Lewis, Jr., and the New Jersey lands to a younger son, Robert Hunter Morris.[5]

Lewis, Jr., served eight years as a member of the New York Council and sixteen years as assemblyman from Westchester, but was best known as judge of the Court of Vice-Admiralty at New York, from 1738 until his death. His first wife was Tryntje Staats, by whom he had three sons and a daughter. She died in 1731, and he remained a widower for fifteen years. On November 3, 1746, at the age of forty-eight, he married Sarah Gouverneur. She was descended from Huguenots who fled their native Hondshoote, a small town ten miles south of Dunkirk, to Leyden in 1594. Nicholas Governeur, a merchant, left Holland to settle in New Amsterdam in 1663. One of his sons, Abraham ("Brom"), became speaker of the New York Assembly. Another son, Isaac, married Sarah Staats, and Sarah Gouverneur was their daughter. Through her mother she was a cousin of her husband's first wife.[6]

[5] On Gouverneur Morris on the Zenger case, see the statement of Dr. John W. Francis, who knew him personally, quoted in William Dunlap, *History of the New Netherlands, Province of New York, and State of New York*, I, 302. On Lewis Morris, library and learning, see Ezra Stiles. *The Literary Diary of Ezra Stiles* (ed. by Franklin Bowditch Dexter), III, 366n.; William Smith, Jr., *The History of the Late Province of New York from Its Discovery to the Appointment of Governor Colden in 1762*, I, 179–80. On his personal habits and oddities, see Beverly McAnear (ed.), "An American in London, 1733–1736," *Pennsylvania Magazine of History and Biography*, Vol. LXIV (April, 1940), 165, 171–72; Jones, *History of New York During the Revolutionary War*, I, 140 n.

[6] McAnear, "An American in London, 1733–1736," *Pennsylvania Magazine of History and Biography*, Vol. LXIV (April, 1940), 181 n. Jeannie F. J. Robi-

In the family home, at half-past one in the morning of January 30, 1752, Sarah Morris gave birth to her only son, Gouverneur. The family Bible, an illustrated Dutch folio bound in embossed pigskin, records that he was christened on May 4 by Parson Samuel Auchmuty, of New York City's Trinity Church. The boy had two older sisters, Isabella and Sarah, and within the next five years two more girls, Euphemia and Catherine, arrived.[7] It would be surprising if he were not a little spoiled. The five children were a family within a family, for their father was past fifty, and his sons by his first marriage—Lewis, Staats Long, and Richard—had grown up and moved away. The older sons disapproved of the second marriage, possibly because it delayed and reduced their inheritances, and were cool to the newcomers.

Gouverneur was an active, athletic lad, fond of sports and of rambles about the estate.[8] He loved the tamed and peaceful beauty of the varied hills, streams, woodlands, and meadows, and in later years he was to buy the patrimony from Staats Long, who was first in line for the inheritance. The manor occupied the southwest portion of what is now New York City's borough of the Bronx. It stretched from the Harlem River on the west to Bungay Creek, today's Intervale Avenue, on the east. Its northern boundary was a diagonal line from the present 165th Street to 180th Street. On the south it bordered on the East River. Down the center of the property ran the Mill Brook, now Brook Avenue, which emptied into the East River, opposite Randall's Island. East of the Mill Brook, on an elevation near the shore of the East River, stood the Morris manor house, with a commanding view of Long Island

---

son and Henrietta C. Bartlett (eds.), *Genealogical Records: Manuscript Entries of Births, Deaths and Marriages, Taken from Family Bibles, 1581–1917*, 150; Monroe Johnson, "The Gouverneur Genealogy," *New York Genealogical and Biographical Record*, Vol. LXX (January, 1939), 134–36.

[7] Robison and Bartlett, *Genealogical Records: Manuscript Entries . . . Taken from Family Bibles*, 151; Martha J. Lamb, *History of the City of New York, Its Origin, Rise and Progress*, I, 576n.

[8] Jared Sparks, *The Life of Gouverneur Morris, with Selections from His Correspondence and Miscellaneous Papers*, I, 4 (hereafter cited as *Morris*).

Sound. The site was slightly south of what is now the junction of 132d Street and Cypress Avenue. The mansion was a two-story, nine-room building with a front porch surmounted by a balcony. Gouverneur's father, as lord of this domain, owned 46 Negro slaves, according to a tally in 1762. His stock numbered 79 cattle, 16 horses, 119 sheep, and 84 hogs. The climate was temperate and fresh. "Fever and ague is there unknown," asserted one of the Morrises, "and . . . persons from other places emaciated by sickness there shortly recover and are speedily reinstated in health and vigor."[9]

Gouverneur grew up in a warm and stimulating atmosphere. There was many an engaging social evening at Morrisania. His father, known for his congeniality, had inherited enough of the family individualism to go about with a hat made of a loon's skin with all its feathers on. Guests were received in the Wilton-carpeted black-walnut parlor, furnished with a settee, silk-bottomed chairs, card table, and teaboard, all made of mahogany. A frequent caller was Judge Morris' long-term friend, Francis Lewis, a prosperous New York merchant who, like the Morrises, was of Welsh ancestry. Lewis' son, Morgan, became an intimate playmate of Gouverneur, who was two years older. One winter, during the father's absence, Morgan and his mother left their home near the

[9] Lewis Morris Memorial to Congress, September 30, 1783, Miscellaneous MSS M. New-York Historical Society. For the correspondence of present streets to the old manor boundaries, see Stephen Jenkins, *The Story of the Bronx, from the Purchase Made by the Dutch from the Indians in 1639 to the Present Day*, 16, 355, 374; Fordham Morris, "Morrisania," in J. Thomas Scharf (ed.), *History of Westchester County, New York, Including Morrisania, Kings Bridge, and West Farms, Which Have been Annexed to New York City*, I, 779. For the location of the manor house, see *ibid.*, I, 520; "Survey Map of South Bronx, 1675," Parke-Bernet Galleries, Inc., *Americana: Printed Books, Manuscripts & Autograph Letters. Including Selections from the Papers of Gouverneur Morris . . .* , *Public Auction, Tuesday, April 7 at 2 p.m.*, frontispiece; "Map of Morrisania and West Farms," in Jenkins, *Story of the Bronx*, 4; A. Everett Peterson, *Landmarks of New York: A Historical Guide to the Metropolis*, 129, 130. For a detailed inventory of the personal property of Lewis Morris, Jr., see *Staats Long Morris, Mary Lawrence and Richard Morris v. Sarah Morris*, 1785, Packet 68, Exhibit D Testimony, New York State Court of Appeals at Albany. The list gives eight rooms in the manor house, to which should be added the unmentioned library.

Battery in New York City to spend the season at Morrisania. Another visitor was William Smith, Jr., a young lawyer just turning thirty, who was already emerging as one of the foremost legal lights of the province and a leader of the Whig Presbyterian forces in politics. He and Morris worked together to foil the plans of the De Lanceys. Morrisania was also enlivened by the frequent Vice-Admiralty Court sessions, which the judge held at home in order to conserve his health.[10] We can imagine Gouverneur sitting in to watch a case being tried and dreaming of his own legal triumphs when someday he might be a lawyer.

His father appears to have made a favorite of Gouverneur, in whom he perhaps detected the qualities which had distinguished the most accomplished Morrises in the past. The older brothers were men of solid worth, but lacking in verve. They had all begun studies at Yale, but in 1746 their father had withdrawn them, after a dispute of some kind which left him permanently embittered toward Connecticut men in general. Lewis, the oldest, settled upon his allotted portion of the family estate west of the Mill Brook and contented himself with the life of a gentleman farmer, to the exclusion of politics. Staats Long embarked on a military career and was wounded while commanding a company under General William Shirley in the French and Indian War. He accompanied Shirley back to England, where he met and married Catherine, Duchess Dowager of Gordon. His subsequent rise in rank was owing more to his connections and good fellowship than to his military talent. The last son, Richard, became a conventionally respectable lawyer, never known for his legal knowledge.[11] Perhaps Gouverneur's growing self-assertiveness and im-

10 Jones, *History of New York During the Revolutionary War*, I, 140 n.; inventory of personal property of Lewis Morris, Jr., and deposition of Francis Lewis, December 31, 1785, in *Morris et al. v. Morris*, 1785, Packet 68, Exhibit D Testimony; Julia Delafield, *Biographies of Francis Lewis and Morgan Lewis*, I, 71, 73; Charles Merrill Hough (ed.), *Reports of Cases in the Vice Admiralty of the Province of New York . . .* , 1715–1788, xxiii.

11 *Ibid.*, xxiii–xxiv; Franklin Bowditch Dexter (ed.), *Biographical Sketches of the Graduates of Yale College*, II, 82–83, 171; O'Callaghan, *Docs. Col. Hist. of N.Y.*, VIII, 187.

periousness of manner was a compensation for the rejection of his half brothers—a determination to excel them and to bend the knee to no one.

For his first schooling young Gouverneur was sent to study under the Reverend John Peter Têtard at New Rochelle.[12] "Dominie" Têtard, as he was called, was a Swiss and a graduate of the University of Lausanne. He had formerly preached to congregations in Charleston and New York. Like other ministers of his day, he added to his slender income by taking in pupils. He taught them French and "the most useful sciences, such as geography, the doctrine of the spheres, etc."[13] Gouverneur mastered his lessons in French so as to speak it fluently, a skill which proved a great asset in later years. For the rest, we suspect that he learned too quickly to find close application necessary. His father saw to it that he turned in a satisfactory performance, as may be inferred from the supervision exercised over Staats Long's studies. The judge would go over his exercises and exact pocket-money fines for mistakes. During his visits home Gouverneur was free again to indulge his fondness for sports and rambles about the manor. He had a companion in his friend Morgan Lewis, who was attending a school close by and who spent many of his Sundays and holidays at the Morris home.[14]

When Gouverneur was nine years old his parents decided to transfer him from the care of Dominie Têtard to more advanced instruction at the Academy of Philadelphia, founded by Benjamin Franklin. It was one of three divisions of the formally entitled College, Academy, and Charitable School of Philadelphia. The

[12] Conversation of Jared Sparks with David B. Ogden [nephew of Gouverneur Morris], March 23, 1831, Letters [really a journal], Sparks Manuscripts, Harvard College Library.

[13] Jenkins, *Story of the Bronx*, 101, quoting a newspaper advertisement.

[14] Sparks, *Morris*, I, 4; a record of two fines exacted of Staats Long Morris, in the back of a notebook, "Lewis Morris, His Book of Arithmetick, Dec. 28, 1738," *Morris et al.* v. Morris, 1785, Packet 68, Exhibit F Testimony; Delafield, *Francis Lewis and Morgan Lewis*, I, 74–75.

academy was the foremost college-preparatory school available, King's College in New York not yet having made similar provision. In Philadelphia, Gouverneur would be under the eye of his Aunt Mary and her husband, Thomas Lawrence, Jr. Lawrence, who had been mayor of the city in 1758, was himself a trustee of the institution; and his father, Thomas Lawrence, Sr., who had been mayor for five terms, had headed the original list of sponsors who had responded to Franklin's call for the establishment of an academy. Gouverneur's uncle, Robert Hunter Morris, had also aided the school's growth, when, as lieutenant governor of Pennsylvania, he had issued the charter on May 14, 1755, which broadened the scope of the academy to include a college.

The training accorded with the prevailing standards for boys of prominent families. Although Franklin the plain pragmatist, had envisioned a utilitarian education, conducted entirely in the best style of the English language, and including mathematics, geography, history, logic, and natural and moral philosophy, these goals had been modified.[15] The curriculum contained the subjects which he recommended, but the ideas of the trustees, "the principal Gentlemen in the Province,"[16] prevailed in subordinating the whole to the study of Latin and the classics; and while the school was officially nonsectarian, a decided Anglican influence reflected the backgrounds of the directors.

Thomas Lawrence, Jr., entered Gouverneur in the academy in 1761. He began attending classes on August 15,[17] in the Academy Building at Fourth and Arch streets, facing on Fourth, from which it was set back and separated by a brick wall. Its grounds reached back two hundred feet to the wall of Christ Church burying

[15] Thomas Harrison Montgomery, A History of the University of Pennsylvania, from Its Foundation to A.D. 1770, 59–60; Francis N. Thorpe (ed.), Benjamin Franklin and the University of Pennsylvania, 71–77; Edward Potts Cheyney, History of the University of Pennsylvania, 1740–1940, 29.

[16] Ibid., 30, quoting Benjamin Franklin.

[17] Sarah Morris, "Waste Book, Commencing 3 July 1762," Morris et al. v. Morris, 1785, Packet 68, Exhibit F Testimony; "List of Scholars entered at the Academy and College up to the Year 1769: Taken from the Earliest Two College Tuition Books," Montgomery, University of Pennsylvania, 546.

ground. The structure had been erected in 1740 to accommodate
the overflow audiences which flocked to hear George Whitefield,
the young visiting Anglican clergyman, whose impassioned and
eloquent sermons touched off a great awakening of religious zeal
throughout the colonies. Now taken over by the trustees for the
use of the academy, it had been divided into two stories. The lower
floor contained the classrooms, and above was a large, fine hall for
academic exercises, with a continuous gallery around three sides
and an organ at one end. The students lived at home or boarded
out, for no dormitories had yet been constructed.

The normal course of instruction at the academy lasted for
three years. Originally, each subject was taught in a separate
room which was designated as a distinct school, and students were
enrolled in such of the schools as their parents selected. By the
time Gouverneur began attending the academy, most of the
studies had been merged in the Latin School and the English
School. The Latin School functioned as the core of preparation
for entrance to the college, although many of the boys never advanced to that stage. The curriculum covered Latin and Greek
grammar and the classics, including Vergil, Caesar, Sallust, the
Greek Testament, Horace, Terence, Livy, Lucian, Xenophon, and
Homer. Mathematics, geography, history, and writing, the legacies
from the defunct schools, also received some attention. The English School, the concession to Franklin's emphasis on perfection
in the use of the mother tongue, was already on the decline.

The master of the Latin School, Professor John Beveridge, was
a Scotsman who had taught in Edinburgh and Wales. He was a
good Latinist, but undignified in bearing and totally devoid of
warmth or sense of humor. Despite his frequent use of the rattan,
he was no match for the schoolboy villainy of Gouverneur's classmates. One of the larger boys, on a bet, twitched the master's wig
from his head, with the excuse of brushing off a spider. Beveridge's
only reaction was, "Hoot mon!" The crowning outrage was a
mass conspiracy, timed to take place when class reconvened after

the lunch hour. Three or four of the boys hid outside the room, awaiting Beveridge's arrival, which was usually a little late. Then, after a calculated number of seconds necessary for him to reach his chair at the upper end of the room, they simultaneously slammed the door and all the window shutters. Inside, with the class now in pitch-darkness, the sixty-odd students raised blood-curdling yells and hurled volumes of Ovid, Vergil, and Horace, but preferably heavier dictionaries, at the head of the classicist, who was groping and crawling for cover. The game was repeated on several succeeding days, until the intervention of the trustees brought it to a stop.

The English School was taught by Ebenezer Kinnersley, a fifty-year-old Baptist clergyman, described by one of his students as "a large, venerable looking man, of no great erudition, though a considerable proficient in electricity." His scientific investigations had earned for him an honorary degree of master of arts (he was not a college graduate) from the College of Philadelphia. He pioneered in the teaching of public speaking and was a strict disciplinarian. The younger boys learned reading and writing, and one day each week were called upon to practice oratory by reciting selections of poetry and prose. The assigned reading included Aesop's fables, an abridged Roman history, and Telemachus. No comparable program of English instruction could be found anywhere in the colonies.

Two of Gouverneur's classmates were his relatives John Lawrence and Redford Ashfield, whom his brother-in-law had also sponsored. Another of Lawrence's wards was Samuel Schuyler, of the New York family. One of the Philadelphia boys was Thomas Morris, brother of the already eminent financier Robert Morris. The chief amusement was foot races around Academy Square, a distance of less than half a mile along Arch, Fifth, Market, and Fourth streets. Samuel Lewis, a Virginia boy, was the undisputed champion. Swimming and skating at the Delaware and Schuylkill rivers were also favorite pastimes.[18]

When Gouverneur had been away at school almost a year, his father became seriously ill at Morrisania. The judge knew the end was near, and on his deathbed he asked that his silver shaving box and the large gold seal ring and pair of gold sleeve buttons which he had always worn be given to Gouverneur as a mark of his affection. He died at three o'clock in the morning of July 3, 1762, at the age of sixty-four. His friend, Francis Lewis, was in the house and remained to assist the widow with the funeral arrangements and the management of the estate. Soon after, the judge's brother, Robert Hunter Morris, now chief justice of New Jersey, arrived to take charge. The usage of the time made the funeral almost a festive affair. The body was buried in the family vault. Then followed a liberal dispensing of food and drink, probably including a number of cases of porter with the judge's initials on the bottles, the gift of his daughter-in-law, the Duchess of Gordon, which had arrived after his death. Mourning rings (costing £53 6s.) and gloves (£2 5s. 4d.) were distributed among relatives and close friends. The total expenses amounted to £127 13s.[19]

The obsequies done with, Chief Justice Morris and Francis Lewis made a beginning at helping the widow straighten out her affairs. The will, dated November 19, 1760, expressed disappointed hopes, and not a little of the bizarre:

My Actions have been so inconsiderable in the World that the most durable Monument will but perpetuate my folly, while it lasts, my desire is that nothing be mentioned about me, not so much as a line in a News Paper to tell the World I am dead

[18] Ibid., 236; Cheyney, History of the University of Pennsylvania, 53–55, 71–80; Alexander Graydon, Memoirs of His Own Time, with Reminiscences of the Men and Events of the Revolution, by Alexander Graydon (ed. by John Stockton Littell), 27–61; J. A. Leo Lemay, Ebenezer Kinnersley, Franklin's Friend, 92–95, 101, 105, 112; Carl and Jessica Bridenbaugh, Rebels and Gentlemen: Philadelphia in the Age of Franklin, 44, 57; "List of Scholars," Montgomery, University of Pennsylvania, 543, 531, 549.
[19] Statement of Gouverneur Morris, April 15, 1786, in Morris et al. v. Morris et al., 1786, Answer, Packet 71, New York State Court of Appeals at Albany; testimony of Francis Lewis, December 31, 1785, and Sarah Morris' Waste Book in Morris et al. v. Morris, 1785, Packet 68, Exhibit F Testimony.

that I have lived to very little purpose my Children will remember with concern when they see the small Pittance I have left them, for Children judge of the Wisdom Goodness and *affections* of their Parents by the Largeness of the bequests coming to them but what I have left them is honestly acquired, which gives me a satesfaction that Ill got thousands cannot bestow.

The judge left a last plea for reconciliation between the children of his first marriage and his beloved second wife:

Differences arising in Family's are always attended with the worst Consequences therefore it is my desire that all my Children use their best Endeavors to Cultivate a good understanding with Each other that they be dutifull to their Mother (which altho she is a Mother in Law [stepmother] to some of them) has done them Equal Justice.

But, fearing the unrelenting bitterness of his son Lewis, he added:

My eldest son may be persuaded not to suffer my wife's bones to be buried in the vault at Old Morrisania, or remove her remains after they have been laid there. In case he should, it is my request that my bones be also removed and laid in some ground in any part of Morrisania east of the Mill Brook.

The will reaffirmed the division of the manor into two estates. The portion to the west of the Mill Brook had already been ceded to Lewis Morris, and that to the east of it was to be retained by the widow during her lifetime, after which it would go to Staats Long Morris. Upon coming into his inheritance. Staats was to award two thousand pounds each to Richard and Gouverneur, and six hundred pounds to each of the daughters by both marriages. Sarah Morris received in her own right two lots on Broadway and joint ownership with the judge's business associate, David Ogden, of a tract on the Passaic River in New Jersey. A number of slaves were given to children and relatives. Gouverneur was to receive "a Negroe Boy called George." The remainder of the slaves were to be sold after Sarah Morris' death. The remaining real estate was to be sold and the proceeds divided among all the children, except Lewis.

Finally, the judge made special note of his plans for Gouverneur's education:

> It is my desire that my Son Gouverneur Morris have the best Education that is to be had in Europe or America but my Express Will and Directions are that he be never sent for that purpose to the Colony of Connecticut least he should imbibe in his youth that low Craft and cunning so Incident to the People of that Country, which is so interwoven in their constitutions that all their art cannot disguise it from the World tho' many of them under the sanctified Garb of Religion have Endeavored to Impose themselves on the World for honest Men.[20]

Thus was carried forward the old grudge, dating from the student days of the older brothers at Yale.

The pressure of business called Robert Hunter Morris back to New Jersey, leaving Francis Lewis to aid the widow Morris in taking the inventory of the personal estate, upon which the future claims of the heirs would be based. The detailed accounting, still in existence, showed that the late judge had left £2,535 in cash and £6,966 in debts owed him. There were 187 pieces of silverware.[21] All the money, plate, slaves, cattle, furniture, and the like were at his widow's disposal for family needs until her death. Her new responsibilities at first left her confused. "Dear Brother, leave me not alone," she implored Morris. He reassured her that "you give too much way to groundless apprehensions, without doing Justice to your own Reason and understanding."[22] Within two

[20] Will of Lewis Morris, November 19, 1760, Liber 23, 426, Surrogate's Office, Hall of Records, New York City.
[21] Inventory of personal property of Lewis Morris, Jr., in *Morris et al.* v. *Morris*, 1785, Packet 68, Exhibit D Testimony.
[22] Sarah Morris to Robert Hunter Morris, August 26, 1762, (Robert) Morris Papers, Box 3; Robert Hunter Morris to Sarah Morris, August 28, 1762, in *Morris et al* v. *Morris*, 1785, Packet 68, Exhibit D Testimony.

years she was deprived of his counsel. He died unexpectedly on January 27, 1764, while attending a rural dance. According to report, he "took out the parson's wife, opened the ball, danced down six couple, and fell dead on the floor, without a word, or a groan, or a sigh."[23]

Meanwhile, in Philadelphia, Gouverneur was finishing his studies at the academy. Beginning in his second year, the scholastic standing of his class dropped sharply. Alexander Graydon, one of the students, wrote:

> With a single exception, we became possessed of the demons of liberty and idleness . . . we cheerfully renounced the learned professions for the sake of the supposed liberty that would be the consequence. We were all, therefore, to be merchants, as to be mechanics was too humiliating; and accordingly, when the question was proposed, which of us would enter upon the study of Greek . . . there were but two or three who declared for it.[24]

It is not likely that Gouverneur was the single exception to the contagion of liberty, but he was no doubt one of those who elected Greek, since he was from the beginning intended for a higher education.

In 1764, after three years at the academy, he was considered ready for admission to King's College in New York. He was then twelve years old, three years younger than the average first-year student. King's was the obvious choice, being near his home and under unofficial Anglican influence. Although a young institution, founded in 1754, it had been put upon a reputable footing during the recently concluded administration of its first president, Dr. Samuel Johnson. The entrance regulations required Gouverneur

---

[23] William Smith, Jr., to Horatio Gates, March 9, 1764, Gates Papers, New-York Historical Society, as quoted in Dunlap, *History of the New Netherlands* . . . , I, 412.

[24] Graydon, *Memoirs*, 40. A complaint of widespread truancy was made to the trustees of the academy on July 13, 1762. Minutes of the Trustees of the College, Academy and Charitable Schools, 1749–69, I, University of Pennsylvania Library Rare Book Room.

to pass an examination based entirely upon the classics. It included Latin and Greek grammar, as well as the translation of Sallust, Caesar's *Commentaries on the Gallic War*, or a portion of Cicero into English and of the Gospels from Greek into Latin.

The college building stood on the outskirts of New York City, at the site bounded by the present Church, Greenwich, Barclay, and Murray streets, and commanded a beautiful view of the Hudson River. The original plans called for a quadrangle, but only one stone wing was ever built. It was a rectangular structure, 180 feet long, three-storied, with a cupola at the center. On the first floor at the three easternmost entrances were the dormitories —twenty-four apartments, each having a large sitting room, study, and bedchamber. At the rear was the dining room. On the second floor, beginning at the westernmost entrance, were the library, laboratory, lecture hall, and museum.

To judge from rules which had been adopted in 1763, Gouverneur's first duty, upon acceptance, was to make a careful copy of the college statutes. They supplied an outline of the life he was to lead for the next four years. Within two weeks he was expected to procure a "proper Academical Habit," to be worn at all times. He would be assigned lodgings at the College Hall, at a rental of four pounds a year. There he would spend his study hours, unless excused, and no late visiting, boisterousness, or gaming would be tolerated; the faculty members reserved the right of inspection at any hour and could force open the door if they were refused admittance. Students were to be properly respectful to upperclassmen and faculty and to abstain from conversation with "persons of bad Fame."

The prescribed daily routine began with morning prayer between five and seven in winter, and six and eight in summer, at a church of the student's choice—in Gouverneur's case it would be the college chapel, where President Myles Cooper officiated at the Anglican service. Then followed three-quarters of an hour for a breakfast of coffee or tea with bread and butter, after which class hours began and continued until the recess of an hour and a half for the noonday meal in the college dining room. There professors and students shared in the weekly regimen of roast beef and pudding on Monday, corned beef and mutton chops on Tuesday, pea porridge and beef steak on Wednesday, corned beef and mutton pie on Thursday, leg of mutton and soup on Friday, and fish on Saturday. Studies then resumed, lasting until evening prayer at six. The scholars dined on bread and butter with cheese or milk or leftovers from the noonday meal. The remainder of the evening was free, until bedtime at nine. Vacation periods were one month after commencement at the end of May, two weeks at Michaelmas, two weeks at Christmas, and two days at Whitsuntide.[25]

For the entire four years of his attendance the course of study which Gouverneur pursued was almost exclusively a classical one. It was a sharp deviation from the scientific and utilitarian education proposed by Dr. Johnson at the time of the opening of King's. His published prospectus, a remarkably advanced expression of eighteenth-century thinking, had announced that the college would

instruct and perfect the Youth in the Learned Languages, and in the Arts of *reasoning* exactly, of *writing* correctly, and speaking eloquently; and in the Arts of *numbering* and *measuring*; of *Surveying* and *Navigation*, of *Geography* and *History*, of *Husbandry*, *Commerce* and *Government*, and in the Knowledge of *all Nature* in the *Heavens* above us, and in the *Air*, *Water* and *Earth* around us, and the various kinds of *Meteors*, *Stones*, *Mines* and *Minerals*, *Plants* and *Animals*, and of every Thing *useful* for the Comfort, the Convenience and Elegance

[25] A History of Columbia University, 1754–1904, Published in Commemoration of the One Hundred and Fiftieth Anniversary of the Founding of King's College, 26; Beverly McAnear, manuscript on the early history of American colleges, in his possession before his recent death; Milton Halsey Thomas, "The King's College Building, with Some Notes on Its Later Tenants," New-York Historical Society Quarterly, Vol. XXXIX (January, 1955), 32–33.

of Life, in the chief *Manufactures* relating to any of these Things.[26]

With Johnson's resignation in 1763, his successor, Myles Cooper, changed all that. Cooper was a Master of Arts and Fellow of Queens College of Oxford, and he had been appointed professor of moral philosophy the year before as the first step in his replacement of Johnson. He scrapped his predecessor's dynamic program and established a new one, founded on the Greek and Roman classics, in line with teaching at Oxford. Included were logic, rhetoric, metaphysics, ethics, English verses and essays, and "moral philosophy," but all that remained of direct rationalistic influence was the study of Hugo Grotius and Samuel von Pufendorf. Probably more science was taught, however, than Cooper's curriculum suggests, for King's had some laboratory equipment, and a professor of natural philosophy was on the faculty. Even in being confined to Grotius and Pufendorf in the study of government, the student was introduced to two widely admired writers on international law, whose political theories rested on the very popular doctrines of the social compact and natural law.[27] Those concepts had been used by the philosopher John Locke to argue that if a ruler did not retain the consent of the governed which was given in the original social compact, the people had the right to depose him. Among American colonials chafing at the yoke of British imperial control, this view was very much alive.

Significantly, the conforming President Cooper did not include the writings of Locke among the required studies. But in point of fact, it made little difference whether he prescribed or banned them. His students had only to look about them to absorb the spirit of controversy. New York was in the grip of a severe business depression, coming in 1764 as the reaction to the termination of the

[26] Samuel Johnson, "Advertisement," May 31, 1754, *History of Columbia University*, 444.

[27] "Plan of Education," adopted by Board of Governors, March 1, 1763, *ibid.*, 450–51; Leonard Krieger, *The Politics of Discretion: Pufendorf and the Acceptance of Natural Law*, 2–3, 88, 106–32, 143–45.

French and Indian War, and destined to continue until 1770. In the midst of the crisis came the news from England that George Grenville's ministry had forced through Parliament the Sugar Act of 1764, designed to support an imperial force of ten thousand men in America for the protection of the frontiers. The measure imposed new taxes on colonial commerce, and in particular it threatened the molasses trade with the foreign sugar islands of the West Indies, a vital means of replenishing the constant drain of money to England. The aroused New York merchants sent protests to Parliament, and the assembly appointed a committee of correspondence to consult with other colonies about appropriate opposition measures.

On April 11, 1765, while still reeling under the Sugar Act, the New Yorkers learned of the passage of the Stamp Act in the previous month. At this news all classes rose to denounce interference in the province's internal affairs. The Sons of Liberty emerged to voice popular sentiment not only against overseas control but also against aristocratic domination at home; and at first the aristocrats were with them, thinking to profit from their support. There followed riots and burnings of stamp shipments. "New York," says a careful student of the period, "was on the verge of civil war."[28] With nonimportation and nonconsumption agreements by merchants and mechanics, and the lawyers' refusal to transact business with stamped paper, economic activity was soon seriously affected. Jubilant relief came for the time being when, on April 26, 1766, a British ship brought the news of the repeal of the Stamp Act. But further troubles developed over the refusal of the assembly to appropriate funds for the support of British troops, in defiance of the Parliamentary Mutiny Act of 1765. On August 11, 1766, British soldiers, in revenge for their loss of cider and beer, assaulted with drawn bayonets a crowd which was erecting a liberty pole on the commons and wounded several persons.

[28] [Alexander C. Flick (ed.)], *The American Revolution in New York: Its Political, Social and Economic Significance*, 19. See also Edmund S. and Helen M. Morgan, *The Stamp Act Crisis: Prologue to Revolution*, 198.

Parliament determined to make an example of the insubordinate colony. In July, 1767, it suspended the lawmaking powers of the assembly until it should provide for the maintenance of the troops. (The act was never enforced, for in the previous month the assembly had already voted three thousand pounds for that purpose.) The issue was to have further repercussions in a mounting tide of disturbances.

At the time of Gouverneur's entrance the faculty of King's College consisted only of President Cooper and Robert Harpur, professor of mathematics and natural philosophy. Cooper was popular, a good mixer and a ready rhymer with a reputation as a wit. A friend of his, the caustic Thomas Jones, penned this description of him:

> His Library sold for £5, the Liquors in his cellar for £150. . . . I knew him well. He was honest, just, learned, and liberal; judicious, sensible, friendly, and convivial; he loved good company, and good company loved him; he was by no means dissipated. . . . I lived with him for several years in the utmost harmony, friendship, and familiarity. Though he was rather hasty in his temper, I scarcely ever saw him in a passion.[29]

Harpur, a graduate of the University of Glasgow, had been appointed in 1761 in spite of misgivings about his Presbyterianism. The students detested him. In 1765 a new professor of natural philosophy was appointed, Samuel Clossy, M.D., of Trinity College in Dublin. Thereafter Harpur confined all his teaching to mathematics.[30]

Gouverneur's entering class contained nine students. They were unevenly and sometimes inadequately prepared for college at their preparatory schools, and at first their progress was slow. Of the

[29] Jones, History of New York during the Revolutionary War, I, 61.
[30] History of Columbia University, 28, 42-43; Minutes of the Governors of the College of the Province of New York in the City of New York in America, 1755-1768 and of the Corporation of King's College in the City of New York, 1768-1770, meeting of October [no day], 1765; McAnear, manuscript on the early history of American colleges.

nine, one dropped out in his second year, "having behaved very indifferently," and two more left in the third year.[31] Among the remainder were several who followed distinguished careers. One was John Stevens, from New Jersey, who was permitted by the authorities to board out at the home of James Duane in the city. Stevens and Gouverneur formed a lasting friendship.[32] Afterward a lawyer by profession, he became famous for his introduction of the steam railway and the screw propeller. Another classmate, Benjamin Moore, entered the Anglican ministry and then served as president of his alma mater. Other prominent names, in different classes during the years of Gouverneur's attendance, were Robert R. Livingston, Egbert Benson, Peter Van Schaack, and John Vardill. Coming from similar social backgrounds, they formed a close community in a day when college education was not widespread, even among the leading families.

Gouverneur was not an industrious student, but he had the gift of absorbing information with a minimum of effort. His favorite studies were Latin and mathematics. In the latter he especially excelled; he could solve complicated arithmetic and scientific problems in his head without recourse to written calculations. He also had a literary flair, with a particular fondness for Shakespeare.[33] He caught the unfortunate fancy of the times for indiscriminate rhyming, but in his prose style he early exhibited a characteristic incisiveness and racy vigor.

In his sophomore year he took part in a student prank which evoked disciplinary action. Three of the students, Gouverneur, Richard Dolier, and John Troup, circulated a "scandalous report . . . virulently attacking the Moral Character" of the despised Professor Harpur. Another student, John Vardill, drew a cartoon graphically portraying Harpur's alleged baseness and posted it in

[31] Herbert and Carol Schneider, *Samuel Johnson, President of King's College: His Career and Writings*, IV, 249–54.

[32] Archibald Douglas Turnbull, *John Stevens: An American Record*, 40.

[33] Conversation of Jared Sparks with Egbert Benson, March 17, 1831, Letters, Sparks Manuscripts, *Sparks, Morris*, I, 5–6.

the College Hall. The furor led the trustees to take action. On May 13, 1766, they conducted hearings, obtained confessions from some unspecified students involved, and concluded that the charges were unfounded. They ordered Vardill to make a public admission of guilt and retraction before the trustees, professors, and tutors in the College Hall the following Tuesday morning, on pain of forfeiting his degree. Dolier and Gouverneur were to be admonished by the president at the same time. There the matter rested, but on February 6 of the next year the trustees accepted Harpur's resignation.[34]

During August, 1766, Gouverneur suffered the first of his physical misfortunes: boiling water from an overturned kettle fell on his right arm and side. The kettle was overturned in what President Cooper described as "a Fit which seized him at his mother's."[35] Just what Cooper meant by a "Fit" is not clear. Possibly it was his term for an antic, since Morgan Lewis was visiting at Morrisania, and no doubt the boys indulged in horseplay. Gouverneur was desperately scalded, but Lewis said that he bore the pain with "a fortitude that would have done honor to an Indian Brave."[36] Dr. Clossy took time from his teaching duties at King's to treat the burn. Gouverneur had to convalesce at home for more than a year until the wound healed. The flesh never grew back normally, leaving only scar tissue.

Upon his return to college, his talent for rapid learning enabled him to rejoin his class. The King's College graduation exercises of 1768 took place on May 17 before an assembly gathered in St. Paul's Chapel in New York. Gouverneur was one of seven recipients of the bachelor of arts degree. The Literary Society, formed

[34] *Minutes of the Governors . . . of King's College*, meetings of May 13, 1766, and February 6, 1767.

[35] Myles Cooper to Samuel Johnson, August 27, 1766, Samuel Johnson Correspondence, III, Columbia University Libraries Special Collections.

[36] Delafield, *Francis Lewis and Morgan Lewis*, I, 75. Julia Delafield was a granddaughter of Morgan Lewis and was present when he told the story of the scalding to Jared Sparks, who omitted it from his biography of Morris. William Pierce, a Georgia member of the Constitutional Convention of 1787, described the burn as being on the right side and fleshless. *DIFUAS*, 102.

by friends of the college to encourage scholarship, awarded him a silver medal.[37] He was chosen to deliver the student commencement address, and his topic was "Wit and Beauty." He spoke in the ornate idiom of the time and the occasion, and with the flowery, descriptive phrases of a sixteen-year-old youth just learning to use uncommon powers of language. But not to stretch the point too far, in this first-surviving product of his pen may be found a glimmer of his developing social outlook. He pictured the human race as ruled by savage passions, save for the softening leaven of the instinct for beauty:

> Philosophers who find themselves already living in Society say that Mankind first entered into it from a Sense of their mutual Wants—that the Passions of Barbarians must have had too great an Influence upon their Understandings to commence this arduous Task Those who were in the prime of Life would never have been perswaded to labour for *their* Support who were past or had not arrived at that State—And even if they *consented* to do it yet the Love of Liberty so natural to all must have prevented both old & young from giving up the Right of acting as they pleased & from suffering themselves to be controuled by the Will of another—Besides Reason unasisted by Beauty would never have smoothed away that Savage Ferocity which must have been an inseparable Bar to their Union.[38]

The love of wit and beauty was more than an adolescent's passing exuberance; the hardheaded view of human nature was the germ of a political philosophy.

[37] *New York Journal,* May 26, 1768; conversation of Jared Sparks with David B. Ogden, March 17, 1831, Letters, Sparks Manuscripts; H. and C. Schneider, *Samuel Johnson,* IV, 254; Lamb, *History of the City of New York,* I, 741; Beverly McAnear, "American Imprints Concerning King's College," *Papers of the Bibliographical Society of America,* Vol. XLIV (Fourth Quarter, 1950), 336.

[38] Gouverneur Morris, Oration on Wit and Beauty (upon graduation from King's College), [New York, 1768], Gouverneur Morris Collection, Columbia University Libraries Special Collections.

The Beginning Lawyer

I T WAS A MATTER of course that young Morris should now consider the law as a career. His natural gifts clearly pointed that way, and his father and grandfather had made outstanding names there before him. The step was a practical one as well, for he could expect an inheritance of only two thousand pounds from his father's estate and but a share of his mother's small property. Accordingly, he entered the law office of the Morris family's old friend, William Smith, Jr., and began an apprenticeship as a law clerk.

The rules of the Supreme Court of Judicature and of the New York Law Society required that he serve a three-year apprenticeship at a fee of £120. With this period of study, and his four years of college, he would meet the qualifications for admission to the bar.[1] Very likely, in keeping with custom, he lodged at his mentor's house at Number 5, Broadway, and ate at Smith's table. Smith had by this time become one of the first lawyers of New York, and in 1767 he had been appointed by the royal governor to a seat in the council of the province. A scholar of considerable learning, he had a large library at his country seat at Haverstraw, in Rockland County, about forty miles north of New York. He had written a highly regarded history of colonial New York which is still a principal source for the period, and was in addition a close student of the Greek philosophers, Hebrew rabbinical writings, mathematics, and medicine. In religion he was a devout Presbyterian. In politics he was one of the "New York Triumvirate," in-

---

[1] Hamlin, *Legal Education in Colonial New York*, 39–41, 163–64.

cluding William Livingston and John Morin Scott, who vigorously opposed the royal authority in the Stamp Act and other controversies. At the same time, with a deep distrust of the common people, he was an uncompromising foe of popular government. He had an analytical mind of the first rank, quick to sense the implications of events and facile in bringing his learning to bear on the subject under discussion. But he was limited by lack of vision, a suspiciousness of human nature which amounted to captiousness, and an intolerance of the political rights of non-Protestants.[2]

Morris' office duties as a law clerk consisted for the most part of oppressive drudgery. With no mechanical means of duplicating documents, not even printed blank forms, there was an endless volume of copying to be done. Some little profit from these labors came in familiarization with legal procedures and the opportunity to consult Smith's personal abstracts, commonplace books, and notes of cases. In the matter of actual instruction, Smith, like most lawyers of the day, left his students largely to their own devices. A second clerk, Peter Van Schaack, a sensitive, warmhearted heir of a patrician Kinderhook family and also a King's College graduate, was finishing his apprenticeship at the time Gouverneur entered the office, and the two became friends, if they had not been such already. Smith rated Van Schaack "the first genius of all the young fellows at New York,"[3] but of his training Van Schaack wrote:

> Believe me, I know not above one or two lawyers in town that do tolerable justice to their clerks. For my part, how many hours

[2] L. F. S. Upton, *The Loyal Whig: William Smith of New York & Quebec*, 50; Dorothy Rita Dillon, *The New York Triumvirate: A Study of the Legal and Political Careers of William Livingston, John Morin Scott, William Smith, Jr.*, 85; "Memoir of the Honourable William Smith, Written by His Son," in Smith, *History of the Late Province of New York*, I, ix–xiii. On Smith's intolerance of Catholics and atheists, see his criticism of the Pennsylvania Constitution of 1776, entry of October 18, 1776, William Smith Diary, William Smith Papers, New York Public Library.

[3] Quoted in Henry Cruger Van Schaack, *Memoirs of the Life of Henry Van Schaack*, 15.

have I hunted, how many books turned up for what three minutes of explanation from any tolerable lawyer would have made evident to me! It is in vain to put a law book into the hands of a lad without explaining difficulties to him as he goes along.[4]

Inattentive as Smith might be to his clerks' daily problems, he did supply an outline, drawn up by his father, for their general course of study which represented the highest standard of its kind yet proposed in New York. As "Sciences necessary for a Lawyer," he advised a background of English, Latin, and French languages; the mathematical tools of arithmetic, geometry, surveying, and bookkeeping; and grounding in geography, history, and logic. In history the student would begin with the view set forth in Bishop Jacques Bossuet's *Discourse on Universal History*, a work which defined government as the necessary restraint on mankind's evil passions, and the best form of government as absolute monarchy tempered by justice and reason. This work was to be followed by study of the histories of ancient civilizations and of England. The readings in the law as such opened with an introduction to Thomas Wood's *Institutes of the Civil Law*, coupled with an abridgement of Samuel von Pufendorf's *The Law of Nature and Nations*. Then came readings in English common law and constitution. The recommended books on the common law were Sir Matthew Hale's *History of the Common Law*, Sir John Fortescue's *Praises of the Laws of England*, Sir Francis Bacon's *Elements of the Common Laws of England* (Volume II), and Thomas Wood's *Institutes of the Common Law*, all works widely used in England and America but very difficult for the newcomer because they gave no systematic survey of general principles. Some of the books were more than a century old and therefore out of date. When the volumes of Sir William Blackstone's *Commentaries on the Laws of England* began to make their appearance in 1765, they supplied the long-desired synthesis and were a boon to students. Since Smith's

[4] Quoted in Hamlin, *Legal Education in Colonial New York*, 43; Henry C. Van Schaack, *The Life of Peter Van Schaack*, 5–6.

outline was written in 1760, it did not include the *Commentaries*, but we know that Van Schaack used them, and undoubtedly Morris did, too. On the constitution, Sir Thomas Smith's *De republica Anglorum* was prescribed. Written in 1565, it saw a balance between the supreme authority of the king and the legal inviolability of the courts, with Parliament functioning in the main as the highest tribunal. While this interpretation reflected the stability of the Tudor reigns, in subsequent internal conflicts it served as a defense of the courts against royal encroachment.

Now that the student had obtained a foundation in the English common law, he was to proceed to more advanced study of natural and civil law. He would read "Bishop Cumberlands Philosophical Enquiry into the Laws of Nature" (probably Richard Cumberland's *De legibus naturae*, published in 1672), the extended writings of Pufendorf, Grotius' *Concerning the Law of War and Peace*, Wood's *Institutes of the Civil Law*, and Domat's *Civil Law According to Its Natural Order*. As a final authority, Smith recommended Matthew Bacon's recently issued *Abridgement of the Law*. "Constantly refer from the Abridgement to Wood & from Wood to the Abridgement," he wrote, "because I would have these Books the Basis or foundation of all your studies." With regard to the apportionment of time to the various subjects:

> I advise that the Morning Hours be applied to the Law & that the After part of the Day be employed in History and such Studies as relieve the Mind. As to the distribution of time for the several kinds of Studies, I know of no general Rule that will suit all Cases.[5]

It was a curriculum built upon the traditional, solid backbone of the common law, but constantly reaching out toward a grasp of general principles. In leaning upon Pufendorf for the natural

[5] William Smith, Jr., "Some Directions Relating to the Law [ca. 1760]," Commonplace Book, Miscellania A, William Smith Papers, New York Public Library, printed in Hamlin, *Legal Education in Colonial New York*, 196–200, with comment on p. 61; Charles Warren, *A History of the American Bar, passim*; George H. Sabine, *A History of Political Theory*, 449–50.

law, Smith made an appropriate choice. Pufendorf's comprehensive treatises were widely respected on both sides of the Atlantic. A practical thinker, Pufendorf interpreted natural law as the product of both reason and experience and the ownership of private property as a natural right. As a compromiser, he sought to reconcile rationalism with Christianity. Although he recognized the right of the people to overthrow a despotic ruler, he defended the perpetuation of social privilege. Here was no extremist position, idealizing human nature or summoning men to revolution, but a respectable answer to the conservative desire for the universal view and at the same time a constructive philosophy emphasizing moral responsibility and peace among nations.[6]

Gouverneur proved to be an apt student of the law. Now that he had settled down to the business of preparing for his lifework, he demonstrated unusual powers of industry and concentration and plowed his way undaunted through the mass of routine. He was on terms of close friendship with Smith, a relationship which may account in a measure for the developing keenness of his thinking. Under Smith's influence his distrust of popular government no doubt deepened, but in Smith's religious prejudices he had no share from the beginning.

Morris applied himself especially to the study of public and private finance. Toward the close of 1769 an anonymous publication appeared, attacking the inflationary nature of a bill to issue loan certificates then before the assembly. The question was momentary, but the argument was so cogent and the grasp of intricate calculations so impressive that when Morris was discovered to be the author he won recognition as an expert, although he was then barely eighteen.[7] His legal abilities, as exhibited in another paper on judicial questions, drew similar notice, as did an eloquent and skillfully reasoned address before a jury. By the

[6] Krieger, *Politics of Discretion: Pufendorf and the Acceptance of Natural Law,* 256–58, 91–92, 143, 222, 153, 164–69.
[7] Sparks, *Morris,* I, 13–15.

close of his apprenticeship, New York already knew him for a talented young man.

King's College awarded him a master of arts degree on May 21, 1771, at a commencement in Trinity Church. The degree was largely honorary, in consideration of individual study beyond the bachelor of arts degree. Several of his old classmates were also recipients, and all of them delivered orations, some in Latin and some in English, before an audience in which sat the governor, the Earl of Dunmore; General Thomas Gage; and the members of the Council. Benjamin Moore, A.B., 1768, who had entered the Anglican ministry, gave the valedictory on "the fatal Effects of misguided ambition," and the others followed with such topics as "Moderation," "Cheerfulness," and "Delicacy."[8] Morris spoke on "Love" as a universal force and expanded on its religious, familial, and patriotic aspects. In the address there is a spirited passage on love of country and liberty:

> What then . . . must be his Love, who has tasted Liberty at the Fountain Head who lives under a Constitution dispensing the Joys of Freedom wherever it prevails who possesses the sacred Rights of a British Subject—Rights torn from the heart of Tyranny nourished with the best Blood of his Ancestors transmitted to him on the Points of their Swords. A Britons Love of Country is firmly fixed on the solid Base of Freedom. . . . O Liberty! Nurse of Heroes! Parent of Worth! best blessing of society! Long—Long—continue to smile upon this happy Soil.[9]

The ardor of these convictions presaged a bold part for their author in events to come.

On October 26 of that year Governor Dunmore issued Gouverneur a license to practice law. The same day he appeared before the Supreme Court of Judicature of the province to take the at-

---

[8] *New York Gazette and Weekly Mercury*, May 27, 1771, as quoted in New-York Historical Society *Collections*, III, 214–16.

[9] Oration on Love [New York, 1771], Gouverneur Morris Collection.

torney's oath. The sitting judges were Robert R. Livingston, father of Morris' friend, Robert R. Livingston, Jr.; and George Duncan Ludlow, of the family of the wife of Morris' half brother Richard. In a festive mood they adjourned to the "House of Samuel Francis [Fraunces]," at the corner of Broad and Pearl streets. There Morris and two other novitiates were duly sworn,[10] and the ceremony concluded, we may presume, with appropriate refreshments and toasts.

Morris was then three months short of twenty, and although all signs pointed to a promising career ahead, he at first considered spending a year in England. "I have thoughts of sailing in the Miller," he wrote William Smith on February 20, 1772:

> I hope to form some acquaintances, that may hereafter be of service to me, to model myself after some persons, who cut a figure in the profession of the law, to form my manners and address by the example of the truly polite, to rub off in the gay circle a few of those many barbarisms, which characterize a provincial education, and to curb that vain self sufficiency, which arises from comparing ourselves with companions who are inferior to us.

Conceding that he had frivolous inclinations, he assured Smith that the trip would not lead him to dissipation: "if it be allowed that I have a *taste* for pleasure, it may naturally follow that I shall avoid those low pleasures, which abound in as great an exuberance on this as on the other side of the Atlantic." But the nub of the plan came out in his closing remark: "I have somehow or other been so hurried through the different scenes of childhood and youth, that I have still some time left to pause before I tread the great stage of life."[11]

Smith, far from convinced, wrote a quick reply to dissuade

---

[10] Minute Book of the Supreme Court of Judicature, April 18, 1769–May 2, 1772, 448–49, Office of the County Clerk, Hall of Records, New York City.
[11] Sparks, *Morris*, I, 16–18.

Morris from the idea. "Remember your uncle Robin [Robert Hunter Morris]," he warned:

> He saw England thrice. No man had better advantages, either from nature or education. He began to figure with 30,000. He did not leave 5000. I know others that never saw the east side of the great lake, who had no other friends than their own heads and their hands, to whom your uncle was in bonds. What! *Virtus post nummos?* Curse on inglorious wealth. Spare your indignation. I too detest the ignorant miser. But both virtue and ambition abhor poverty, or they are mad. Rather imitate your grandfather [Governor Lewis Morris], than your uncle. The first sought preferment *here*, and built upon his American stock. The other *there*, and died the moment before shipwreck. . . .
>
> Upon the whole, I must refer you to your mother. She must spare a great deal before you can resolve with prudence. And when the guineas lay at your feet, think! think! think! I love you with great sincerity, or I should not be so much puzzled.[12]

These arguments apparently took root. Morris discarded his notions of travel for the time and turned in earnest to building a legal practice in New York City.

By British standards, the province of New York provided the closest approximation to an aristocracy in America. Somewhat as "at home" in England, there was the combination of an influential landed gentry with a wealthy merchant group, centered about a thriving seaport in a temperate climate. The location of the province at the geographical and military center of British power in America brought the upper classes into frequent contact with British influences, particularly in New York City, where the royal governor, soldiery, and civilian holders of crown appointments were daily reminders of the imperial connection.

New York, with a population of 18,726 whites and 3,137

12 February 25, 1772, *ibid.*, I, 19.

Negroes, according to the census of 1771, was in eighteenth-century America accounted a city of size. Occupying the southern tip of the island of Manhattan, it extended northward only to Catherine and Reade streets.[13] At the southernmost point stood the governor's mansion, facing northward on Bowling Green. Above the green began the central thoroughfare of Broadway, which extended to the common at the city limits. It was a wide, paved street, lined on both sides with regularly spaced young poplar and elm trees. Sidewalks had been built as far as Vesey Street, the site of the lovely St. Paul's Chapel, which had been erected in 1766 but was as yet without the spire which would be added after the Revolution. The diverging streets were generally narrow and poorly paved. On the west they led directly to the Hudson River, with few interruptions of north and south roads. In the opposite direction, toward the East River, the pattern was irregular. Since 1762 the streets had been lighted at public expense, with lamplights on posts. Water was still a matter of private concern, and wells were so impure that the drinking supply was hawked about on carts. Still in the planning stage was a large public well to be built at Broadway and Chambers Street, from which an engine would pump water through wooden pipes to the consumers.

In the more densely populated areas the city had the urban appearance of three-storied, brick houses, built wall to wall, although often with spacious gardens at the rear. Northward they were spaced farther apart, with frequent stretches of greenery. There were many surviving structures of Dutch style, with the gable ends facing the street. The homes of the wealthy were situated not only in the more fashionable parts of town but also among stores, lawyers' offices, and workshops, for such locations implied no loss of prestige. The most lavish of the mansions were in the Georgian style, based upon the English adaptation of the

[13] Evarts B. Greene and Virginia D. Harrington, *American Population Before the Federal Census of 1790*, 102.

classical. They were usually square, brick houses with pillared doorways and semicircular fanlights. Near the governor's residence, in the "Court End," the passerby encountered the names of De Lancey, De Peyster, Cruger, and Livingston. Ascending Broadway, one noted the homes of the Kennedy, Watts, Livingston, and Van Cortlandt families.

"An acquaintance with the manners of the principal families of New-York, before the present troubles," wrote a cultivated New Yorker from England in 1779, "gives a good idea of those in the *towns* in England."[14] Well-to-do New York homes maintained a high standard of comfort and luxury in their spaciousness, decoration, and furniture. Each wealthy family had Negro slaves who served as footmen and maids and in other servant occupations. In 1770, sixty-two persons, of whom thirty-four were merchants, owned carriages. New Yorkers dressed in the best London style, if a year late. Like the Londoners, New Yorkers had their coffeehouses, social clubs, and dancing assemblies. Like the London public entertainment places the Vauxhall Gardens and Ranelagh, there was a Vaux Hall, overlooking the Hudson between Chambers and Warren streets, where tea was served and wax figures were exhibited under the supervision of Samuel Fraunces; and a Ranelagh, the scene of concerts and fireworks, at the northern outskirts of town, above Reade Street. Since 1752 there had been seasons of theatrical repertory.[15]

The New Yorker set great store by common sense, the popular rendering of eighteenth-century rationality. He was usually a churchgoer, but his religion was likely to be an intellectual rather

---

14 Peter Van Schaack, as quoted in Van Schaack, *Peter Van Schaack*, 162.
15 Theophilus F. Rodenbough, "New-York During the Revolution, 1775–1783," in James Grant Wilson (ed.), *The Memorial History of the City of New-York, from Its First Settlement to the Year 1892*, II, 469–79; John Austin Stevens, "Life in New-York at the Close of the Colonial Period," *ibid.*, II, 445–68; Virginia D. Harrington, *The New York Merchant on the Eve of the Revolution*, 11–46; Evarts B. Greene, "New York and the Old Empire," in Alexander C. Flick (ed), *History of the State of New York*, III, 143.

than an emotional experience. Many of the well-to-do, including many of Dutch ancestry, were joining the Anglican church as the most fashionable one. Common sense was deemed sufficient equipment for a mercantile career, and few boys other than those intended for the law or the ministry received a college education. Common sense suggested that life be made enjoyable, and that enjoyment included the bountiful pleasures of the table and the bottle. It was no unusual thing to develop gout from excessive indulgence in those pleasures, and it was no disgrace to grow tipsy at a party. Much the same picture could be drawn of English urban life.

Still, New York was not London, even discounting size. There, as everywhere else in America, the great fact of existence was the availability of unoccupied land, and with it unparalleled opportunity, even for the poor. Fortunes were to be made or enlarged, and few men rested content with their holdings. Social divisions, although distinct, were therefore flexible. The artisan might be distinguished from his bewigged superior by his leather apron, but he was not prohibited from discarding it. The New York aristocracy was a newer and more virile one than that of England.

The intellectual horizon was chiefly limited to politics, for there was too much to be done to permit leisure for the intensive cultivation of letters and the arts. Here and there a studious lawyer developed a reputation for learning, but he was the exception. Professional men of letters could not flourish, for there were no church livings, civil pensions, or private patrons to support them, and not enough public interest to encourage them. Politics was the very real concern of the leading citizens, both as a means of obtaining added land grants or appointments to office and as the instrument for assuring domination of colonial society. There was probably more self-government in the colonies than in England itself. The distance from the mother country had enabled New Yorkers to build their own "power of the purse," thereby reducing the royal governors to a subordinate status. But if there was more self-government, there was also a greater popular demand for a share in it.

Young Morris, come of age, quickly drew notice in the professional and social life of New York. Arresting in appearance, he was over six feet tall and well proportioned. He had light-brown hair, worn in a queue, and blue eyes. His features were dominated by a prominent nose with a high ridge. His mouth was generous, spiritedly drawn up at the corners. The upper lip was a trifle long. The lower lip protruded slightly. A strong, full chin gave balance to the handsome face.[16]

It was already obvious that he had a superior mind and a rich imagination. Bred to the social graces, he had also grounded himself even more thoroughly in classical literature than was common at the time. With a carefully cultivated voice "of much compass, strength, and richness," he could be charming as a conversationalist and as an orator.[17] "He is witty, genteel, polite, sensible, and a judicious young fellow, and has more knowledge (though still a youth) than all his three other brothers put together," wrote the New York Loyalist Judge Thomas Jones, a chary dispenser of compliments.[18] Once, in a rare moment of self-revelation, Morris admitted, "I speak too often and too long. . . . To my Sorrow I add that I am by no Means improved in my public Speaking."[19] Outwardly, however, he exhibited an uninhibited, jaunty brilliance, which his detractors were to take for conceit and arrogance. Biographers and historians have attributed the quality to his French ancestry, but we know now that, even on his mother's side,

[16] Morris was the same height as George Washington and served as a model for Jean Antoine Houdon's statue of him which stands in the Virginia state capitol in Richmond and, in duplicate, before Independence Hall in Philadelphia. Entry of June 9, 1789, GMDFR, I, 109, 109n. On the color of Morris' hair, see Howard Swiggett, *The Extraordinary Mr. Morris*, xiii, 4.

[17] James Renwick, *Life of Dewitt Clinton*, 161. Renwick knew acquaintances of Morris and had perhaps seen and heard Morris himself in later life.

[18] Jones, *History of New York During the Revolutionary War*, I, 140n.

[19] To Robert Morris [a cousin, not the financier], October 20, 1778, (Robert) Morris Papers, Box 3.

he was probably in the greatest proportion of Dutch descent. A more plausible explanation would combine the factors of innate high spirits, the individualism for which the Morrises were noted, a desire to excel over unfriendly half brothers, and the drive of a young aristocrat with the prospect of only a modest inheritance to make his own way in the world.

Morris' legal practice grew in part through the clientage of family and friendship connections. He acted for his mother in lawsuits pertaining to the Morrisania estate, and even his oldest brother, Lewis, brought cases to him. From his law register (now in the Library of Congress), giving what appears to be a partial list of his cases, and from the description of Jared Sparks, who had access to additional records in 1831, it appears that the business throve.[20] His fees were in some instances as high as two and three hundred pounds. Among the opposing lawyers with whom he matched wits was young John Jay, who represented a defendant in an action begun in June, 1772. "This Cause put off at Circuit for small Mistake in Notice, one word being used for another of which Mr. Jay took ungenerous Advantage," noted Morris in his register. The litigation dragged on for more than a year, until on September 6, 1774, "Case went off for Want of Jury."[21] In two other cases, growing out of disputed election contests, Jay was again the opposing counsel. In July, 1773, Morris applied to the court for writs of mandamus to require the mayor, aldermen, and commonalty of the borough of Westchester to admit one Gilead Honeywell to the office of alderman and one Isaac Legget to the office of common councilman. Morris won both cases when the writs were awarded in the July, 1774, term.[22]

A sign of his standing in his profession was his admission to the exclusive legal society, the Moot, on March 4, 1774. Among

[20] Law Register, Papers of Gouverneur Morris, Library of Congress; Sparks, *Morris*, I, 20.

[21] Law Register, 2, Papers of Gouverneur Morris. See also briefs of Gouverneur Morris and John Jay, Gouverneur Morris Manuscripts, Parke-Bernet sale lot 61, acquired by Columbia University.

[22] Law Register, 14–15.

the older members were Morris' mentor, William Smith, Jr.; Morris' half brother, Judge Richard Morris (who had succeeded to his father's position); Benjamin Kissam; and William Livingston. The younger members included John Jay, Robert R. Livingston, Jr., James Duane, Egbert Benson, and Peter Van Schaack. The prestige of the club was so great that the decisions made in the debates at its meetings acquired something of legal authority. Discussion of party politics, however, was permanently out of order and ground for a member's dismissal.[23]

Morris' legal activities branched out into commercial enterprises. As aide to his mother, he made a trip to New England in October, 1772, the purpose of the trip, as briefly explained in her account book, being "to examine into the affairs of People bound to the Estate."[24] He served as agent in an advertised sale of New York houses belonging to his uncle, Nicholas Gouverneur.[25]

In October, 1773, Morris made his first venture into land speculation. At an auction in New York City he purchased a tract in the Kayaderosseras patent, in what is now Saratoga County, New York. It was part of the estate of John Broughton, and the price was £777 14s. 6d. In lieu of cash, Morris advanced a £475 bond which belonged to his mother. The bond was an obligation of Broughton himself, contracted before Sarah Morris' marriage and retained by her afterward in accordance with the terms of a prenuptial contract. Morris never paid his debt to Broughton. On June 1, 1784, a court action declared the bond forfeited and charged Sarah Morris with the difference, including interest, of £49 19s. 9d., which she paid.[26] Since it is not known that she

[23] Theodore Sedgwick, Jr., *A Memoir of the Life of William Livingston*, 151n.–52n.; Van Schaack, *Peter Van Schaack*, 14.

[24] Entry of October 20, 1772, Sarah Morris, Waste Book, in *Morris et al.* v. *Morris*, 1785, Packet 68, Exhibit F Testimony.

[25] *Archives of the State of New Jersey; Tenth Volume of Extracts from American Newspapers Relating to New Jersey*, 1773–1774, 1st series, XXIX, 398–99.

[26] Testimony of William H. Ludlow, December 3, 1785, in *Morris et al.* v. *Morris*, 1785, Packet 68; Gouverneur Morris, *The Diary and Letters of Gouverneur Morris*, (ed. by Anne Cary Morris), II, 385. For a description of the Kay-

raised any protest, the entire transaction appears to have been in the nature of a gift.

The Morris family unit at Morrisania was dwindling. In 1762, the oldest girl, Isabella, had married Isaac Wilkins, an Anglican minister and King's College graduate, class of 1760. The couple lived at Morrisania for one or two years and then purchased a modest home on a lonely neck of land projecting into the ocean east of the Morrisania estate, at what is now Clason's Point in the Bronx. The youngest sister, Catherine (nicknamed Sarah), married her paternal cousin Vincent Pearse Ashfield, a New York shipping merchant and seafarer.[27] Euphemia, with whom Morris was closest, was wed in 1775. They remained a closely knit group, however. Morris was always on affectionate terms with his sisters and brothers-in-law, and in the years ahead they were to prove ready to help each other generously.

Morris' social life was as gay as the pressures of work would permit. The round of entertainment in the fashionable circle of New York, paced by the pleasure-loving British army officers, offered many allurements. Many years later Morris recalled that the example of those officers "could not but dispose young people to levity and mirth, more than is suited to the condition of those who must earn their living by their industry."[28] He belonged to the select Social Club, which included his closest friends, John Jay, Robert R. Livingston, Egbert Benson, Morgan and Francis Lewis, Peter Van Schaack, and John Stevens. During the winter

aderosseras patent, see Ruth L. Higgins, *Expansion in New York, with Especial Reference to the Eighteenth Century*, 28–29.

[27] Gouverneur Morris Wilkins, "Isaac Wilkins, D.D., 1739–1830," in William B. Sprague (ed.), *Annals of the American Pulpit*, V, 462–67; Jenkins, *Story of the Bronx*, 407–408; Elizabeth Morris Lefferts, *Descendents of Lewis Morris of Morrisania*, Chart E; [New York State], *Names of Persons for Whom Marriage Licenses Were Issued by the Secretary of the Province of New York Previous to 1784*, 272.

[28] Gouverneur Morris, "A Discourse Delivered Before the New-York Historical Society, . . . 6th December, 1812." New-York Historical Society *Collections*, II, 139.

they passed Saturday evenings at Sam Fraunces' tavern, and in the summer they met in their clubhouse at Kip's Bay.[29]

Among the Livingstons whom Morris met was Catherine, one year older than he, the daughter of William Livingston, former law partner of William Smith, Jr., and future governor of the state of New Jersey.[30] A group of letters which Morris wrote to "Kitty" between 1771 and 1773 has been preserved. In the first letter he adopts a light and flippant tone but sends two verses which suggest a deeper interest:

> Love thou tender Foe to Rest—
> Soft Disturber of the Mind
> Ease at Length my troubled Breast
> Sweet Tormenter now be kind
>
> Ah no more with fierie Delight
> Rudely thus my Senses tear
> Blast no more with Tears each Night
> & each Day with harsh Despair—[31]

In another letter, of May 24, 1772, he asks for a lock of her hair, promising to "wear it devotedly as a sacred Relick." On August 1, 1772, he writes:

> Whenever you shall again write . . . be sure to let me know your Dreams for by them shall I form a *Guess* of what passes in your waking Mind   If it is true that what most employs our most earnest Attention in the Day becomes always the Subject of our nocturnal Consideration it will follow that you are if possible more frequently in my Mind than I know of for I certainly dream of nothing else.

Most revealing of all is a letter of August 16, 1772, in which he says that he loves her, even though she will not accept him:

[29] John Moore, "List of Members of the Social Club," in Wilson, *City of New-York*, II, 474n.

[30] Edwin Brockholst Livingston, *The Livingstons of Livingston Manor*, 553–54.

[31] November [no day], 1771, Livingston Papers, Massachusetts Historical Society. All other letters quoted between Morris and Catherine Livingston are from the same collection.

Every Day & every Hour I feel a more violent Inclination to enjoy your Company & Conversation & perceive that I take no Pains whatever to quell these Emotions tho it is a thousand to one that I shall find them extremely troublesome for you acknowledged that once you warmly loved (Susan [her older sister] says five Times)   It is therefore clear that I am a Fool & that you are a Judge   how uncomfortable a hopeless Passion of this Kind is.

No further explanation is offered. Perhaps Morris could not propose marriage, since he was not yet financially secure. At any rate, he did not waste away, for, he had written Kitty, "I am (as you know) constitutionally one of the happiest among Men."[32] On January 11, 1773, in a resigned farewell, he wrote, "I wish you the full Fruition of your own Wishes for as many Years as your Life may consist of." Fifteen years later Kitty married Matthew Ridley, a prominent, English-born, Baltimore merchant and a friend of Morris.[33]

By the beginning of 1774, at the threshold of political upheaval, Morris still seemed far removed from the active part he was to take. Then starting his twenty-third year, he was working hard at the law, impatient of the close application which financial necessity had forced upon him, and disclaiming political ambitions with a youthful air of disillusionment. To a friend, a Mr. Penn, of Philadelphia, he wrote:

Politics I dislike, and only look on with pity, while the madness of so many is made the gain of so few, exclaiming with poor Hamlet, "What's Hecuba to him, or he to Hecuba?" Religion —the very word demands respect, and, as B—— says of his wife, "I speak of her with reverence." Love—as dull as a tale twice told. Friendship—gone to pay Astraea a visit; her votaries so few that the world knows them not. Business—it has so transformed, and transmigrated, and almost transubstantiated me, as hardly to leave the memory of what I was.

[32] August 1, 1772.
[33] Sedgwick, *William Livingston*, 411–12.

And to Mrs. Penn:

> What a terrible life do I lead. Worse than at Philadelphia. There I was all night up it is true, but it was in company, making merry. Here up all night writing, and like his grace the Duke of C. "nobody with me but myself." Pity it is you are not here —balls, concerts, assemblies—all of us mad in the pursuit of pleasure.[34]

[34] To Mr. [first name not given] Penn and Mrs. Penn, January 7, 1774, Sparks, *Morris*, I, 20–21.

A Conservative Path to Revolution

HE YEAR 1774 was a turning point in the fortunes of New York. Turmoil arose once more, this time over the tea tax; and the Sons of Liberty reappeared as a radical and decisive force. Encouraged by the news of the Boston Tea Party, a New York crowd had its own tea party. On April 22 it boarded the ship *London* in New York harbor and dumped eighteen cases of tea overboard.

Many conservatives had before this gone on record against the tea tax, but the outbreak of violence raised in their minds the dreaded specter of mob rule. If there was to be a popular resistance movement, they decided, they must gain control of it themselves at the next opportunity.

On May 2 news arrived of the closing of the port of Boston. The radicals issued a call for a public meeting at Fraunces Tavern on May 16. The conservatives determined to attend in force, and they planned their strategy in advance. They would propose the immediate appointment of an executive committee of fifty men, to be elected as a group; and they would be ready with a slate of names for blanket approval, before the radicals could have time to draw up one of their own.

On the appointed day a crowd assembled which was so large that it adjourned to more spacious quarters at the Exchange. It soon became clear that the radicals had detected the secret designs of the conservatives. They insisted that the candidates be voted upon individually, and an open contest followed. When the balloting was over, the conservatives emerged with a slim majority of twenty-seven to twenty-three. Among the conservatives chosen were Morris' Social Club associates John Jay, Peter Van Schaack, and James Duane. A second public meeting on May 19, at Fraunces Tavern, confirmed the election and added another member (Francis Lewis, the friend of the Morris family), naming the group the Committee of Fifty-one.[1]

In the face of these events, young Morris' professed detachment from politics disappeared. He attended the second meeting and the next day dispatched to a friend a description of it. "I stood in the balcony," he wrote, "and on my right hand were ranged all the people of property, with some few dependents, and on the other all the tradesmen, &c. who thought it worth their while to leave daily labor for the good of the country." The spectacle of an aroused populace disturbed him deeply. "The mob begin to think and reason. Poor reptiles! it is with them a vernal morning, they are struggling to cast off their winter's slough, they bask in the sunshine, and ere noon they will bite, depend upon it." No amount of political maneuvering, he warned, would halt the advance of the "mobility," as long as inflammatory issues persisted. The only hope lay in a settlement of American differences with Britain. "I see, and I see it with fear and trembling, that if the disputes with Britain continue, we shall be under the worst of all possible dominions. We shall be under the domination of a riotous mob." Not that Morris did not sympathize with the struggle for colonial self-government; he insisted that the responsibilities following from political liberty could be appreciated and exercised only by the gentry. The crowd, he said, might "roar out" such words as liberty, property, and religion, but it could not comprehend them. These were terms really comprehensible only to the gentry, who "kept the dictionary of the day, and like the mysteries of the ancient mythology, it was not for profane eyes or ears. As the basis for reconciliation with Britain, he frankly advocated colonial acceptance of mercantile regulation, which,

[1] Carl L. Becker, *The History of Political Parties in the Province of New York, 1760–1776*, 112–15. See also Alfred F. Young, *The Democratic Republicans of New York: The Origins, 1763–1797*, 11–16.

he maintained, would not stifle American trade, as the merchants feared. The British, in the interest of their own gain, must allow a profit to the American merchant, or both the trade and the profit would disappear:

> A safe compact seems in my poor opinion to be now tendered. Internal taxation to be left with ourselves. The right of regulating trade to be vested in Britain, where alone is found the power of protecting it. . . . Some men object, that England will draw all the profits of our trade into her coffers. All that she can, undoubtedly. But unless a reasonable compensation for his trouble be left to the merchant here, she destroys the trade, and then she will receive no profit from it.[2]

In advocating compromise, Morris voiced the virtually unanimous sentiment of the conservatives. Yet within one year from the date of his letter to Penn, he and many of the same conservatives were leading an armed rebellion against Britain. Their struggle to wrest the popular movement from the radicals found them adopting radical methods themselves. The Committee of Fifty-one stimulated the election of similar committees in other counties of the province and formed an association with them in the hope of subordinating the urban radicalism of New York City to the conservatism of the rural districts. The association then sent delegates to the First Continental Congress, called to meet on September 1, 1774, in Philadelphia. There, away from the pressure of local clamor, the conservatives expected that sober counsel would prevail. A compromise plan of colonial union proposed by Joseph Galloway of Pennsylvania, however, was defeated by one vote. Instead, on October 20 the Congress adopted the Continental Association, binding all the colonies to rigorous measures of nonimportation, nonexportation, and nonconsumption of British goods. And among the signers of the association were the New York delegates, including John Jay and James Duane, who had previously endorsed the Galloway plan.

[2] To [first name not given] Penn, May 20, 1774, Sparks, *Morris*, I, 23-26.

Although the signing of the association was in effect an open break with Britain, the conservatives still thought of themselves as British subjects peaceably defending their rights. Six months later, on April 19, 1775, a British military force fired upon a band of minutemen lined up across the Lexington green and left eight of them dead. The conservatives, whether they liked it or not, were now British subjects in rebellion.

If the rights were to be won, the rebellion must succeed. Representatives of the various colonies met in the Second Continental Congress in Philadelphia on May 10, with Lewis Morris, Robert R. Livingston, and Francis Lewis among the New York delegation. They organized an army with George Washington at its head, dispatched troops to New York, and recommended seizure of the crown officers there.

In civil war there is no middle ground. Morris, forced to take sides, chose for the Patriots. Like most other conservatives, he hoped for compromise as much as ever and considered the resort to arms as merely an extreme step forced upon the colonists by the tide of events. But as between America and Britain, he stood with America. He was young, and the Revolution was in one sense a young man's movement. His family, on both the Morris and the Gouverneur sides, had been ardent defenders of self-government; and he saw his grandfather's defense of freedom of the press as a link with the Revolution. "The trial of Zenger, in 1735," he afterward said, "was the germ of American freedom—the morning star of that liberty which subsequently revolutionized America."[3] As early as his graduation address at King's College, he had proudly numbered himself among those "who can boast the glorious Title of free born Americans."[4] He was an American before he was a Briton.

[3] Statement of John W. Francis, who was personally acquainted with Morris, as quoted in Dunlap, *History of New Netherlands* . . . , I, 302.

[4] Oration on Wit and Beauty (upon graduation from King's College) [docketed "Oration When Graduated Bachelor of Arts before I was 17 Years old. 1768"], Gouverneur Morris Collection.

His decision strained close family ties. His mother took the part of the Loyalists. One brother-in-law, Isaac Wilkins, the leader of the Westchester Loyalists and a power among the die-hard faction of the provincial assembly, was forced by popular wrath to flee the colony to England. Another Loyalist brother-in-law, Vincent Pearse Ashfield, was imprisoned for a time by the Patriots and later allowed to depart for England. Only Samuel Ogden, who married Morris' sister Euphemia on February 5, 1775, in a ceremony at Morrisania, joined the Patriots. Morris' maternal uncles, on the other hand, were Whigs in the family tradition. Isaac Gouverneur, a merchant in the Dutch West Indian island of Curaçao, sent a brace of nine-pound cannon to the New York Patriots.[5]

Morris' half brothers were also divided in allegiance. Lewis Morris alone was an early and active Patriot. Richard wavered unhappily for some time before declaring for the American cause. Staats Long, now a British general in England, remained with the crown but resigned his commission rather than fight his countrymen. The British War Office, respecting his feelings, refused to accept the resignation and assigned him to Minorca and other posts in the Mediterranean.[6]

Having made his choice, Morris abandoned the role of bystander. He entered actively into the insurgent movement in Westchester County, where his social position immediately placed him in the front rank. On May 8, 1775, fifteen days after New York learned of the Battle of Lexington, a group of freeholders met at White Plains to elect representatives from Westchester to a proposed Provincial Congress of New York. The predominant sentiment in the county was Loyalist, but the Patriots,

[5] Isaac Wilkins, *My Services and Losses in Aid of the King's Cause During the American Revolution*, 8; Sprague, *Annals of the American Pulpit*, V, 464; Garret Abeel to New York Provincial Congress, June 24, 1776, *JPC*, II, 239; A. Van Doren Honeyman (ed.), "Extracts from American Newspapers Relating to New Jersey for the Year 1775," *Archives of the State of New Jersey*, 1st series, XXXI, 54; Peter Force (ed.), *American Archives*, 4th series, III, 1307.
[6] GMDFR, I, 460n.

under the leadership of Morris' brother Lewis declared themselves the official voice of the people. One of the elected delegates was Gouverneur Morris.[7]

The Provincial Congress convened on May 23 at the Exchange in New York City. For all his youth—he was then twenty-three—Morris took a prominent role from the start. "Gouv Morris cuts a figure—I think him a very fine young fellow," wrote his colleague from Dutchess County, Richard Montgomery, the future hero of Quebec.[8] Morris' literary and financial talents won quick recognition. They were much needed, for the congress exercised both the legislative and the executive functions and was chronically undermanned by absenteeism. In one sense the entire Revolution was the work of a small band of resolute men who persevered in the face of the apathy about them.

The first problem of the congress was to procure funds. Since no revenue was in sight, it appointed a committee on May 26, including Morris, "to take into consideration the expediency of emitting a Continental Paper Currency." The next morning Morris had a thorough and lucid report ready for the committee to present to the congress. He accepted the necessity of the measure and recommended that the Continental Congress issue the entire sum and distribute it among the colonies. Each colony would be accountable for its share, but the Continental Congress would discharge any debt in default. Morris moved that discussion of the document be postponed for three days and that merchants be invited to attend. At the appointed hour of nine o'clock in the morning of May 30, the report was "fully debated and considered."[9] Morris delivered a speech which left a powerful impression, and the report won unanimous acceptance. It was sent to the Continental Congress, where it was put into effect. From this

[7] Henry B. Dawson, "Westchester-County, New-York, during the American Revolution," in Scharf, *Westchester County*, I, 243–59; Force, *American Archives*, 4th series, II, 529, 832.
[8] To Robert R. Livingston, June 3, 1775, Bancroft Transcripts, Robert R. Livingston Papers, 1775–77, p. 33, New York Public Library.
[9] Force, *American Archives*, 4th series, II, 1254, 1258, 1262–64.

time on, Morris was the recognized financial expert of the Provincial Congress. His friend Egbert Benson wrote afterward that "Mr. Morris appeared to have comprehended it [paper currency] throughout, and as it were by intuition. He advanced and maintained opinions new to all. There was none who did not ultimately perceive and acknowledge them to be just."[10]

Side by side with preparations for war went overtures for peace. The conservatives, and some future Loyalists, still hoped that a show of resistance would bring Britain to her senses. On June 2 the Provincial Congress appointed a committee to formulate a plan of reconciliation to be submitted to the Continental Congress, and Morris was one of the members. Determined to do all in his power to promote a workable compromise, he pressed upon his colleagues a long draft of a report, "to which," he wrote Jay, "they could make no Objections excepting that none of them could understand it."[11] Then he brought in a shorter plan, a condensation of the first, which recommended insistence upon the colonial right of self-taxation; parliamentary regulation of empire trade, but payment of all duties to colonial treasuries; and completely voluntary contributions to the defense of the empire, either by colonial assemblies or a continental congress with a president appointed by the crown. This plan the committee accepted but added two paragraphs which Morris very much opposed. One called for the repeal of all acts objected to by the Continental Congress in its association of October 20, 1774, and of all subsequent Parliament restrictions on colonial trade and fishery. The other decried "the indulgence and establishment of popery all along the interior confines of the old Protestant colonies,"[12] a reference to the Quebec Act of 1774, which extended the province of Quebec south to the Ohio River. Morris feared that excessive demands such as these might cause rejection of the

[10] Quoted from a "short sketch of the character of Gouverneur Morris" by Egbert Benson, in Sparks, Morris, I, 39n.–40 n.

[11] June 30, 1775, quoted in Theodore Roosevelt, Gouverneur Morris, 35–36.

[12] Force, American Archives, 4th series, II, 1312, 1315.

plan in England, and he considered the statement on Catholicism as "most arrant Nonsense." He fought it, he said, "untill I was weary it was carried by a very small Majority and my Dissent entered."[13]

When the report reached the floor of the Provincial Congress, he attempted to have the undesirable articles removed. Failing to do so, he secured the adoption of a motion that no one article be considered so essential to the others as to exclude the idea of accommodation without such article and that no part of the report be obligatory on the representatives in the Continental Congress.[14] He wrote Jay that "provided our essential Rights be secured on solid Foundations we may safely permit the British Parliament to use big sounding Words."[15] The New York delegates to the Continental Congress, upon receipt of the report, accepted the hint in Morris' proviso and shelved the entire scheme.[16]

While the conservatives in the Provincial Congress were striving for peace, the crowds in the streets were precipitating new incidents which invited war. A disturbance arose over James Rivington, English-born printer of *Rivington's New York Gazetteer*, otherwise known as "Rivington's Lying Gazette." He had published aspersions on the Sons of Liberty which, by early March of 1775, had aroused protests from as far away as New York's Ulster County, New Jersey, and Rhode Island. On March 8 the Committee of Fifty-one sent Philip Livingston and John Jay to demand of Rivington the authority for a false statement he had printed and afterward referred the matter to the Continental Congress. On May 10, before that body could act, a mob—from which the King's College Loyalist president, Dr. Myles Cooper, had just narrowly escaped in his night clothes over the back fence of his house—turned its wrath upon Rivington. He was saved only by

[13] To John Jay, June 30, 1775, quoted in Roosevelt, *Gouverneur Morris*, 35.
[14] Force, *American Archives*, 4th series, II, 1327.
[15] June 30, 1775, quoted in Frank Monaghan, *John Jay*, 72.
[16] New York Delegates to the Provincial Congress, July 6, 1775, LMCC, I, 155-56.

the exertions of two good friends. Thereupon he discovered some merit in the Patriot cause, published a "short apology," and signed the "Association," a loyalty pledge prescribed by the Provincial Congress.[17]

Morris stepped in to plead forbearance for Rivington, by writing to influential acquaintances in Philadelphia to press for a favorable disposition of his case there. To General Charles Lee he wrote:

Not one month ago and Whiggism was branded with Infamy. Now each person strives to show the Excess of his zeal by the madness of his actions. The British Court shall soon behold its warmest Advocates driven from their Country miserable Exiles. This may produce good effects. But other matters now warmly agitated are replete with Mischief. Among other things Rivington is placed in the woful Dilemma to fly hence into Bankruptcy or become a Victim at the altar of popular vengeance. I venture to predicate the consequence of these proceedings. Pity, which however it may be overcome is never totally banish'd from the human heart—Pity will at length resume her seat— she will usurp upon Reason and sit in Judgment. . . .

You will oblige me then if in the Circle of your acquaintance you endeavor to prevent any mischievous Resolutions against this unfortunate Printer, who is now I verily believe a sincere Penitent.[18]

And to Richard Henry Lee:

I am informed that the Committee of this City have drawn up a Representation of Mr. Rivington's Case for the Animadversions of that respectable Body of which you are a Member. The Consequence of this Step will undoubtedly strike your

[17] Lorenzo Sabine, *The American Loyalists, or Biographical Sketches of Adherents to the British Crown in the War of the Revolution*, 557–59; O'Callaghan, *Docs. Col. Hist. of N.Y.*, VIII, 297; Broadus Mitchell, *Alexander Hamilton*, I, 74–75.
[18] [May, 1775], "The Lee Papers," New-York Historical Society *Collections*, I, 178–79.

Mind. It is the giving a new Power to the Congress our Association hath given them the legislative and this now tenders them the judicial Supremacy.

. . . A mild and favorable Sentence will conciliate the Opinions of Mankind. . . . The History of his conduct is simply this. His Company his Acquaintances his Friends were warm Advocates for the Power of *Government*. Indifferently wise his Mind took a wrong Biass from Interest Deference for the Sentiments of others & Opposition—A Tool in Prosperity. A Cast off in Adversity. He solicits the Assistance of that Body which his Press has aspersed. Magnanimity will dictate to that Body the true Line of Conduct.[19]

The Continental Congress merely returned the case to the New York Provincial Congress, which then relented with a resolution, on June 7, that Rivington "be permitted to return to his house and family, and that this Congress do recommend to the inhabitants of this colony, not to molest him in his person or property."[20]

This action, it developed, gave him but a brief respite. For a time he was sufficiently in the good graces of the Provincial Congress to serve as the official printer, but before long he resumed his press war on the Sons of Liberty. At this, Isaac Sears, one of the Sons of Liberty leaders whom Rivington had particularly assailed, assembled an armed force of seventy-five men in Connecticut, and on November 23 they crossed over to New York City, destroyed Rivington's press, and carried his type back to Connecticut for manufacture into bullets. Shortly afterward, Rivington departed for England.

In a more explosive incident, on June 6, Morris had a direct encounter with the mob. On May 26 the British warship *Asia*, armed with sixty-four guns, had arrived off the Battery with orders

[19] May [n.d.], 1775, Correspondence of Richard Henry Lee and Arthur Lee, I, American Philosophical Society.

[20] Force, *American Archives*, 4th series, II, 1284. See also Arthur M. Schlesinger, *Prelude to Independence: The Newspaper War on Britain, 1764–1776*, 224–27; Sidney I. Pomerantz, "The Patriot Newspaper and the American Revolution," in Richard B. Morris (ed.), *The Era of the American Revolution*, 61–65.

for the evacuation of the last contingent of troops, the "Royal Irish" regiment under the command of Major Isaac Hamilton. On June 3 the Provincial Congress requested the people "not to obstruct the embarkation of the said troops, but to permit them to depart this City peaceably."[21] The British kept the date of departure a secret to avoid disturbances, and June 6 opened auspiciously, a bright, cheerful day. But by noon word of the troop movement reached "a few persons who were then assembled at a Mr. Jesper Darkes [Jasper Drake's] who keept a public house in Water Street near Beekman slip where the most zealous partisans in the cause of Liberty used to have dayly and nightly meetings." According to report, the British were carrying with them several carts loaded with spare arms. The self-appointed watchdogs decided that the troops were acting in violation of a measure passed by the Committee of Fifty-one, which permitted the British to leave, but without spare arms. The "zealous partisans" thereupon set out to halt the troops. Marinus Willett, a veteran of the French and Indian War, was the first to catch up with the procession of one hundred soldiers and five carts, at the corner of Beaver and Broad streets. He seized the reins of the horse drawing the first cart, explaining his action in no uncertain terms to Major Hamilton and David Mathews, a passerby and future Loyalist mayor, who took Hamilton's side.

At this point Morris walked up and joined Hamilton and Mathews. "He was a Whig of very respectable Connections and tho young of Brilliant talents—To be opposed by Mr. Morris stagard me," wrote Willett later, "and I doubt whether all my Zeal and Enthusiasm would have supported me had it not been for the arrival at that Critical moment of John Morine Scott." Scott was a well-known lawyer and a leading radical of the Committee of Fifty-one. "You are right Willett," he called out loudly, "the committee have not given them permission to carry off any spare arms." That decided the issue for Willett and for the crowd that

[21] Force, *American Archives*, 4th series, II, 1290.

had gathered around. At Scott's suggestion Willett jumped on a cart and harangued the troops to the effect "that if it was their desire to join the Bloody business which was transacting near Boston, we were ready to meet them in the Sanguin field, But that if any of them felt a repugnance to the unatural work of sheding blood of their Countrymen and would recover their arms and march forward they should be protected."[22] One soldier came forward, but the others marched off. The citizen throng, now in firm possession of the five loaded carts, led them triumphantly up Broadway.

Morris, however, had no intention of yielding to the judgment of the mob. Four days later, on June 10, he arose in the Provincial Congress to announce: "I move that the Arms and military Accoutrements taken from His Majesty's Troop on Tuesday last, be restored."[23] The motion was carried, nineteen to four.

Still another trouble spot of popular agitation developed at the Canadian border. According to reports which reached the Provincial Congress on May 26, radicals from the northern New York counties had made raids into the province of Quebec. The conservatives wished to avoid such incidents, which would aggravate relations with the crown. To placate the Canadians, the Provincial Congress sent them an open letter, written by Morris, with fifteen hundred copies printed in French and five hundred in English. The letter disclaimed responsibility for the invasion but appealed for Canadian support, asserting opposition to the "ministerial tyranny" of Parliament but not to the imperial connection.[24]

Continuance of the policy of moderation became increasingly difficult as time wore on. Despite the best efforts of the conservatives, the possibility of conciliation rapidly receded, and the controversy moved closer to full-scale warfare. An embarrassing

[22] All quotations in the account of the Willett incident are from "Colonel Marinus Willett's Narrative," in Henry B. Dawson (ed.), *New York City During the American Revolution, Being a Collection of Original Papers*, 61–65.

[23] Force, *American Archives*, 4th series, II, 1274.

[24] P. V. B. Livingston, President, to the Inhabitants of the Province of Quebec, June 2, 1775, *ibid.*, 893.

situation developed when both George Washington and Lord Tryon, the British governor of New York, were scheduled to pass through New York City on the same day. To prevent them from meeting, the Provincial Congress sent a duplicate guard of honor to each. Fortunately, the two men kept out of each other's way. Morris was on two committees which arranged Washington's brief reception.

Within the Provincial Congress tempers wore thin, and tension between the conservatives and the radicals heightened. The minutes of August 4, 1775, record:

> Mr. John De Lancy [afterward a prominent Loyalist], having insulted Mr. [John Morin] Scott, a member in this House, while the Congress was sitting, by calling him a scoundrel, and attempting to run his fist in his face,
> Ordered, That Mr. John De Lancey be reprimanded by the President for his conduct, and that he ask the pardon of this Congress for his offense.[25]

Spurred on by necessity, the congress adopted more drastic measures. Recruitment began for a contingent of three thousand troops and for a militia force. Imports were regulated. On September 2, Philip John Schuyler's troops at Ticonderoga began moving northward to Canada, led by Richard Montgomery during Schuyler's illness.

Morris viewed the military operation with something less than enthusiasm. On October 13, 1775, he wrote his friend Robert R. Livingston: "Schuyler Men are undisciplined and ill provided the Yorkists officered by the vulgar for the most Part the soldiers from this Town not the Cream of the Earth but the Scum." He expected the expedition to conquer Montreal, but if not, he said, "let them eat Snow at st Jeans [St. Johns]."[26]

The Provincial Congress was now suffering from declining at-

25 Ibid., 1318.
26 Robert R. Livingston Papers, Library of Congress.

tendance. On November 4 it voted adjournment and the election of a new congress, to meet November 14.

Morris had worked so earnestly for reconciliation in the first Provincial Congress that his Loyalist brother-in-law Vincent Pearse Ashfield still hoped to see him side with the crown. Ashfield wrote Isaac Wilkins on November 4: "I hope Governor Morris may not be returned to serve upon the next Congress, as he has done nothing in the last that can bring the resentment of Government upon him. I have used all my influence to get him off, but cannot."[27]

Morris did not serve in the new congress. Whether he declined or failed of election is not known. By February, 1776, however, he was distinctly anti-British, and he applied for a commission in the "New York Line" of the Continental Army. Some of the gentry had formed a private plan to raise a battalion of fifteen hundred men for nine months, and Morris was to have been a lieutenant colonel. The Provincial Congress rejected this offer, preferring to proceed with its own program of recruitment. "We are going to raise a new battalion," wrote Frederick Rhinelander to Peter Van Schaack. "Colonels Lasher and Gouverneur Morris are candidates for the command. As both the gentlemen have great merit, it is hard to tell which will succeed."[28] John Lasher, a shoemaker in civilian life, was already a colonel in the militia and an active radical in New York City politics. The congress attempted a compromise by designating Lasher as colonel and Morris as lieutenant colonel and forwarded the list of nominations to the Continental Congress at Philadelphia.[29]

---

[27] Quoted in Richard Arthur Roberts (ed.), *Calendar of Home Office Papers of the Reign of George III, 1773–1775, Preserved in the Public Record Office,* IV, 482.

[28] February 23, 1776, Van Schaack, *Peter Van Schaack,* 54.

[29] Sparks, *Morris,* I, 89n.; Jones, *History of New York during the Revolutionary War,* I, 101; Nathaniel Woodhull to John Hancock, February 28, 1776, New York State Papers, I, 180–84; Papers of the Continental Congress, No. 67, National Archives; Force, *American Archives,* 4th series, V, 317.

But Morris would not agree to this arrangement. He felt that the refusal of the Provincial Congress to accept the application of the other gentry, in the private plan for raising a battalion, made it unethical for him to agree to be an exception. He therefore sent a letter to his half brother Lewis, then sitting in the Continental Congress, asking him to use his influence to prevent ratification of the nomination. "You well know," he wrote, "that the Offers of my Service were merely for the Benefit of the general Cause conscious that my little Abilities were more adapted to the Deliberations of the Cabinet than the glorious Labours of the Field." After explaining his reason for declining the nomination, he haughtily added that he was "very sorry to find that a herd of Mechanicks are preferred before the best Families in the Colony."[30] As it turned out, the Continental Congress turned down all the New York nominations, on the ground of reserving to itself the right of making them.[31]

The second Provincial Congress lasted for only six months. Elections were held for a third Provincial Congress, and Morris was once again chosen a delegate from Westchester County. By May 15, 1776, he was back in his old seat.[32] The conflict had now deepened, past the stage of compromises. The Continental Congress had ordered eight thousand men to defend New York City. Thomas Paine had published his pamphlet *Common Sense*, arguing powerfully for independence. On May 15 the Continental Congress advised the colonies to elect new governments, thereby moving for independence in all but name.

Morris had worked unsparingly for reconciliation, but he was a realist. He recognized simply that the crisis had come and that the momentum of the Revolution could produce no other answer

[30] February 26, 1775, Thomas A. Emmet Collection, New York Public Library. This letter must have been misdated for 1776, for the Continental Congress was not in session in February, 1775.

[31] Nathaniel Woodhull to John Hancock, July 11, 1776, New York State Papers, I, 232.

[32] Force, *American Archives*, 4th series, VI, 1306, 1310.

than independence. In an intimate letter to Peter Van Schaack, on September 8, 1778, he wrote:

> Could the American contest have been decided without blood, I should have been happy. While the appeal lay to reason, I reasoned; when it was made to the sword, I thought it my duty to join in the great issue. While reconciliation appeared practicable, I labored for reconciliation. When the breach was so widened that no hope remained of cure, I solemnly pledged my faith to support the independence of my country, which had then become essential to her liberties.[33]

When on May 24, 1776, the Provincial Congress took up the question of forming a new government, Morris opened the discussion with what was recorded as "a long argument showing the necessity of the measure, and that this is the crisis in which it should be done."[34] He developed his thesis with brilliant persuasive powers, clothed in a sparkle of language surpassing anything he had yet written. "There is a common Story of a certain Juggler," he told the congress, "who would undertake to cut off a Man's Head, and clap it on again so neatly as to cure him without a Scar." The bond with Britain had in actual fact been severed and could never be restored on its former footing. Parliament, he now maintained, could not be trusted to observe any compromise. The colonies were already exercising the prerogatives of independence which remained to be declared only in name:

> Coining Money, raising Armies, regulating Commerce, Peace, War, All these Things you are not only adepts in, but Masters of. . . . Some, nay many Persons in America, dislike the Word Independence. For my own Part, I see no reason why Congress is not full as good a Word as States General, or Parliament.

Then, in a striking anticipation of the nationalistic principles

---

[33] Quoted in Van Schaack, *Peter Van Schaack*, 131; *Goodspeed's Catalogue* 271. See also Gouverneur Morris, *An Oration, Delivered on the 19th day of May, 1812, in Honor of the Memory of George Clinton, Late Vice-President of the U.S.*, 7.

[34] Force, *American Archives*, 4th series, VII, 1332.

he was to advocate at the Constitutional Convention of 1787, he sketched a glowing preview of the new republic. Liberty would be secured by a national congress, whose members would be elected annually from small districts and ineligible for re-election within a three-year period. Separate colonies would no longer exist, and the westward settlements would be peaceably integrated with the seaboard. Population would increase, for "free republican States are always most thickly inhabited," commerce would flourish, education would spread, and America would rise as "an Asylum from Oppression" to all peoples. He even brought himself to say that aristocracy must surrender some of its privileges for the sake of the new nation.

But Morris did not propose "to hire a Number of Men to go and bawl Independence along the Continent." He wanted no incitement to a popular upsurge, such as might overturn the existing social order. His plan was to secure independence by obtaining secret treaties of recognition with the powers of Europe. The people were to be kept uninformed until the new government was firmly established:

> I would send Ambassadors to the European Courts, and enter into Treaties with them. Every Thing like Independence, should form secret Articles; the Rest I would give to the World as soon as it was completed. This Measure, will both discourage, and preclude, impertinent Enquiry. And when the People of this Country enjoy the solid Advantages which arise from our Measures, they will thank us for the Deception.[35]

What were his listeners to make of this speech? Pleading passionately for independence, he yet counseled against openly declaring it. Was he, after all, unable to reconcile himself to the loss of the steadying effect of the imperial connection? Or was

---

[35] Oration on necessity of declaring independence from Britain [probably 1776], Gouverneur Morris Collection. The content of this speech leaves no doubt that it was delivered in the debates on the formation of a new government. Force, *American Archives*, 4th series, VI, 1332. This was also the conclusion of Carl Becker in *Political Parties in New York*, 267n.

his appeal a skillful delaying tactic, designed to win time for the election of a more conservative legislature to draw up a state constitution? So it appeared, when he followed his speech with a motion for the popular election of a new body of "persons to frame a Government." At this, his old radical opponent, John Morin Scott, immediately arose with a countermotion that "this Congress have power to form a government."[36] After almost a week of debate, Morris won. On May 31 the Provincial Congress issued a call for the election of a new congress to succeed itself, with power to decide the question of a constitution.[37] The decision on independence was deferred until then.

In the meantime Morris was busy with important committee assignments. On May 18 the Provincial Congress had named him one of a "Secret Committee" to confer with General George Washington on all significant matters. Washington had arrived in New York City on April 13, with a force of eight thousand men, to repel the expected attack of Lord Howe's fleet and army. Morris relayed Washington's messages to the Provincial Congress,[38] and thus began what was to develop into a lifelong friendship between the two men.

Morris also served on a committee of the congress to recruit two battalions of Continental troops for three months. Many years later, in 1814, he related an incident in this connection. Information reached the committee that the steward of the manor of Livingston, a sworn Tory, had committed most of the Livingston tenants to service with the British forces, in return for the promise that they would receive full ownership of their lands in fee simple. He was arrested and condemned to instant death.

[36] Force, *American Archives*, 4th series, VI, 1332. The "general committee" of the "mechanics in union" of New York City also expressed "astonishment" at doubts that the existing Provincial Congress was not authorized to draft a constitution. This committee demanded, as protection against "oligarchy," that a referendum be held after the constitution was formulated. William M'Euen to delegates of the Congress, June 14, 1776, in H. Niles (ed.), *Principles and Acts of the Revolution in America*, 442–43.

[37] Force, *American Archives*, 4th series, VI, 1351–52.

[38] *Ibid.*, 1313, 1318, 1319, 1348.

Morris, however, intervened with the shrewd suggestion: "Fit out a sloop . . . , take the man down in it to the Manor of Livingston, call out the tenants, and hang him in their presence."[39] The execution was carried out, and the next week, when a military draft call was issued throughout the province, the manor of Livingston was the only area to supply its full quota at once.

In raising one of the battalions, the committee resorted to a stratagem. As Morris explained the matter in an official letter to Washington, the committee persuaded an independent battalion of New York City militia to enter Continental service, with assurances that no duty would be required beyond twenty miles outside the limits of the province and probably not farther than the outskirts of New York City itself. But, Morris pointed out, the agreement had not been committed to writing, nor had the committee reported it to the Provincial Congress, "the Propriety being inferred by a Resolution of the honorable the Continental Congress." Consequently, he broadly hinted, Washington might deploy the troops as he saw fit.[40]

The best efforts of the committee could not secure the required total of troops. Many New Yorkers preferred service in the New England forces, to which the Continental Congress gave higher pay. The New York congress protested against the discrimination with no result. At last, determined to present its case forcefully, it sent Morris to Philadelphia, bearing a letter dated June 7 to John Hancock, the presiding officer. The mission was successful. The Continental Congress raised the pay of the New York troops to a level with those of New England, and Morris was back in New York after a week's absence.[41]

[39] Edward Everett, "Eighteen Hundred Fourteen," *Old and New*, Vol. VII (January, 1873), 50. This is a recollection, written in 1855, of a visit with Morris at the end of 1814.

[40] Samuel Townshend and Gouverneur Morris to George Washington [May 30, 1776, Morris' handwriting], Papers of George Washington, Library of Congress.

[41] Nathaniel Woodhull to John Hancock, June 7, 1776, New York State Papers, I, 364–66; Force, *American Archives*, 4th series, VI, 1379–81, 1406.

New duties awaited him as a member of a committee recently formed by the Provincial Congress to try suspected Loyalists. The increasingly harsh politics of the Patriots and news of the impending arrival of British forces under General Sir William Howe had emboldened the Tories to forcible resistance. Ominous rumors magnified the picture of their activities. On June 12 a mob roamed the streets of New York on the hunt for Tories. The congress deplored the outbreak but stiffened its own attitude. Within two weeks of its first meeting on June 15 the new committee was confronted with the Hickey Plot, a conspiracy with a threatening ring. The committee called the defendants and witnesses to appear at the hearings in the courtroom of City Hall. The story unfolded before the investigators, John Jay, Philip Livingston, and Morris, was of a scheme to raise an underground Loyalist force prepared to assist the anticipated British force in a conquest of New York City. Governor Tryon had supplied the money and direction from his safe retreat aboard the *Duchess of Gordon* in New York Harbor, and New York's Tory mayor, David Mathews (Morris' former ally in the street encounter with Marinus Willett), had recruited and paid the plotters. Mathews was arrested at his home in Flatbush at one o'clock on the morning of June 22. The most vicious of the lot was judged to be Thomas Hickey, one of Washington's guards, an alleged deserter from the British army and passer of counterfeit money. He was sentenced at a court-martial and hanged on June 28 before a crowd of nearly twenty thousand.[42]

In the case of Hickey and his fellows the duty of the judge was obvious, but it was scarcely so in many others, where disloyalty was more a question of sentiment than one of action. The congress had ordered the committee to arrest and examine a number of suspected persons, specifically named. If not cleared of sus-

---

[42] *Ibid.*, 1370, 1154–79; *Minutes of a Conspiracy against the Liberties of America, passim*; Douglas Southall Freeman, *George Washington, a Biography*, IV, 115–20; Benson J. Lossing, "Washington's Life Guard," *Historical Magazine*, Vol. II (May, 1858), 130–31.

picion, they could be released only upon parole of the committee. The suspects included prominent men whose only offense was that they had not declared themselves for the Patriot cause; among them were Morris' half brother Richard and his old friend and teacher William Smith.[43] Richard Morris won acquittal and eventually, if reluctantly, joined the Patriots.

Smith was to prove a confirmed Loyalist. Testimony to the divisions of civil war was Morris' signature to the summons, dated June 27, 1776, which ordered Smith to appear before the committee on Saturday, July 6, at ten o'clock, "TO SHEW CAUSE, (if any you have) why you shoul'd be considered as a friend to the American cause."[44] An express rider, Sampson Dyckman, served the summons on July 1. "It was in Part printed and delivered unsealed by Dyckman in the Presence of My Brother Thomas & Colo. Hay at Mr. Hay's House," noted Smith in his diary. By then the Provincial Congress had adjourned to White Plains, a move brought on by the news that General Howe had landed at Sandy Hook on June 28. Smith, who had not received word of any new meeting place for the committee before which he was to appear, substituted a written reply "& directed my Servant to Gouverneur Morris, one of the Committee & formerly a Clerk in my Office, at Morrisania or wherever he could be found." The letter stated that Smith still confidently expected a "Pacification" of the "unnatural & destructive War" and wished until then to remain neutral. It declared his "Friendship to the Rights and Liberties of this Country" and pledged his "Attachment to her Fortunes & Interests within the Power of the Congress," but opposed the complete repudiation of parliamentary authority. He wrote, in part:

I have always considered the two Countries as under a great

[43] Force, *American Archives*, 4th series, VI, 1368–70; entry of May 21, 1777, William Smith Diary; Otto Hufeland, *Westchester County During the American Revolution, 1775–1783*, 90.

[44] Entry of July 1, 1776, William Smith Diary. The summons is in a folder, marked "Corres," William Smith Papers, 198–206.

Covenant, which gave Great Britain a general Sovereignty over the Colonies, limited by the first Expectations we had raised, by the whole Series of her Conduct in Grants, Charters, Statutes & Legislative Establishments And thought her very Favors created Rights because they inspired Confidence exciting to Adventures, Expences and Hazards advancive of the National Glory, Strength and Dominion. I wished to see this Covenant drawn out into explicit Articles to insure a Government and Conduct in Future conducive of the general Prosperity of the Empire. I expected the Desideratum from Great Britain. I expected it from America. But my Hopes of a speedy Agreemt. were, I confess, abated when My Countrymen adopted the Opinion that it was requisite to our Safety to exclude the Houses of Parliament from all Authority in Cases affecting the internal Policy of the Colonies. And from the Day I read the Declaration of Rights in 1774, I have longed to see it explained into an Enumeration of Articles for internal Establishments essential to the Felicity of the Colonies and Consistant with the common Weal of the Empire. I have frequently expressed my Sentiments upon this Subject to many Gentlemen with whom I stood connected by the Ties of Blood and Friendship, Members of the Continental as well as provincial Congress. I can not suppress the Convictions of my own Mind. I am not to expect that others should conform to Mine. I submit to the Majority, wishing still for such Explanation.[45]

Smith's servant found Morris at Morrisania that night. The next day Morris gave him a reply for delivery upon his return the same evening. Speaking only for himself, Morris gently but bluntly wrote that, although the committee would probably accept Smith's explanation, he was not happy with it. He frankly preferred that Smith be required to take sides, and he pointed out that future claims to high office would depend upon the decision made then. The letter follows:

[45] To Leonard Ganservoort, Philip Livingston, Lewis Graham, Gouverneur Morris, Thomas Tredwell, and Thomas Randal, July 4, 1776, *ibid.*

MORRISANIA, 5t July 1776

DEAR SIR:

Last Night I recd your Letter directed to the Committee of Congress and took the Liberty to open and peruse it. The Intention of Congress in issuing those Summonses was to discriminate between the Friends and Foes of America and to take Security for the Preservation of a perfect Neutrality by the latter. The View was a little more enlarged, for besides the Attention to the public Interests and the Tenderness to Individuals which in some Measure influenced their Conduct, they expected to give their Friends and the Friends of Mankind an Opportunity of declaring with a loud Voice their Attachment to the Rights of Humane Nature. I shall observe to you my Friend, that your Abilities and Virtue, while they ingaged the Esteem of your Countrymen, have given them a Title to call for your Services. If it were decent or useful, I would add that at this Moment when the Ties between Britain & America are haggled away by the Sword of War, the future Consequence of every Gentleman in the Country depends upon the Decision of his present Conduct. But however the People may dispose of their Offices and Honors, they will at least give the Applause which is due to each generous Effort of the Patriot and, should even that be denied, they will never take away that sweet Consciousness of Integrity which warms the Bosom of that Man who risks all for the Benefit of Mankind.

You see my Wishes for you and I hope you will believ that they flow from the Heart of Friendship. I fear the Committee will be satisfied with your Letter. It is what I do not wish but rather that it may be put in your Power to cross over into the Road whither you are beckoned by your Countrymen. My Respects wait on Mrs. S. and the Rest of your Family, to whom I pray you present my Love and tell Bill I have got a fine Horse for him to ride when he comes to see me.

I am, Sir,
Your most obedt. humble servt.
GOUVR. MORRIS.[46]

[46] July 5, 1776, *ibid.*

Smith was perhaps too vain to sense any affront in Morris' appeal to his ambitions for political advancement. He only concluded that "This Youth who has Parts" had "joined the popular Party to obtain the Emoluments he supposed to be in their Gift."[47] The congress did not get around to Smith's case again until eleven months later, when the Committee of Safety paroled him to the manor of Livingston, the estate of his father-in-law.[48] After a prolonged period of indecision, he threw in his lot with the Loyalists and, oddly enough, was permitted to cross the enemy line to New York City, where the British made him chief justice of the province.

As the Revolution became clearly defined, old ties were severed, and with them went many of the old graces of a disappearing way of life. "The Social Club may be literally said to be drummed out of town," wrote Dr. John Jones, a friend of Morris, to James Duane of the Continental Congress. "If you do not shed a few sympathetic drops . . . I shall pronounce you to be a false hearted man, which I would not do for one half of my estate in Socialborough."[49] Yet some bonds would not be broken. Who could bear malice toward gentle Peter Van Schaack for remaining with the crown? He had defended colonial rights during the preliminaries of the controversy but had shrunk before the extreme step. The congress at first paroled him, but in 1778 he was banished to England. When he saw the order, signed by his former law clerk, Leonard Gansevoort, Jr., he exclaimed, "Leonard! you have signed my death-warrant; but I appreciate your motives."[50] Before departing, he sent a farewell letter to Morris. Morris compassionately replied with the reasonableness and the rationality which characterized his approach to the resistance movement:

[47] Entry of January 9, 1780, William Smith Diary.
[48] JPC, I, 960; William Smith, *Historical Memoirs from 16 March 1763 to 9 July 1776 of William Smith* (ed. by William H. W. Sabine), 6–7.
[49] April 14, 1776, "The Duane Letters," Southern Association *Publications*, VII, 254, quoted in Edward P. Alexander, A *Revolutionary Conservative: James Duane of New York*, 73n.
[50] Quoted in Van Schaack, *Peter Van Schaack*, 110.

I would to God, that every tear could be wiped away from every eye. But so long as there are men, so long it will and must happen that they will minister to the miseries of each other. . . . It is your misfortune to be one out of the many who have suffered. In your philosophy, in yourself, in the consciousness of acting as you think right, you are to seek consolation, while you shape your old course in a country new.[51]

[51] September 8, 1778, *ibid.*, 131–32. On Morris' humane attitude, see also his letter to his cousin Robert Morris, December 3, 1777, (Robert) Morris Papers, Box 4.

CHAPTER IV

HE FOURTH Provincial Congress convened at White Plains on July 9, 1776. Morris had been re-elected from Westchester County. The removal from New York to White Plains was a step which Morris had proposed. John Jay, arriving in New York on July 1, was dismayed to find the congress gone, and he criticized Morris for the move. He feared that it would retard the prosecution of Tory conspirators and create a public impression of leniency toward privileged persons. He complained about Morris bitterly to Robert R. Livingston:

> I returned to this City about Noon this Day from Elizh. Town, & to my great mortification am informed that our Convention influenced by one of G. Morris vagrant Plans have adjourned to the White Plains to meet there Tomorrow. This precipitate ill advised Retreat I fear will be not a little injurious to the publick. The Prosecution of the Late Discoveries of Gov. Tryons Plot will be delayed, & may it not by our Enemies be imputed to a Design of keeping the Necks of some of our Citizens out of the Halter? . . . I begin to lose Patience. This Stroke of Morrissania Politics quite confounds me.[1]

These objections seem hardly worth the indignation which Jay worked up over them, for the committee of the Provincial Congress to investigate Loyalists continued meeting at City Hall in New York at least as late as the middle of July,[2] and in any case

[1] July 1, 1776, Robert R. Livingston Papers, 1765–1776, Library of Congress.
[2] Gouverneur Morris to George Washington, July 14, 1776, Papers of George Washington.

the advancing British troops were shortly to drive the congress from White Plains as well.

The elections had produced a mandate from the voters for independence. On July 9 the Provincial Congress unanimously authorized the New York delegates to the Continental Congress to join the rest of the states in ratifying the Declaration of Independence. Lewis Morris was one of the four New Yorkers who thereupon signed the immortal document. The Provincial Congress now officially changed its name to the Provincial Convention of the State of New York and on August 1 appointed a committee of thirteen, including Gouverneur Morris, to report a constitution for the new government. Consideration of the plan on the floor had to be postponed, amid the press of administrative problems.

Financial matters, in particular, could not wait. Morris, now a recognized expert, served on a committee of three to "report upon the mode of auditing and passing the public accounts of this State, and such other matters as may be necessary for the regulation of the treasury."[3]

Early in September he absented himself from the convention for three months. No explanation was offered. Even to his friends his absence seemed a dereliction of duty. On October 10 Robert R. Livingston wrote to Edward Rutledge, member of the Continental Congress from South Carolina: "Gouverneur thro' what cause God alone knows has deserted in this hour of danger retired to some obscure corner of the Jerseys where he enjoys his jest and his ease while his friends are struggling with every difficulty and danger & blushing while they make apologies for him which they do not themselves believe."[4] Rutledge, equally pained, replied:

I am amazed at Governeur! Good God what will mankind come to! Is it not possible to awaken him to a sense of his Duty? Has

[3] JPC, I, 540.
[4] *Illustrated Catalogue of Important Revolutionary Letters: The Unpublished Correspondence of Robert R. Livingston, First Chancellor of New York, to be Sold Without Reserve or Restriction, by Order of the Owner James R. Keene . . . January 25th, 1918*, No. 97.

he no one Virtue left that can plead in favour of an oppressed & bleeding Country?—Has he no Friendship for those who are standing so opposed as you & Jay are to the attacks of open and secret Enemies? one would think he would find a solid Satisfaction in acting and even suffering with such Men in such a Cause—Does he desire to live for ever in obscurity or would he prefer being 'dam'd to ever lasting Fame,' to a life devoted to his Country?[5]

It developed that Morris was staying at Boonton, New Jersey, probably with his sister Euphemia and her husband, Samuel Ogden, who owned a slitting mill there, at which implements were manufactured for the Patriots. Morris wrote the convention on October 13:

A series of accidents too trifling for recital, have prevented me the pleasure of attending the Convention according to my serious intention for upwards of a month past. Among the last, let me mention the loss of all my horses. As soon as I can find one of them or purchase another, I shall hasten to the Fishkills.[6]

He did not, in fact, return until December 9,[7] and there is no record of the reasons for his delay.

Much had happened in his absence. Washington's armies, after the battles of Long Island, Harlem Heights, White Plains, and Fort Washington, had yielded New York City to the British. Morris' own Westchester County had become the no man's land to be so vividly described in James Fenimore Cooper's novel *The Spy*—torn between the advances and retreats of both sides and ravaged by lawless bands of freebooters.

The Provincial Convention, after stopping at several meeting places in the wake of the British, had found temporary sanctuary in the relatively remote town of Fishkill. Sessions were being held in the Dutch Reformed Church (which is still standing). Morris

[5] October 19, 1776, *ibid.*, No. 98.
[6] *JPC*, II, 323; *ibid.*, I, 796.
[7] Force, *American Archives*, 5th series, III, 364.

resumed his share of the endless committee assignments. Finance and commerce continued to claim him. There were also constant requests for drafts of official letters from his facile pen. One day would find him writing adroitly to Governor Jonathan Trumbull of Connecticut, protesting against a Connecticut embargo on New York trade:

> The Committee have too good an opinion of the Legislature of Connecticut to suppose that they had it in idea to cut off the communication between this State and the seaports to the eastward of us, in order to reduce the price of commodities in those ports.[8]

On another day, in response to a complaint against a band of marauding thieves at Cortlandt Manor, he would be acidly advising that "a few examples of capital punishment, will be of more use than several companies of rangers."[9]

On February 11, 1777, the convention decided to move once more, this time to Kingston, on the west side of the Hudson River, in Ulster County. The first meeting there was set for February 19.

Morris rode to Kingston in company with James Duane and Robert R. Livingston. On their way they stopped at Livingston Manor, where they found William Smith, paroled there by the convention. Smith listened skeptically to the talk of the Patriots' doings. "The enthusiasm of those who lead the People at this Day if not counterfeited is astonishing," he noted in his diary. Smith's wife asked whether military recruits were responding to the call with alacrity. "Slow enough," replied Morris, adding guardedly that there was no dearth of men.[10]

The principal business scheduled for the convention at Kingston was the consideration of a state constitution and bill of rights. Notices were sent to the various counties, urging the attendance

[8] *JPC*, I, 764, 772.
[9] *Ibid.*, I, 785.
[10] Entry of February 15, 1777, William Smith Diary.

of all delegates; there had not been sufficient members at Fishkill to make up a quorum, and those present had been obliged to act only as the Committee of Safety.

The committee to draw up a constitution, which the convention had appointed on August 1 of the previous year, had not yet formulated its report. According to the analysis of a recent scholar, of the thirteen members of the committee, six were conservative, five were moderate, one was radical, and one was indeterminate.[11] Morris, John Jay, Robert R. Livingston, James Duane, and John Morin Scott served on the committee. Morris had attempted to block the naming of Scott, his old antagonist, with whom he had been feuding over candidates for the command of the Westchester militia, on the ground that the Provincial Congress had passed a resolution denying seats to military officers (Scott had been commissioned a brigadier general), but Scott's appointment had been confirmed by the narrow vote of twenty-one to twenty.[12] Jay was the head of the committee. According to William Jay, his son and biographer, late in February, 1777, he retired to "some place in the country" and prepared the first draft of the report. Livingston and Morris are credited with having given him substantial assistance,[13] but specific evidence of their contribution is lacking. They took a prominent part afterward, in the discussions on the floor.

Morris' political ideas had by this time taken permanent form. He was barely twenty-five, but the record of his position in the debates at Kingston clearly foreshadows the views he was to advocate in the Constitutional Convention of 1787. He had set down the basic principles of his political philosophy in a paper written in 1776, on the meaning of liberty, a philosophy which recognized the importance of political liberty but emphasized the necessity of imposing some restraints upon it as a matter of both

11 Bernard Mason, *The Road to Independence: The Revolutionary Movement in New York, 1773–1777*, 246–47.
12 *Ibid.*, 214–15; Flick, *American Revolution in New York*, 81, 83.
13 Charles Z. Lincoln, *The Constitutional History of New York*, I, 496–98.

expediency and reason. His developing philosophy had two basic premises: (1) that human nature is shortsightedly selfish and should be subject to restraint and (2) that the institution of private property is the foundation of society. It was his view that property fosters commerce, which gives a "mighty Spring" to the "progressive Force" of society. Government, as the protector of society, must therefore safeguard property and commerce by enforcing laws for the performance of contracts, redress of injuries, and punishment for crimes. This government, however, must rest on the rule of law, not on an erratic despotism. The rule of law depends basically upon political liberty, or the consent of the people. But complete political liberty, which he defined as "the Right of assenting to and dissenting from every Public Act by which a Man is to be bound," could endanger property. Man's selfishness would thereby be unleashed. To Morris it followed that, while a measure of political liberty is a prerequisite to the rule of law, there must also be limitations on that liberty itself.

All this was not to say that Morris was a misanthrope and a materialist. He believed that the only happy life is the virtuous one and that the virtuous life consisted in obeying the golden rule. Unfortunately, men would not voluntarily conform to this creed. Government, whose object is "to promote the Happiness of the People," must consequently force them to do so. Morris plainly had little use for the eighteenth-century concept of natural rights, which he interpreted as the unfettered freedom of the individual. "He who wishes to enjoy natural Rights must establish himself where natural Rights are admitted. He must live alone."[14] The only "natural" law of life was that men must live in society, and the only "natural" rights were those which experience had shown necessary for the preservation of society.

Consideration of the new constitution began at Kingston on March 12, 1777, with the reading of Jay's report. The convention

[14] "Liberty: Several Essays on the Nature of Liberty—Natural, Civil, Political. An Outline (?)" [1776], Gouverneur Morris Collection.

chamber was cramped, and the air was so foul with odors from a prison in the basement of the building that after a few days Morris moved that "the members be permitted to smoke in the Convention Chamber to prevent bad effects from the disagreeable effluvia arising from the jail below."[15] The proposed constitution was a brief one, and its details were based upon the antecedent provincial government. It provided for a governor and a bicameral legislature consisting of a senate and an assembly. The colonial judicial system and local governments were retained virtually unchanged. The chief questions to be decided had to do with the extent of the governor's powers and the degree of popular representation in the legislature.[16]

Morris advocated a strong executive. He supported a motion that the governor be given a qualified veto power over legislation, but Robert R. Livingston secured the passage of a substitute measure which vested the power in a council of revision, consisting of the governor, chancellor, and judges of the supreme court. Morris also favored giving the governor the complete power of appointment. This idea was so unpopular that it was overwhelmingly voted down. Instead, the convention adopted a scheme which Jay had devised during an evening's conversation with Morris and Livingston at their lodgings. The power of appointment was vested in a council of appointment over which the governor presided, but with only a casting vote.[17] The governor's authority was thus severely limited. New Yorkers had had too much experience with royal governors to accept a strong executive, even one of their own choosing.

When the section on the legislature came up for discussion, Morris attempted to restrict the popular vote. He moved to strike

15 *JPC*, I, 842.

16 Two drafts of the proposed constitution are printed in Lincoln, *Constitutional History of New York*, I, 496–556. The draft written by Jay has not been found. See also Mason, *Road to Independence*, 224–29.

17 *JPC*, I, 834, 836, 860, 862; Lincoln, *Constitutional History of New York*, I, 533; John Jay to Robert R. Livingston and Gouverneur Morris, April 29, 1777, John Jay Papers (microfilm), Columbia University Libraries Special Collections.

out a provision for election of the assembly and senate by ballot and favored retaining the old method of viva voce. Jay secured the defeat of this move. Morris succeeded, however, in raising the voting qualification from a simple freehold to a freehold of at least twenty pounds.[18]

Guarantees of fundamental liberties were included in the constitution. A stubborn contest arose over the article on religious toleration. Jay, the descendant of Huguenot forebears who had been driven from France to America, declared that he wished "to erect a wall of brass around the country for the exclusion of Catholics."[19] He introduced two motions to that effect which were defeated and then a third, more moderate, which received widespread support. In a veiled manner it stated that "the liberty hereby granted shall not be construed to encourage licentiousness or be used to disturb or endanger the safety of the state."[20] Morris, always a firm believer in religious liberty, refused to accept even that general provision, for fear that it might be interpreted to apply against Catholics. He attacked it with every tool and stratagem his ingenuity could devise. First he attempted to disqualify the motion by moving that the sense of it was the same as Jay's earlier one. This effort failing, he secured postponement of further consideration of the article.[21] Eleven days later, on April 1, he brought in an amendment to Jay's motion which altered it to read that "the liberty of conscience hereby granted, shall not be so construed as to excuse acts of licentiousness, or justify practices inconsistent with the peace or safety of this State."[22] With a slight change of wording he had transformed Jay's implied threat to freedom of worship into a specific recognition of liberty of "conscience." The amendment won unanimous acceptance.

Jay, still inflexible, then introduced an amendment to the section on naturalization, requiring all new citizens of the state to

[18] Lincoln, *Constitutional History of New York*, I, 507–14; *JPC*, I, 836, 866.
[19] Quoted by Morgan Lewis in conversation with Jared Sparks, August [no day], 1831, Letters, Sparks Manuscripts.
[20] *JPC*, I, 845.   [21] *Ibid.*, 846.   [22] *Ibid.*, 860–61.

"abjure and renounce all allegiance and subjection to all and every foreign King, prince, potentate, and state, in all matters ecclesiastical as well as civil."[23] Morris fought the amendment hard, but his motion to eliminate it was twice voted upon and twice defeated. Ten years later the issue became insignificant when the federal Constitution reserved the power of naturalization to the national government.

Morris strove to commit the state to abolition of slavery after the war. His mother was a slaveowner, and under the terms of his father's will he would receive a slave upon her death, but he was devoted to the principle of personal liberty. On April 17 he made the following motion in the convention:

> And whereas a regard to the rights of human nature and the principles of our holy religion, loudly call upon us to dispense the blessings of freedom to all mankind: and inasmuch as it would at present be productive of great dangers to liberate the slaves within this State: It is, therefore most earnestly recommended to the future Legislatures of the State of New-York, to take the most effectual measures consistent with the public safety, and the private property of individuals, for abolishing domestic slavery within the same, so that in future ages, every human being who breathes the air of this State, shall enjoy the privileges of a freeman.[24]

On the question of slavery Jay fully shared Morris' conviction. He had left the convention, however, because of the death of his mother, and on this occasion it was Robert R. Livingston who opposed Morris' liberal view. Livingston secured the defeat of the measure by a vote of thirty-one to five.[25]

---

[23] *Ibid.*, 852–53, 860–61. Also on Morris and religious freedom, see his support of a petition of Pennsylvania Moravians, protesting the use of their *Gemeinhaus* as a powder magazine. Entry of May 11, 1778, diary of the Rev. George Neisser, pastor of Moravian Congregation of York, Pennsylvania, "Items of History of York, Penna., during the Revolution," *Pennsylvania Magazine of History and Biography*, Vol. XLIV, No. 4 (1920), 315, 317,
[24] *JPC*, I, 887.
[25] Lincoln, *Constitutional History of New York*, I, 553–54.

The constitution which emerged from the debates was, like all successful constitutions, the product of compromises. The delegates had had their differences. One of them, Colonel Peter R. Livingston of Albany, had reported to William Smith:

There are Dissentions. [John Morin] Scott, a perfect Leveller & opposed by the Landed Men. Jay not so much inclined to Democracy. Robt. R. L. [Livingston] still less so. Gouvr. Morris & P. R. L. [Peter R. Livingston] for the Govr.'s having a Negative in Legislation.[26]

But when the constitution was presented to the convention for approval, all the members voted for it, with the sole exception of Peter R. Livingston. It went into effect immediately, without submission to the people.[27]

Morris, although disappointed in the weakness of the executive, accepted the constitution as a necessity. He never expected perfection in human affairs. He summed up his views in a letter to Alexander Hamilton:

That there are Faults in it is not to be wondered at for it is the Work of Men perhaps not the best qualified for such Undertakings. I think it deficient for the Want of Vigor in the executive unstable from the very Nature of popular elective Governments and dilatory from the Complexity of the Legislature. For the first I apologize by hinting the Spirit which now reigns in America suspiciously Cautious. For the second because unavoidable. For the third because a simple Legislature soon possesses itself of too much Power for the Safety of its Subjects. God grant that it may work well for we must live under it.[28]

Without waiting for new elections, the convention appointed the important state officials necessary for the functioning of the government under the constitution. Robert R. Livingston be-

26 Entry of April 11, 1777, William Smith Diary.
27 *JPC*, I, 892.
28 May 16, 1777, Alexander Hamilton Papers, Library of Congress.

came chancellor, to the mortification of John Jay, who had wanted the office.[29] Jay was made chief justice. Morris, according to information which reached William Smith, refused to accept any office. "Gouvr. Morris will have no Office; objects his Youth and unsettled Condition in Life. . . . It gives no Umbrage. He told them plainly He had done enough to hang himself & therefore they need not be jealous of him."[30] Until a governor, senate, and assembly could be elected, the convention appointed a fifteen-member Council of Safety. Morris was one of the fifteen.[31]

Four days later, on May 7, Morris introduced a measure which might properly have been included in the constitution itself. It was a resolution for "remitting all quit rents due, and forever abolishing all quit rents within this State."[32] The quitrents formerly due the kingdom of Great Britain had already been appropriated by the state after the signing of the Declaration of Independence. Morris' resolution would have abolished them, as well as those due Patriot landowners. The resolution kindled long debates and was finally referred to a committee, whose members included John Jay and John Morin Scott, where it was buried. So democratic a proposal coming from Morris was perhaps a surprise, but it was in accord with his insistence on the unrestricted right of private property. He could support popular interests when he considered them good for society. His effort to remove the outmoded, feudal imposts was far ahead of his time. Not until 1846 were they abolished, and then only after a bitter political battle.[33]

Morris was now a key figure in the state government. Peter R. Livingston told William Smith that "R. R. L. [Robert R. Livingston], Scott, Jay & G. Morris rule in the Council at Kingston.

[29] Conversation of Morgan Lewis with Jared Sparks, August [no day], 1831, Letters, Sparks Manuscripts.

[30] Entries of May 5 and May 21, 1777, William Smith Diary.

[31] JPC, I, 910.

[32] Ibid., 913, 914.

[33] Edward P. Cheyney, "The Antirent Movement and the Constitution of 1846," in Flick, History of the State of New York, VI, 317.

The Rest seem to leave every Thing to them."[34] On May 13 the convention balloted for a new slate of delegates to the Continental Congress. Morris was elected, in company with Philip Schuyler, Philip Livingston, James Duane, and William Duer.[35] More than five months were to elapse, however, before the legislature would see fit to release him from state assignments; the duties in Kingston appeared more important than representation in Philadelphia.

Indeed, with the approaching threat of General John Burgoyne's army from the north, it was an open question whether there would be a New York State at all. The over-all British strategy was to seize the Hudson River–Lake Champlain line of communication, with its lateral Mohawk River branch, thus subjugating New York and cutting off New England from the other states. Burgoyne was to ascend Lake Champlain and follow the Hudson to Albany, there to meet a smaller force under Colonel Barry St. Leger, coming by way of the St. Lawrence River, Lake Ontario, and the Mohawk Valley. Sir William Howe, moving up the Hudson from New York City with a fleet and an army, would join the other two commanders at Albany, thereby closing the trap.

Burgoyne, with a well-trained army of about eight thousand men, invaded northern New York on June 1, 1777. He appeared before Fort Ticonderoga on July 1, facing three thousand Patriots under General Arthur St. Clair. Four days later Burgoyne made the Patriots' position untenable by occupying a commanding elevation at Mount Defiance and sent them in retreat across Lake Champlain, down toward Castleton and Fort Edward.

The alarmed New York legislature appointed a committee of Robert R. Livingston and Abraham Yates to visit General Schuyler at his headquarters and inquire into the defeat. On July 10,

---

[34] Entry of May 21, 1777, William Smith Diary. Antagonism persisted between John Morin Scott and the other members. Don R. Gerlach, *Philip Schuyler and the American Revolution in New York, 1733–1777*, 305–306.

[35] *JPC*, I, 931,

Morris was substituted for Livingston, whose father had just died. William Smith, hearing of the replacement, remarked with his usual acerbity: "Perhaps he [Livingston] disliked the dangerous Service of an Enquiry into the Misconduct of the Generals by which the Fort was supposed to be lost and readily took Hold of his Brother John's going a Volunteer from Albany to Fort Edward & his Mother's Fright for Excuses."[36]

Morris set out on the trip before Yates, who was to join him later. On July 14 he wrote from Albany that he had been detained there by continual rains and would leave within an hour for Fort Edward. He added what must have aroused misgivings in the Council of Safety, that he intended to take whatever steps the emergency of the army might require: "Having no powers, I shall do what I think is best, and trust to the Council to confirm it, or hang me. But whether Mr. Yates will join in pursuing that line of conduct is very uncertain."[37] He was taking it upon himself to act as a representative rather than as an emissary of the council.

He arrived at Fort Edward at noon on July 16. Burgoyne's army was then at Whitehall, twenty miles to the north. The total Patriot force, reported Morris, consisted of twenty-six hundred Continental troops and two thousand militia, with a small body of five hundred men to the west. "Excepting the General [Schuyler], and Genl. Sinclair [St. Clair]," he wrote, "you have not a general officer here worth a crown."[38] The Patriots were in dire straits.

The day after his arrival at Fort Edward, he and Schuyler made an excursion to Saratoga. He quickly sensed the tactic which was to prove the key to American success: to wear out the enemy in an exhausting march through the forest. "I will venture to say," he wrote the Council of Safety, "that if we lay it down as a maxim, never to contend for ground but in the last necessity, and to leave

36 Entry of July 19 [1777], William Smith Diary.
37 JPC, I, 997.
38 To the President of the Council of Safety, July 16, 1777, ibid., 511.

nothing but a wilderness to the enemy, their progress must be impeded by obstacles, which it is not in human nature to surmount."[39] He would advise Schuyler accordingly.

At the same time, he warned the council, steps should be taken to combat the lukewarm, or even disaffected, spirit of the population in the counties west and east of Schuyler's army. Westward, in Tryon County, the Loyalists were numerous and active, and recruits, though urgently needed, were not being contributed to General Nicholas Herkimer's undermanned force at Cherry Valley. "It is really terrible," declared Morris, "that matters of such infinite importance must be put to the hazard for the sake of men who have not spirit to assemble in their own defence." He suggested that a police force of one hundred militia be sent there from the Patriot counties of Ulster and Dutchess. Eastward, in the Grants, where the settlers were claiming recognition of a new state of Vermont, a British agent was assiduously flattering the Vermonters with offers of confirming their land titles and making Vermont a separate British province. "Very many of those villains," observed Morris, "only want a New-England reason, or if you like the expression better, a plausible pretext, to desert the American States, New-Vermont among the rest."[40]

But the legislators in Kingston were more interested in a plausible account of the defeat of Ticonderoga that could be published to calm the popular fears than in Morris' advice on questions of strategy. Even his friends Livingston and Jay were among his critics. Livingston drafted a strong official letter of admonition.[41] Jay wrote privately, explaining that Schuyler's enemies, in the absence of evidence to the contrary, were blaming the general for the loss of Ticonderoga. "We are silent, because we have nothing to say; and the people suspect the worst, because we say nothing."[42]

[39] July 17, 1777, *ibid.*, 508.
[40] To the President of the Council of Safety, July 21, 1777, *ibid.*, 1004.
[41] Pierre Van Cortlandt [president of the Council of Safety] to Gouverneur Morris, July 19, 1777, *ibid.*, 1004.
[42] July 21, 1777, Sparks, *Morris*, I, 1333.

The rebuke nettled both Morris and Yates, and with some cause, for their original instructions had said nothing about writing reports for public consumption. They sent a tart reply in a style that was clearly Morris'. It appeared, they wrote, that the prime object of their mission was "to write the news."[43] They pointedly quoted the council's directive, expressed in general terms, authorizing them to confer with Schuyler upon measures for the aid of his army. The desired information about the defeat at Ticonderoga, the letter concluded, could not be forwarded because Schuyler himself was not able to furnish it. But Morris and Yates would depart for Kingston the next morning to report in person.

Upon receiving the letter, the offended council, on motion of Jay, resolved that it was "disrespectful and unsatisfactory" and recalled Morris and Yates.[44] In any event, the council had already appointed Morris to another committee five days previously. He and John Sloss Hobart were to discuss paper-money inflation with representatives of the New England states at a meeting in Springfield, Massachusetts, on July 30. A letter, drafted by Jay, had instructed Morris to proceed there immediately "and not by your absence occasion delays."[45]

The message reached Schuyler's headquarters at Moses Creek on July 25, the day after Morris had left for Kingston. Schuyler sent it on, but either it did not overtake Morris on his journey or he chose to disregard it. He arrived in Kingston on July 28 and reported at once to the council. Now, verbally, he depicted the predicament of the northern army in a way that he had not been able to by letter. Burgoyne, he said, undoubtedly had ten thousand men. Schuyler's militia forces, restive under prolonged absence from home, were unreliable. Little help could be expected from the counties of Gloucester, Cumberland, and Charlotte, which were largely Loyalist. Without reinforcements Schuyler

---

[43] July 23, 1777, *JPC*, I, 1016.
[44] *Ibid.*
[45] July 22, 1777, *ibid.*, 1010.

could not stop Burgoyne's advance. Should the northern and western agricultural areas fall to the enemy, it would mean the loss of the entire state.[46] It was an appalling picture. William Smith heard from Walter Livingston that "Gouvr. Morris and R. R. L. [Robert L. Livingston] were hopeless last Sunday [July 27]."[47]

In view of the crisis, Morris asked the council to relieve him of his assignment to Springfield and instead send him to Washington's headquarters to request reinforcements for Schuyler. The council agreed and delegated the coolheaded Jay to accompany him. They departed the next day, July 29.[48]

They found Washington and his army on the march through Pennsylvania, in what was to be a futile effort to head off the northward advance of Howe's superior army of sixteen thousand troops toward Philadelphia. Washington informed Jay and Morris that he could not spare more than the two brigades he had already ordered to Schuyler's aid. Knowing that force was not enough, the two men continued on to Philadelphia, hoping to induce the Continental Congress to send militia from Maryland, Pennsylvania, and New Jersey.[49]

On the day they arrived in Philadelphia, too late to intervene, the Continental Congress resolved to replace Schuyler with Horatio Gates as commander of the northern army. Morris later wrote Schuyler that, although he had been opposed to the change, there was no overlooking the insistence of Gates's New England partisans that their troops would not march under Schuyler.[50] Morris

[46] Philip Schuyler to Gouverneur Morris, July 25, 1777, Schuyler Letter Book, November 19, 1776–July 1, 1778, New York Public Library; John Jay to Philip Schuyler, July 28, 1777, John Jay Papers; JPC, I, 1019; John McKesson to George Clinton, July 29, 1777, PPGC, II, 145.

[47] Entry of July 31, 1777, William Smith Diairy.

[48] Gouverneur Morris to Philip Schuyler, August 27, 1777, Gouverneur Morris Collection; JPC, I, 1019; John McKesson to George Clinton, July 29 [1777], PPGC, II, 146.

[49] Robert Benson to George Clinton, August 20, 1777, containing a copy of the memorial which Jay and Morris submitted to the Continental Congress, ibid., 235–36.

[50] August 27, 1777, Gouverneur Morris Collection.

and Jay submitted their request to the Congress in the form of a memorial. While they were waiting for a reply, they received an importunate letter from the New York Council of Safety, dated August 12, urging them to impress upon the Congress the desperate plight of the state. Burgoyne's army, the letter read, was on the point of taking Albany and loosing the whole Six Nations of the Iroquois Indians on the frontiers. The northern troops were "so dispirited that they hardly dare look the enemy in the face. They are unused to Indians, and have the greatest dread of them." Most of the forces at Albany were occupied in suppressing Loyalist insurrections. If immediate aid was not sent, "the poor remains of this State must inevitably fall into the hand of the enemy."[51] Armed with these facts, Jay and Morris succeeded in obtaining what Morris described as "such reinforcement for the northern armies, as will enable Gates to act with éclat, if he has spirit and understanding sufficient for that purpose."[52] On August 16 the Congress directed Washington to send five hundred riflemen to the relief of the Northern Department. He obediently dispatched a crack regiment under Colonel Daniel Morgan. By August 20, Jay and Morris were back in Kingston, after a long and tedious trip.[53]

The new constitution of the state now began to function. General George Clinton of Ulster County, a favorite with the common people, had been elected governor. The convention gave way to a newly chosen senate and assembly. Morris sat for Westchester County in the assembly. Why he was placed in the lower house is not clear. Perhaps it was because he was expected to leave as soon as possible for service in the Continental Congress.

The military predicament of the state continued to worsen. Kingston itself became endangered, as a British army under Sir

51 JPC, I, 1038–39.
52 To Philip Schuyler, August 27, 1777, Sparks, Morris, I, 141.
53 JCC, VIII, 649; Lynn Montross, The Reluctant Rebels: The Story of the Continental Congress, 1774–1789, 211; Robert Benson to George Clinton, August 20, 1777, PPGC, II, 232; JPC, I, 1046.

Henry Clinton, on October 5, belatedly started up the Hudson River from New York to meet Burgoyne. Within three days Clinton cleared the way to Albany by capturing Fort Montgomery, Fort Clinton, and Fort Constitution in the Highlands. If Clinton and Burgoyne joined forces, the doom of New York State would be sealed.

But Burgoyne had already been defeated at Saratoga. The news of the British disaster disheartened Clinton. He turned back to New York, but not before a small force under General John Vaughan set fire to Kingston on October 15. The old wooden houses were easy victims of the flames. Morris, staying to help the townsfolk flee, extracted a touch of humor from the tragedy:

> The alarm in the town exhibited more of the Drolerie than the Pathos of Distress. The good Dominie and his Yefrow by the Help of the pale and astonished Antoine and the gallant Mr. Brush blowing between Resolution & palid Fear load about half a Ton upon my waggon and then eight of them children included were dragged only slowly—before they went Willy squealed Sally bawled Adam played tricks and the Yefrow like Hecuba at the taking of Troy [cried] Mau Mau Mau.[54]

At the last minute Morris, accompanied by John Morin Scott, came upon a wealthy widow, Mary Cooke Elmendorph, who had refused to leave her large stone house on what is now Fair Street. They persuaded her to go; but a story persists that Mrs. Elmendorph, famed for her hospitality, had attempted to appease the enemy by having a sumptuous meal ready for them and that they ate it and then burned the house.[55]

Burgoyne officially surrendered to Gates on October 17. Although there was some grumbling at Hurley, where the state gov-

---

[54] To Robert R. Livingston, October 13, 1777, Robert R. Livingston Papers, New-York Historical Society, quoted in George Dangerfield, *Chancellor Robert R. Livingston of New York, 1746–1813,* 103.

[55] Entry of November 3, 1777, William Smith Diary; Mary Elizabeth Forsyth, "The Burning of Kingston," *Journal of American History,* Vol. VII (July, 1913), 1145.

ernment had set up temporary quarters, that Gates had let Burgoyne off too easily,[56] all Patriots breathed a great sigh of relief.

During the lull which followed, Morris took up his pen to write a lighthearted, rhymed note to Mrs. James Ricketts (the former Sarah Livingston, of Elizabethtown), the wife of a conspicuous Tory:

> Dear Madame, Your fair sister Sue
> Commands me write, and write to you.
> Her kind request I'd fain have parried,
> And reason good, for you are married!
> Then too, with politics and nonsense
> I've lost my rhyming talents long since;
> But since, in time and reason's spite,
> I'm doomed for my sins to write,
> And what is harder still, I deem,
> Preclude from my favorite theme—
> Phoebus disdaining to inspire me
> And Cupid not allowed to fire me,
> For should he play me such a trick it's
> Ten to one 'twould anger Ricketts!
> In such a case I needs must choose
> (A Hobson's choice) to write the news.
> Know then, the great Burgoyne's surrounded,
> His arms magnanimously grounded.
> I'd tell you, if I was a Tory,
> That Howe had gained much greater glory,
> He's taken Philadelphia City,
> For which the honest man I pity,
> Because he is so high in air
> That if his Knightship don't take care
> He'll get so terrible a tumble
> As e'en his Quaker friends will humble.
> Your friends are all in health and spirit
> And we shall conquer, never fear it!

[56] Entry of October 19, 1777, Samuel Blachley Webb, *Correspondence and Journals of Samuel Blachley Webb*, (ed. by Worthington C. Ford), I, 232.

Your sisters, as some folks relate,
Have each of them secured a mate,
But would you know if this be truth
Ask Nature and her handmaid Youth.
For me, I'm as I used to be,
I'm often wounded, always free
The servant of the common weal.[57]

Morris had been chosen a delegate to the Continental Congress on May 13. The appointment had expired, but on October 3 he was reappointed and on October 22 was requested "immediately to repair to Congress to relieve Mr. Duane."[58] The assignment caught him embarrassingly short of funds, for he anticipated that his salary would not cover inflated living expenses during an absence of at least five months. He was forced to ask the Council of Safety for an advance from the treasury, explaining that "I have already expended so much in the public service as to impair my finances."[59] The council ordered an advance to him of five hundred dollars.

[57] Margaret Armstrong, *Five Generations: Life and Letters of an American Family*, 1750–1900, 11–12. Margaret Armstrong believed the letter to have been written in winter of 1779, but the events discussed clearly place it in the fall of 1777.

[58] JPC, I, 1072, 931; Pierre Van Cortlandt to Gouverneur Morris, October 22, 1777, Gouverneur Morris Collection.

[59] October 24, 1777, JPC, I, 1073.

CHAPTER V

HREE MONTHS elapsed between the issuance of the order for Morris to relieve James Duane at the Continental Congress and his appearance there on January 20, 1778. The hard-pressed New York delegation, so decimated by ill health and the demands of personal business that the state was sometimes without representation, had sent insistent appeals for his attendance. But he had dallied with the Ogdens at Boonton, New Jersey.[1]

He found the Congress, driven from Philadelphia by Howe's army, established in inadequate quarters at the little town of York, Pennsylvania, a farming community of eighteen hundred on the western shore of the Susquehanna River. "Believe me," wrote Cornelius Harnett, a delegate from North Carolina, "it is the most inhospitable scandalous place I was ever in."[2] Oliver Wolcott of Connecticut reported that private lodgings were not to be had and that "a single Man exclusive of Horskeeping cannot probably live under at least ten pounds per Week."[3]

Congress assembled in the modest courthouse on the square. In the courtroom, heated by a massive wood stove, President John Hancock sat at the judge's bench, the delegates occupying rows of seats before him. Only about twenty-one members were in resi-

---

[1] *JCC*, X, 65; William Duer to George Clinton, November 9, 1777, Dreer Collection, Letters of Members of the Old Congress, Historical Society of Pennsylvania; James Duane to George Clinton, November 23, 1777, *PPGC*, II, 539, 560; Francis Lewis to Pierre Van Cortlandt, January 5, 1778; *LMCC*, III, 15; Gouverneur Morris to Robert R. Livingston, December 1, 1777, Robert R. Livingston Papers, New-York Historical Society.
[2] To William Wilkinson, December 28, 1777, *LMCC*, II, 562n.
[3] To Mrs. Wolcott, February 18, 1778, *ibid.*, III, 90.

dence, and of these sometimes no more than nine were on the floor to represent as many states.[4]

Morris' talents were already known in York. Robert Morris, a delegate from Pennsylvania and the future "Financier of the Revolution," observed that the newcomer possessed "first rate abilities" and added sagely, "I think he will be immensely usefull if he pursues his objects steadily (for I have been told his only blemish is being a little too whimsical)."[5] The two Morrises, unrelated, were to become fast friends.

On his first day of attendance in the Congress, Morris received an assignment of considerable importance. He and Charles Carroll of Carrollton, Maryland, were named additional members of a committee which had been formed earlier to confer with Washington on the reorganization of the army. Washington had written a letter to the Congress on December 23, 1777, depicting the hardships of the "naked and distressed Soldier" at Valley Forge, asked to "occupy a cold bleak hill and sleep under frost and Snow without Cloaths or Blankets."[6] The quartermaster general, Thomas Mifflin, had provided no supplies whatever since July, 1776. In these straits, Washington had said, nothing less was required than a complete overhaul of the organization of the army to reform all abuses; and he had recommended the appointment of the conference committee on which Morris was now to serve. Congress clothed the committee with sweeping powers to "form and execute" a plan, in conjunction with Washington, to reduce the number of battalions in service, remove and replace officers in the civilian departments of the army who were guilty of "misconduct, negligence, or incompetency," remove "all just causes of complaint relative to rank," determine what reinforcements were necessary,

[4] Montross, *The Reluctant Rebels*, 209–10; Henry Laurens to John Rutledge, January 30, 1778, *LMCC*, III, 63.

[5] To Richard Peters, January 25, 1778, General Wayne Papers, Historical Society of Pennsylvania, quoted in Clarence L. Ver Steeg, *Robert Morris, Revolutionary Financier, with Analysis of His Earlier Career*, 82.

[6] George Washington, *Writings of George Washington*, (ed. by John C. Fitzpatrick), X, 192.

recommend changes in the regulations of the various departments, and "adopt such other measures as they shall judge necessary for introducing economy and promoting discipline and good morals in the army."[7]

Morris left York for Valley Forge in company with John Harvie, a fellow committee member from Virginia. They crossed the Susquehanna and, on January 24, arrived in Lancaster, where they took overnight lodgings at an inn. While there Morris became involved in an incident, the consequences of which were to plague him more than a year afterward. A British convoy, permitted by Washington to pass through the American lines with supplies of clothing and medicine for British prisoners, had stopped at the inn in which Morris and Harvie were staying. The British paid their tavern bill in a sum of gold and silver agreeable to the keeper. Because of the severe depreciation of American currency, the bill was considerably lower than the official exchange value of the charge in paper money which Americans were obliged to pay. One of the American officers attached to the convoy thereupon demanded that the bill be recalculated at the exchange rate established by the Council of Pennsylvania. That meant that the British would have to pay what they considered an exorbitant price. The British objected that Washington had assured them they need pay only *reasonable rates* and, seeing two members of the Continental Congress present, appealed to Morris and Harvie for support.

It was an explosive question, bearing upon conflict between congressional and state jurisdiction. Resentment had already arisen over an earlier discovery of a bag of counterfeit American bills of credit in one of the wagons of the convoy. Morris, however, seeing a threat to the national prestige, did not hesitate to interfere. The case, he said, "was alone to be determined by the Law of Nations," for the British "were not subject to the municipal Laws of the separate States so long as they demeaned themselves

[7] JCC, X, 40.

consistently with the Terms they had either tacitly or expressly agreed to." He also sat down in the public room of the tavern and dashed off a letter of protest to Thomas Wharton, Jr., president of Pennsylvania.

When Morris arrived at Valley Forge a day or so later, a fellow committee member, Joseph Reed of Pennsylvania, took him to task for having written the letter. Reed censured it as imprudent, saying that Morris should instead have spoken in person to Wharton (the Pennsylvania Council was then sitting in Lancaster). Morris replied that he was not personally acquainted with Wharton. Reed finally closed the long altercation by observing with a smile that Morris had acted hastily and "would not do it if it was to do again."[8]

Reed's criticisms were but a foretaste of the reaction to the affair in York. The Congress received a strong complaint from Wharton about the action of Morris and Harvie (who had apparently concurred with Morris), and congressional sentiment sided with Wharton. In the meantime, however, Washington had written a letter to the Board of War expressing disapproval of retention of the British convoy for reasons similar to those Morris had advanced. This, and the fact that Morris and Harvie were not present to defend themselves, prevented Wharton's sympathizers from pressing a motion of censure against them.[9]

At Valley Forge, Morris met the Marquis de Lafayette, the twenty-year-old French nobleman who had come to America

[8] All quotations in the account of the incident at Lancaster are from Gouverneur Morris to Joseph Reed, April 9, 1779, Manuscripts of Joseph Reed, VI, 1779, New-York Historical Society, printed in LMCC, IV, 150–51.

[9] Daniel Roberdeau to the President of Pennsylvania (Thomas Wharton, Jr.), January 26, 1778, and January 30, 1778, Pennsylvania Archives, 1st series, VI, 201–202; George Washington to Board of War, January 26, 1778, Washington, Writings, X, 351–52; Washington to William Stephens Smith, January 27, 1778, ibid., 356; Washington to Horatio Gates, January 27, 1778, ibid., 355; deposition of James Christy, February 3, 1778, Pennsylvania Archives, 1st series, VI, 233; Pennsylvania Council to Board of War, February 16, 1778, ibid., 268; Robert L. Brunhouse, The Counter-Revolution in Pennsylvania, 1776–1790, 47.

seven months earlier and was now a protégé of Washington. Morris was "deeply surprised at the mature Judgment and solid Understanding of this young Man."[10] Lafayette had just been named to head a northern army to invade Canada. He was unhappy, however, that the Congress and its Board of War had appointed General Thomas Conway, a French officer of Irish birth, as his second-in-command. He detested Conway (whom he believed a leader in the rumored Conway Cabal, to replace Washington with Gates as commander in chief). He preferred General Alexander McDougall (formerly a leader of the New York radicals) or, as a second choice, Baron de Kalb. He pressed his objections in a letter to Henry Laurens, adding that he thought it unwise to place two foreigners in charge of the Canadian expedition and even declaring himself willing to serve under McDougall.[11]

Lafayette showed his letter to Morris and found that Morris thoroughly agreed with him. In fact, Morris had already recommended McDougall for the post before leaving the Congress at York. After the conversation Morris himself wrote to Laurens. He emphasized the unfavorable popular reaction that might result from the appointment of the foreigner Conway. "Liberality in vulgar minds," he said, as usual making no secret of his distrust of human nature, "is not common even in America." And he suspected that Conway might, for his own advancement, be more interested in a reconquest of Canada for France than in the success of the American cause:

It deserves the Consideration of Congress whether in Case an Accident should happen to the Commander in Chief it would be prudent to trust a Person whose object it is to push his Fortunes in France with an opportunity to imbue the Minds of

10 To the President of Congress (Henry Laurens), January 26, 1777 [1778], *LMCC*, III, 50.

11 [January 26, 1778], *ibid.* 60n. On jealousy and partisanship as motivations of Lafayette, see Bernhard Knollenberg, *Washington and the Revolution, a Reappraisal: Gates, Conway, and the Continental Congress*, 43, 210–13.

the Canadians with a Love of the Grand Monarque who may as probably like Canada as any of his Predecessors.[12]

Laurens did not welcome the news that Lafayette had taken Morris into his confidence. "Forgive me Dear Marquis," Laurens wrote, "for expressing some regret that you disclosed any part of them [the contents of Lafayette's letter to him] to a gentleman who though very Sensible appears to me, and has given some proof, to be often guardless and incautious."[13] Laurens nevertheless agreed with Lafayette and Morris, and when Lafayette went to York and threatened to take all his countrymen officers back to France, the Congress gave in and replaced Conway with the Baron de Kalb—McDougall had declined, pleading poor health. Lafayette then set out for Albany to take command.

By now, however, Morris had become disenchanted with the advisability of the venture. In that view he may have been encouraged by Washington, who had privately disapproved of the idea from the start. Morris and the other members of the committee at Valley Forge reviewed the whole project and agreed that it should be abandoned. On February 11 Morris prepared a letter in their name to Laurens, opposing the scheme as a doubtful enterprise which would overextend military and supply lines. The futility of the expedition became only too obvious to Lafayette when he arrived at Albany and saw the poorly equipped, dispirited troops. He had no alternative but to report to the Congress that the invasion was foolhardy. That shelved it. As for Conway, he had hastened to Albany before the Congress could notify him of his replacement by Baron de Kalb. When the plan proved a fiasco, he grew so disgruntled with his prospects for advancement that he arrogantly attempted to pressure the Congress for preferment by submitting a letter of resignation. To his chagrin, the

[12] January 26, 1777 [1778], *LMCC*, III, 50–51.
[13] January 28, 1778, *ibid.*, 59–60.

Congress accepted his resignation, and that was the end of his military career in America.[14]

Morris found that the task of reorganizing the army was a staggering one. He wrote John Jay:

> Congress have sent me here in Conjunction with some other Gentlemen, to regulate their army, and in Truth not a little Regulation hath become necessary. Our Quarter-Master and Commissary Departments are in a most lamentable situation. . . . Our Troops,—*Heu miseros!* The Skeleton of an Army presents itself to our Eyes in a naked, starving, Condition, out of Health, out of Spirits.[15]

But three weeks later, with indomitable spirit, he wrote Robert R. Livingston, "This is the Seed Time of Glory as of Freedom."[16]

The congressional committee set itself up at Moore Hall, a mansion about two and a half miles north of Washington's Valley Forge headquarters. Francis Dana of Massachusetts was chairman, and he and Morris were the dominant members. The others were Nathaniel Folsom of New Hampshire and Joseph Reed. Charles Carroll, who had been appointed with Morris, had been called home by his wife's illness and never made an appearance.[17]

Before all else, the committee took up the problem of the desperate shortage of supplies. Astonishingly, the army was at this time without a quartermaster general or a commissary general in camp—the former, Thomas Mifflin, had resigned, and the latter,

---

[14] Freeman, *George Washington*, IV, 598; Committee at Camp to President of Congress, February 11, 1778 [draft in Morris' handwriting], Papers of the Continental Congress, No. 33, fol. 121; Louis Gottschalk, *Lafayette Joins the American Army*, 135–38, 195–96; conversation of Jared Sparks with the Marquis de Lafayette, November [no day], 1828, Historical MSS, European I, 178–79, Sparks Manuscripts.

[15] February 1, 1778, John Jay, *The Correspondence and Public Papers of John Jay*, (ed. by Henry P. Johnston), I, 173–74.

[16] February 22, 1778, Robert R. Livingston Papers, New-York Historical Society.

[17] Washington, *Writings*, X, 362; John Henry, Jr., to the Governor of Maryland (Thomas Johnson, Jr.), January 27, 1778, LMCC, III, 55.

Joseph Trumbull, was too ill to fill his position. The committee at once sent letters to the Congress, recommending the appointment of Philip Schuyler as quartermaster general and Jeremiah Wadsworth, a Connecticut businessman, as commissary general. Schuyler was unacceptable to the Congress, and the post went to Nathanael Greene, Washington's most valued general. Wadsworth was confirmed and also proved to be an excellent choice.

The committee also undertook to direct an immediate organizational reform of the tangled supply system. Morris, with his financial and administrative talents, took over the greatest part of this work. The various commissary branches were ordered to inventory their stocks and list their personnel, new rules were instituted, and requests were sent to the several states for provisions. The committee toiled on into the middle of March, handling a wealth of detail, including officers' complaints and decisions on promotions.[18]

One of the supply officials with whom Morris came in contact was Robert Lettis Hooper, Jr., deputy quartermaster general. Like Morris, Hooper had fallen into difficulties with the Pennsylvania Council of Safety, which had accused him of using army wagons to transport private merchandise. The charges against Hooper were afterward substantiated, but he was at first upheld by the Board of War. Thus emboldened, he sought out the Pennsylvania official who had drafted the complaint, Attorney General Jonathan D. Sergeant, and gave him a physical beating. Sergeant, a small man, had no chance against the much larger Hooper, and he later refused to complete an affidavit which he had been preparing against Hooper. Hooper then wrote a letter to Morris, whom he took for a sympathizer (Sergeant had been one of Washington's detractors), boasting that, "as he had horsewhipped

---

[18] The Committee of Conference, Minutes, January 28, 1778, through March 12, 1778, *ibid.*, 61–62, 65, 68–69, 71, 73, 80, 83, 86, 89, 91–92, 101, 104, 109, 115; Francis Dana to the President of Congress, January 28 and 29, 1778, Papers of the Continental Congress, No. 33, fol. 71; Freeman, *George Washington*, IV, 572–85.

the Attorney General, he proposed to go through with the Council and should not stop at the President of the State."[19]

The story was too rich for fun-loving Morris to keep to himself. He gleefully showed Hooper's letter to a group at camp, including the members of the committee and Washington himself. But Reed, the Pennsylvanian, saw no humor in the situation. He took deep offense and immediately demanded the letter from Morris. Morris refused, declaring that it was private and should not be surrendered without its writer's consent. Reed could do nothing but fume and send a report to the Pennsylvania council. A warrant was issued against Hooper for libel, but General Greene refused to release him for appearance in court.[20] A year later Morris was to hear repercussions of the incident.

In the committee's work on the strictly military reorganization of the army line, it had for guidance a comprehensive report prepared by Washington. His recommendations called for improvement of morale among the officers by guarantee of half pay for life upon retirement and pensions for widows, recruitment of infantry by drafts from state militia forces, increase in the size of cavalry regiments, and revamping of the quartermaster and commissary departments. All these recommendations the committee accepted and transmitted to the Congress in substantially the same form that Washington proposed. In the committee's reports the long tables of organization of the infantry, artillery, cavalry, provost, and corps of engineers are in Morris' handwriting, suggesting that he worked closely with Washington in the discussions.[21]

[19] Joseph Reed to the Continental Congress, April 14, 1779, JCC, XIII, 453n.–54n.; Thomas Wharton, Jr., to Thomas McKean, February 15, 1778, Pennsylvania Archives, 1st series, VI, 266–68.

[20] Gouverneur Morris to Joseph Reed, April 9, 1779, LMCC, IV, 151; Roberdeau Buchanan, Genealogy of the McKean Family of Pennsylvania, with a Biography of the Hon. Thomas McKean, 60.

[21] Arrangement of Army, March 1(?), 1778, Plan for Establishment of a Corps of Engineers and Arrangement of the Engineering Department, March 3(?), 1778, USR 1778, March 1–June 10, Library of Congress; Papers of the Continental Congress, No. 33, fol. 99, 103; JCC, XI, 538–43; Freeman, George Washington, IV, 583–86.

The frequent contacts between Washington and Morris at this time permitted Morris' acquaintance with the general to ripen into friendship. Morris, who accepted few men without reservations, formed an early admiration and even veneration for Washington, in whom he found the embodiment of the aristocratic virtues of self-command, moderation, and devotion to the public service. The two men shared similar social backgrounds. Washington liked Morris, respected his talents, and perhaps found his irrepressible self-assurance engaging.

Morris' attachment was the more sincere because it was not slavish. He sided with his committee against Washington in a major difference about the terms of negotiations then under way for an exchange of prisoners with the British. Washington wished simply to arrange for the release of as many American soldiers as possible with the least delay. The committee wished to include civilians in the exchange. Rather than permit every captured citizen to be considered a "rebel unexchangeable," guilty of treason under English law and thus to be treated more rigorously than military prisoners, the committee insisted that an exchange of civilians must be the *sine qua non* of any agreement.[22] There were other reasons, involving national military policy and finance, and the committee assigned Morris to draft an exposition of those reasons for Washington to study.

The paper, written by Morris, was never submitted. It was superseded by a conference with Washington, where presumably its contents were verbally communicated. As a disquisition on statecraft, it is a remarkable document. Beginning with fundamentals, Morris lectured Washington that "interest alone (and not Principles of Justice or Humanity) governs Men" in diplomatic negotiations and that Americans therefore must distinguish their interest from that of the British. The British, he said, very much desired the exchange of military prisoners. They were short

[22] Committee of Conference to George Washington, February 11, 1778, *LMCC*, III, 81.

of manpower because of the overextension of their forces in posts seized all along the Atlantic seaboard. They were also short of money, and a congressional resolution requiring them to pay in specie for the subsistence of their men in American hands was distressing them. At the same time the British did not want to exchange civilians, because they intended to make acceptance of civil office under the revolutionary government extremely dangerous.

The Americans, on the other hand, were not desperate for men. The capture of Burgoyne's army, and the respite that feat had provided, made it likely that they could bring a large force into the field sooner than the British. British payments for maintenance of their captured men would bring a much needed flow of coin into Patriot coffers. In the meantime, imprisoned Patriot soldiers would be ensured comfort by a Patriot policy of retaliatory treatment to British prisoners; while if they were exchanged, they would only scatter through the country and add little to the size of the Patriot armies. It was therefore not desirable to exchange enlisted men. Patriot officers, civil servants, and sailors, however, were in short supply, and it was to the American interest to exchange them. And above all, the exchange should be the cornerstone of any agreement. Insistence on these points, Morris admitted, might prevent an understanding, but if so, the British would suffer more than the Americans. "And at any rate," he concluded, "should the Exchange be ever so desirable the best Way to bring it about will be by apparent Indifference whether it ever takes Place."[23]

These were hardly views that Washington could accept. He was interested primarily in maintaining the morale of a fighting army, a consideration which the civilian committee of Congress did not fully appreciate. In a sense, the dispute raised the ques-

[23] Committee of Conference to George Washington [a draft in Morris' handwriting], March 9(?), 1778, ibid., 115-20.

tion of the subordination of the military to the civilian authority. In this case, Washington ultimately won his point.

The committee concluded its business at Valley Forge on about March 30, 1778.[24] Morris did not return immediately to the Continental Congress at York. Taking time out between legislative missions had, it seems, become a habit with him. Soon William Duer of the New York delegation was writing to Robert Morris:

> It is said that my Friend Gouverneur Morris is at your *Chateau* [at Manheim, Pennsylvania]. for the sake of our Country, . . . entreat him to push on and come with him yourself. From a want of Representation in the State of New York, and several other Embarrassments we cannot bring as many members absolutely essential to our Safety, without you, especially the Establishment for the Army. . . . If G. Morris should be at Lancaster, pray write him in the most pressing Terms, to come forward.[25]

There is no record of Gouverneur's whereabouts at this time, but on April 15 he was back on the floor of the Congress.

Once there, he took up the cause of the army reforms which Washington had requested at camp. Of those reforms the most important and controversial was the measure providing for half pay for life for army officers. Washington insisted that this was absolutely essential to stem the flow of daily resignations of commissions. Opponents of the bill maintained that the Congress, formed only for the purpose of waging war, had no authority to create a peacetime establishment and that the proposal would introduce that anathema of the eighteenth century—a standing army. The forces on both sides of the issue were almost evenly divided. The opposition maneuvered to defeat the bill by moving

[24] *Ibid.*, 164.
[25] April 12, 1778, *ibid.*, 164–65.

that it be referred to the states, where it would surely fail. Morris, acting in close touch with Washington, informed him on May 1 that, of the states represented, "the Yeas will be Massa'ts Rhode Island, Connec: Jersey, and South Carolina the Nays will be N York Maryland Virginia and Georgia. Pensilvania is in a mighty flimsy Situation on that Subject having indeed a mighty flimsy Representation."[26]

In other words, the fate of the bill depended upon the vote of Pennsylvania. Here there was a ray of hope. If the still-absent Robert Morris could be prevailed upon to attend Congress in time, he might swing the Pennsylvania delegation. On May 11, Gouverneur sent Robert an urgent message, telling him that, of the three sitting delegates from Pennsylvania, two were opposed to the half-pay measure and that he must come to York at once to save the day: "James Smith assures . . . that his *worthy* Colleague Jonathan B. Smith hath absolutely declared off upon the Half Pay Business. Clingan is of the true Eastern Stamp and Clay. . . . Think one Moment and come here the next." William Duer added a post-script in similar vein, pressing Robert to "be here by Eleven o'Clock to Morrow."[27] Two days later, on May 13, the motion to submit the half-pay measure to the states came up for a vote, and Robert Morris was in his seat. The motion was defeated by six states to five. Pennsylvania voted in the negative, and Robert Morris' was the deciding ballot in the delegation split of two to one.[28] A compromise bill, changing the life payments to seven-year payments, was then passed unanimously on May 15.[29]

26 *Ibid.*, 213.

27 *Ibid.*, 230–31. James Smith, Jonathan Bayard Smith, and William Clingan were members of the Pennsylvania delegation to the Continental Congress. *Ibid.*, lviii.

28 The vote in the Pennsylvania delegation was: Robert Morris and James Smith, no; William Clingan, aye. JCC, XI, 495–96. Tabulations of eight congressional votes on half pay for life for officers, showing Gouverneur Morris' consistent championship of the measure and demonstrating solid bloc support from the New England states, New York, Maryland, and Virginia, are given in Herbert James Henderson, Jr., "Political Factions in the Continental Congress, 1774–1783" (Ph.D. dissertation), 175, 176.

29 JCC, XI, 502–503.

Washington, learning the news from Gouverneur, was gratified. The remaining reform was the regimental reorganization of the army. "For Godsake My dear Morris," Washington wrote, "let me recomd. it to you to urge the absolute necessity of this measure with all your might."[30] Morris strove willingly. He made enemies in the Congress in the process; but, he told Washington, he considered himself "an Advocate for the Army. I loved them from Acquaintance with some Individuals and for the Sufferings which as a Body they had bravely and patiently endured."[31] By June 4 the reorganization plan was completed, and Morris had the satisfaction of drafting the resolution to transmit it to Washington.[32] Washington had no stauncher ally in the Congress. Their one difference, over the terms of prisoner exchange, was removed when Morris yielded the point. On May 23 he wrote that the Congress had agreed not to ask for an exchange of civilians: "Congress having determined on the Affair of the Prisoners, and (in my opinion wisely) dropt for the present all Mention of Citizens; you will probably be enabled to negotiate a Cartel."[33]

Before the legislation for army reform had been completed, Morris was already deeply involved in equally crucial questions of foreign policy. On April 20, five days after he had returned to York, the Congress received a letter from Washington, enclosing a parliamentary bill, sponsored by Lord North, which conceded the colonial claim to exclusive self-taxation and provided for the appointment of commissioners to treat with the Americans. Both Washington and the members of Congress immediately suspected the bill of being a Trojan horse. Morris prepared a report, which was adopted and published by the Congress, rejecting the British bait in no uncertain terms.[34] The gist of his report was that no

---

[30] May 18, 1778, Washington, *Writings*, II, 412.

[31] To George Washington, October 26, 1778, LMCC, III, 463–64.

[32] Morris to Washington, June 9, 1778, Papers of George Washington; *JCC*, XI, 570.

[33] *LMCC*, III, 261.

[34] Edmund C. Burnett, *The Continental Congress*, 322–24; *JCC*, X, 374–80; Gouverneur Morris to John Jay, May 3, 1778, LMCC, III, 219.

negotiations were possible unless the British "either withdraw their fleets and armies, or else, in positive and express terms, acknowledge the independence of the said states."[35] Henry Laurens, for once well pleased with Morris, wrote that "this little clause of 7 Lines . . . certainly contains a complete answer to the Laborious performances of Lord North and the Labours of the blood thirsty Tryon."[36]

What the members of the Congress did not yet know was that Britain's belated effort at conciliation was a last-minute attempt to forestall the ratification of treaties which had been concluded by commissioners of America and France in Paris on February 6. On April 27 the Congress received a hint that "some preliminaries of a treaty have lately gone to France."[37] The next day Morris wrote to John Jay, shrewdly guessing the truth:

Great Britain seriously means to treat. . . . If the minister from France were present as well as him from England, I am a blind politician if the thirteen States (with their extended territory) would not be in peaceable possession of their independence three months from this day. . . . Probably a treaty is signed with the house of Bourbon ere this; if so, a spark hath fallen upon the train which is to fire the world.[38]

On the evening of Saturday, May 2, after the Congress had adjourned for the Sabbath, President Henry Laurens hastily summoned the members to a special meeting. He announced the arrival of a messenger from Paris, bringing treaties of alliance and commerce with France. The Patriots greeted the news with unrestrained joy. Independence was now assured. Americans needed no longer risk hanging as the price of liberty.

But if victory was within reach, the struggle to grasp it was still

[35] JCC, X, 379.
[36] To John Laurens, April 28, 1778, LMCC, III, 195. See also Henry Laurens to George Washington, June 9, 1778, PPGC, III, 433-34.
[37] George Johnstone to Robert Morris, February 5, 1778, quoted in Burnett, Continental Congress, 330; JCC, X, 398n.
[38] LMCC, III, 199-200.

far from over. The British commissioners appointed by Parliament to negotiate Lord North's proposals for conciliation were on their way to America, and their honeyed promises might win over weak hearts. To forestall that possibility, the Congress assigned Morris to prepare for publication a warning address to the people, to be distributed throughout the country and read in churches of all denominations immediately after worship services.[39] The address set forth in glaring colors the infamies of the British and denounced the British overtures as efforts to "lull you with the fallacious hopes of peace, until they can assemble new armies to prosecute their nefarious designs." It exhorted Americans to prepare for one last, supreme effort:

> Arise then! To your tents! And gird you for the battle! It is time to turn the headlong current of vengeance upon the head of the destroyer. They have filled up the measure of their abominations, and like ripe fruit must soon drop from the tree.

Morris, still the enthusiast for northern conquest, urged the Patriots on to Canada:

> Expect not peace, whilst any corner of America is in possession of your foes. You must drive them away from this land of promise, a land flowing indeed with milk and honey. Your brethren at the extremities of the continent already implore your friendship and protection. It is your duty to grant their request. They hunger and thirst after liberty. Be it yours to dispense to them the heavenly gift. And what is there now to prevent it?[40]

Only independence, the address maintained, would assure future security, for the British would never consider themselves bound by any agreement to keep faith with those they called rebels. Then Morris, hoping to capitalize on the aroused patriotic fervor, pleaded for financial as well as military sacrifice. If the Americans

[39] JCC, XI, 471, 474–81; Burnett, Continental Congress, 334–35.
[40] JCC, XI, 478–79.

would lend money to the Congress, replace state currencies with a single Continental issue, curb luxury spending, and strengthen their armies, victory would be certain. Both the style of the address, florid but piercing, and the treatment of financial matters show why Morris had by now become probably the foremost publicist of the Congress.

The British negotiators, the Earl of Carlisle, William Eden, and George Johnstone, arrived in Philadelphia on June 4. Eden brought with him letters of introduction (which he was never able to present) to Morris, John Jay, Robert R. Livingston, and James Duane. The letters had been written by John Vardill, a Loyalist exile in London who had been a fellow student of theirs at King's College.[41] On June 13 the Congress received the British proposals in writing, wrapped in a packet with triple seals depicting a fond mother embracing her returning children. President Laurens immediately began reading the message. On the second page he came to a passage referring to the French alliance as an "insidious interposition of a power which has, from the first settlement of these colonies, been actuated with enmity to us both." At once Morris interrupted and moved not to proceed further, "because of the offensive language against his most Christian majesty."[42] His object was to send the letter back with contempt and force the commissioners to remove the objectionable portion, thereby creating the impression that Britain was reduced to imploring peace from America. For three days the Congress debated the motion and ended by rejecting it and voting to complete the reading of the letter. The task of preparing a reply was then delegated to a committee of five, consisting of Morris, Richard Henry Lee, Samuel Adams, William Henry Drayton, and John Witherspoon. Lee, Witherspoon, and Morris all wrote drafts of a report. All agreed that the British advances must be rejected, both be-

[41] "Memorial of John Vardill, 16 November 1783," in Lewis Einstein, *Divided Loyalties: Americans in England During the War of Independence*, 412.
[42] *JCC*, XI, 605–606; Gouverneur Morris to John Jay, June 23, 1778, LMCC, III, 316.

cause of the language used against the king of France and because of the absence of recognition of independence. The committee adopted Morris' version, evidently because of its superior literary merit and dignity. "Nothing but an earnest desire to spare the further effusion of human blood," it read, "could have induced them [the Congress] to read a paper containing Terms so opprobrious to his most Christian majesty, the good and great ally of these states, or to consider propositions so derogatory to the honor of an independent nation."[43] On the floor of the Congress the expression "Terms so opprobious" was changed to the softer "expressions so disrespectful." The remainder of the reply received unanimous approval on June 17.

Morris had tempered his wording to suit the mood of the Congress. He wanted it further impressed upon the British commissioners that the united Patriots throughout the country would countenance no agreement short of unqualified independence. What he could not say officially he communicated anonymously in an address to the British commissioners, signed "An American," which the *Pennsylvania Gazette* published on June 20. Scornfully he told them that Americans no longer needed or wanted the British connection, that mutual affection and trust were gone, and that America, with the aid of France, possessed the strength to maintain its independence.[44] The argument was much the same as that of his appeal for independence before the New York Provincial Convention in 1776.

The address served to emphasize what the Congress had already made clear—that there was no turning back from the road to independence. As if to symbolize that determination, word arrived on June 20 that the British had evacuated Philadelphia, the capital city. The Congress held its last meeting in the cramped quarters at York on June 27 and adjourned to reassemble in Phil-

[43] *JCC*, XI, 615. For Lee's and Witherspoon's drafts, see *LMCC*, III, 296–97.
[44] The manuscript of this address is in the Gouverneur Morris Collection. See also Morris to Jay, June 23, 1778, *LMCC*, III, 315–16.

adelphia, with a public celebration .planned for the second anniversary of the Declaration of Independence on the Fourth of July.[45]

[45] *JCC*, XI, 626, 641, 662; *Pennsylvania Packet*, July 6, 1778.

The Precocious Nationalist

CHAPTER VI

I N 1778, PHILADELPHIA, with a population of about thirty-eight thousand people, was the undisputed metropolis of America. Before the Revolution it had ranked after London as the second city of the British Empire. Its neat, wide, tree-lined streets were "straight as a string"[1] and laid out in a precise, checkerboard pattern. Thriving commerce and public spirit had made it a model community for its time. The simple, uniform houses were all of brick. The paved streets were kept clean during the day by a garbage-removal system under municipal contract and at night were lit and patrolled by paid constables.[2] Philadelphia was a center of wealth and budding culture. Libraries, newspapers, and educational, scientific, medical, and charitable institutions had been established on a firm footing. The Quaker influence had created a tolerant atmosphere, and in the homes of leading merchants the earlier, austere way of life had been relaxed in favor of fine clothes, good food, and convivial society.

During their occupation the British had found the city hospitable. British specie had filled the merchants' pockets, and the attentions of courtly British officers had warmed many debutantes' hearts. The Patriots had raged at reports of the gaiety. Morris had even considered levying tribute upon the city but abandoned the

---

[1] Marquis de Barbé-Marbois, *Our Revolutionary Forefathers: The Letters of François, Marquis de Barbé-Marbois During His Residence in the United States as Secretary of the French Legation, 1779–1785* (tr. and ed. by Eugene P. Chase), 129.
[2] Carl Bridenbaugh, *Cities in Revolt: Urban Life in America, 1746–1778*, 33.

idea when Washington wrote him that he would not entertain the thought of punitive measures.[3]

The home of the Congress was the red-brick State House (now Independence Hall), whose tower Benjamin Franklin was reported to have compared to a microscope half out of its case.[4] The British had used the building as a hospital and left it in deplorable condition. A nauseating stench arose from a square pit nearby into which the dead bodies of men and horses had been thrown. The necessity of removing the corpses and the filth kept the Congress from reassembling until July 7.[5]

The members had barely settled down to business when they learned that a French fleet under the command of the Comte d'Estaing had arrived in Delaware Bay and that on board the flagship was a minister plenipotentiary to the United States, Conrad Alexandre Gérard. Within three days Gérard arrived in Philadelphia and presented his credentials to President Laurens. The plainest republican swelled with pride at the thought that in three years the new nation had advanced to the point of receiving an emissary from the most powerful monarchy in Europe. But what form should the reception ceremony take? It was the first occasion of its kind, and the Republic must conduct itself with fitting dignity. The Congress appointed a committee—Morris, Richard Henry Lee, and Samuel Adams—to devise the appropriate protocol. "Would you think," wrote Adams, "that one so little of the Man of the World as I am should be joyned in a Committee to settle Ceremonials? It is however of some Importance that we agree upon Forms that are adopted to the true *republican* Principles; for this Instance may be recurrd to as a Precedent in Futurity."[6] The committee went to Gérard himself for advice. He outlined the general diplomatic procedure followed in Europe

[3] Washington to Morris, May 29, 1778, Washington, *Writings*, II, 485; Morris to Washington, June 9, 1778, Papers of George Washington.

[4] Barbé-Marbois, *Our Revolutionary Forefathers*, 130.

[5] Henry Laurens to the President of South Carolina [Rawlins Lowndes], July 15 [1778], LMCC, III, 332–33.

[6] To James Warren, July 15, 1778, *ibid.*, 332.

but declined to express any opinions regarding the particular ceremony applicable to the organization and functions of the Congress.[7]

Morris, schooled in the polite conventions, then wrote a report for the committee which the Congress accepted with minor changes.[8] It went into great detail regarding the military honors to be accorded Gérard, the exact procedure for conducting him into the presence of the Congress, and the manner of receiving him there. Settling these questions, wrote committee member Lee, was a "work of no small difficulty."[9] Certainly the committee members gave their task great thought, as indicated by the specification that the president's chair was to be placed on a stage two feet above the floor, while the envoy's chair was to be placed on a stage raised eighteen inches. (The Congress sensibly disregarded that provision.) The most significant section of Morris' report was a stipulation that any representative of a foreign power must deliver all communications to the president in writing, failing which it would "be from the constitution of Congress impracticable for him to receive an immediate answer."[10] This provision served notice that the president of Congress had only nominal functions and that the Congress reserved to itself the executive power of control over the conduct of diplomacy.

It was almost a month before the State House was restored to a condition deemed fitting for the official reception of the minister. On August 6, with much formality, the momentous ceremony took place. President Laurens, surrounded by the delegates, sat on a platform in a mahogany armchair before a large table covered with green cloth. Two members of Congress presented Gérard to the assembly. Gérard bowed to the president and to the house, and they bowed in return. He addressed them in

[7] Conrad Alexandre Gérard to Comte de Vergennes, July 18, 1778, Conrad Alexandre Gérard, *Despatches and Instructions of Conrad Alexandre Gérard, 1778–1780* (ed. by John J. Menge, 171.
[8] JCC, XI, 698–701, 707–708.
[9] To Thomas Jefferson, July 20, 1778, LMCC, III, 342.
[10] JCC, XI, 701.

French, expressing the esteem and affection of France. Laurens read a prepared reply in English and was so nervous that he barely managed to get through it. More bowing, and the ordeal was over. All present then repaired to the City Tavern on Second Street for a lavish dinner, arranged by a committee of Reed, Dana, and Morris at a cost of $1,424. The diners drank twenty-one toasts, to the accompaniment of band music and the firing of cannon.[11]

The arrival of Gérard spurred the British commissioners to fresh efforts to win the American states back into the fold. On July 11 they sent an open letter to the Congress, challenging the authority vested in it by the Articles of Confederation to make treaties with foreign nations. Morris drew up a resolution as a proposed reply, stating that only a formally titled ambassador or minister plenipotentiary appointed by the king of England could have authority to treat with the United States and that the commissioners were not so empowered.[12] The Congress, however, disdained to make any answer at all. But Morris wanted no stone unturned to make the American position clear. He returned to the newspapers with a second article, signed "An American," in the *Pennsylvania Packet* of July 21. "It is a most diverting circumstance," he told the commissioners bitingly, "to hear you ask Congress what power they have to treat, after offering to enter into a treaty with them, and being refused."

The commissioners, growing desperate, now discarded all restraint. They attempted to bribe members of Congress with offers of high office and even cash rewards, and they appealed directly to American public opinion. Morris replied with another "An American" article in the *Pennsylvania Packet* of September 19, asserting the futility of the commissioners' challenge. He said that "at least two-thirds" of the population were unflinching

11 Timothy Pickering to Mrs. [Rebecca] Pickering, August 7, 1778, in O. Pickering, *Life of Timothy Pickering*, I, 235; Elias Boudinot to Mrs. Boudinot [August 8, 1778], LMCC, III, 363, 362n.; JCC, XI, 733, 753–57, 814; *Pennsylvania Packet*, August 6 and August 11, 1778.

12 Gouverneur Morris, Proposed Resolves [July 18(?), 1778], LMCC, III, 338; Burnett, *Continental Congress*, 352.

Patriots, including both plain people and large landowners. He told the commissioners that "the principles of your opponents are republican, some indeed aristocratic; the greater part democratic, but all opposed to Kings."[13]

Morris' articles attracted the attention of the French minister, who sent a copy of the second one to the French minister of foreign affairs, Comte de Vergennes, in Paris, with the explanatory note that its author was "a young man of twenty-eight, a delegate from New York, named Gouverneur Morris, descended from a Dutch family. . . . he is a man full of merit and energy, with whom I am trying to become intimate."[14] Gérard, closely watching the course of the negotiations, took particular interest in a separate demand made by the British commissioners for the immediate release of Burgoyne's captured army. France wanted the troops held in America, in order to prevent their deployment in Europe. To that end Gérard informally counseled the Congress to reject the commissioners' demand on the ground that they did not have powers to negotiate the question; the Saratoga Convention, to be legal, first had to be ratified by Parliament. Congress followed his advice and rejected the demand.[15] On October 20, Morris assailed the commissioners again with an "An American" letter in the *Pennsylvania Packet*. He charged that the envoys were not authorized to conduct negotiations about the prisoners and that, moreover, the British could not be trusted not to use the released troops against the United States. Gérard informed Vergennes that the article had the sanction of the Congress.[16]

[13] The manuscript of this article is in the Gouverneur Morris Collection. The public appeal of the Earl of Carlisle, Sir Henry Clinton, and William Eden, dated August 26, 1778, was printed in *Pennsylvania Packet*, September 12, 1778, and read in Congress on August 31, 1778. See also Weldon Brown, *Empire or Independence: A Study in the Failure of Reconciliation, 1774–1783*, 273–77; John F. Roche, *Joseph Reed: A Moderate in the American Revolution*, 133–42.

[14] September 24, 1778, Gérard, *Despatches and Instructions*, 311. Gérard's error in Morris' age, which was twenty-six, was a slip of the pen, for in an earlier dispatch he had referred to Morris as a "young man of twenty-six very much esteemed for his talents." To Comte de Vergennes, July 19, 1778, *ibid.*, 175.

[15] *Ibid.*, 97, 220; JCC, XI, 776, 885, 880–83, 897.

[16] October 25, 1778, Gérard, *Despatches and Instructions*, 350.

Rebuffed at every step, the commissioners turned to a last desperate resort. On October 3 they published a "Manifesto and Proclamation," offering a general pardon to all Americans who would accept conciliation and threatening dire punishment to all who did not. The paper was to be distributed throughout the states by vessels sailing from New York under flags of truce. In reply, the Congress issued a manifesto of its own on October 30, written by Morris. It proclaimed the justice of the American cause, attacked the British attempt to intimidate the Patriots, and warned that if the threats were carried out the Congress would "take such exemplary vengeance, as shall deter others from a like conduct."[17] Morris capped the controversy with a white paper for the Congress, a lengthy, official pamphlet, entitled *Observations on the American Revolution*, which documented not only the negotiations with the Carlisle commission but also the entire course of the Revolution. Its cataloguing of British oppression and American resistance was perhaps a little stale, but the message was resolute. In probably the most violent passage he ever penned, Morris threatened London with the torch and the people of Britain with the scalping knife:

> ... the towns on her coast are at least as defenceless as ours; and their citizens, unused to arms, are utterly incapable of repelling an assault. A small sum of money would wrap their metropolis in flames, ... and the dreaded scalping-knife itself may, in the hands of our riflemen, spread horror through their island.

He concluded with a call to national greatness and humanitarianism—a vision which he loved to evoke again and again, all through his life:

> The portals of the Temple we have raised to Freedom, shall be thrown wide, as an Asylum to mankind. America shall receive to her bosom and comfort and cheer the oppressed, the miser-

[17] *JCC*, XII, 1082. A conclusive identification of Morris as the author of the American "Manifesto" is in *LMCC*, III, 377 n. For the British "Manifesto," see *JCC*, XII, 1013.

able and the poor of every nation and of every clime. The enterprise of extending commerce shall wave her friendly flag over the billows of the remotest regions. Industry shall collect and bear to her shores all the various productions of the earth, and all by which human life and human manners are polished and adorned. In becoming acquainted with the religions, the customs and the laws, the wisdom, virtues and follies, and prejudices of different countries, we shall be taught to cherish the principles of general benevolence. We shall learn to consider all men as our brethren, being equally children of the Universal Parent—that God of the heavens and of the earth, whose infinite Majesty, for providential favour during the late revolution, almighty power in our preservation from impending ruin, and gracious mercy in our redemption from the iron shackles of despotism, we cannot cease with gratitude and with deep humility to praise, to reverence and adore.[18]

The Congress later ordered the printing of thirteen hundred copies of the pamphlet, at a cost of $2,986.[19] The departure of the commissioners for England put an end to further acrimony.

From the beginning to the end of this war of words, it had been Morris who had written the proclamations of the Congress. "*I have drawn and expect to draw, almost if not all the publications of Congress of any importance,*" he had written Robert R. Livingston. That this was more than an idle boast is attested by the records of the Congress. Edmund C. Burnett, the esteemed authority on the history of the Congress, states that "the *Journals* contain a good deal of evidence to show that this is not quite such an exaggeration as it might at first blush seem to be."

The volume of work was oppressive, and during the stifling days of August, Morris' usually gay spirits had drooped under the burden. "The every day minutia are infinite," he had told Livingston. "From Sunday morning to Saturday night I have no exercise unless to walk from where I now sit about fifty yards to Congress

---

[18] Committee of Congress, *Observations on the American Revolution*, 131–32.
[19] JCC, XII, 1063; *ibid.*, XIII, 421.

and to return. My constitution sinks under this and the heat of this pestiferous Climate." Nor could his limited income stand the strain of inflated living costs. "I think I cannot much longer attend," he wrote Livingston eleven days later. "The depression here rapidly increasing hath arrived to such a pitch that I am confident my expenses are between 15 and 20 dollars per day. . . . In times like the present I dare not, I cannot quit my post though to continue at it is big with ruin. Should I leave the State unrepresented I shall be censured by all."[20] Yet somehow, with the aid of his attorney's fees, he stayed on. There was talk that he had become involved in trade, but he insisted that he abstained as a matter of principle, as long as he remained in Congress.[21]

The French alliance instilled vigor into the entire conduct of American foreign relations. The Congress appointed Benjamin Franklin minister plenipotentiary to the court of France, the same rank that Gérard held in America. (Franklin was still in Paris, where he had served as one of the three commissioners appointed to negotiate a treaty of alliance with France.) A committee led by Morris was directed to prepare a letter of credence and instructions for the new envoy.[22]

In their preliminary work on the instructions the committee members wanted to place particular emphasis on a provision directing Franklin to invite French support of an attack on Quebec. Lafayette, who was to deliver the instructions to Franklin personally, had proposed the expedition and hoped to lead it. Canada continued to exert a special fascination upon Americans,

[20] Morris to Livingston, August 17, 1778, *LMCC*, III, 377, 377n.; Morris to Livingston, August 28, 1778, Robert R. Livingston Papers (Bancroft Transcripts), II, 143–45, New York Public Library.

[21] Charles Carroll of Carrollton to William Carmichael (?), May 31, 1779, *LMCC*, IV, 239; Gouverneur Morris to Robert R. Livingston, February 22, 1778, Robert R. Livingston Papers, New-York Historical Society; Gouverneur Morris to Peter Van Schaack, September 8, 1778, in Van Schaack, *Peter Van Schaack*, 132.

[22] *JCC*, XII, 901, 908.

even though one invasion had already been defeated and plans for a second abandoned. Anticipating French opposition to the project, Morris took a preliminary draft of the instructions to Gérard in the hope of winning him over. Gérard received the plan coldly; France had no desire to become involved in a costly, drawn-out war of conquest. But the French envoy expressed his opposition discreetly, for fear of antagonizing American zealots.

Morris gave voice to Americans' suspicions that France's objections were dictated by the Spanish government, which hoped to make Canada a perpetual enemy and thereby divert American attention from the Spanish Mississippi River domain. Gérard, who was working closely with an unofficial Spanish observer in Philadelphia, Juan de Miralles, replied that America had given Spain reasons for alarm because of the recently established American settlements on the banks of the Mississippi in the Natchez country. Morris assured Gérard that America had no designs on the Mississippi territory. Many of his colleagues, he said, opposed expansion on the ground that if the new American populations of the Northwest were granted free access to both the Mississippi and the St. Lawrence, they might declare themselves independent of the United States. When Gérard pointed out that several delegates had advocated joint American-British control of Mississippi navigation, Morris took it upon himself to say that this sentiment was a minority one, motivated in some cases by personal interest in the new settlements. Gérard accepted Morris' assurances for the moment but was to discover that they did not reflect the majority opinion of the Congress.[23]

In their conference on the draft of Franklin's instructions, the

---

[23] Gérard, *Despatches and Instructions*, 104; Edward S. Corwin, *French Policy and the American Alliance of 1778*, 243–48; Richard B. Morris, *The Peacemakers: The Great Powers and American Independence*, 220–21. Also on Morris' willingness to limit America's western boundaries, first by giving up some of the Northwest Territory and later by stopping at the Appalachian Mountains, see his draft, n.d., JCC, XIII, 341, and draft, n.d. (but after October 18, 1780), in Samuel Flagg Bemis, "Canada and the Peace Settlement of 1783," *Canadian Historical Review*, Vol. XIV (June, 1933), 283n.–84n.

two men also discussed a proposed recommendation to drive the British from American seaports and establish an American navy. Gérard unequivocally opposed the idea. Not only was it impractical, he said, but it would transfer British naval operations to European waters, an outcome which France could only conclude was desired by America for selfish reasons. In a conciliatory manner Morris agreed to strike out the provision.[24] Neither that point, however, nor the proposal to invade Canada did Morris and the committee ultimately concede.

The final draft of the instructions, submitted by the committee to the Congress and accepted on October 26, directed Franklin to assure France of America's inflexible determination to continue the war but also to insist that Articles XI and XII of the treaty of commerce, which provided discriminatory privileges for the French West Indian molasses islands in trade with the United States, be expunged as "inconsistent with that equality and reciprocity which form the best surety to perpetuate the whole." The French acceded to this demand at Versailles, in September, 1779. Concerning Canada, Franklin was to "constantly inculcate the certainty of ruining the British fisheries on the banks of Newfoundland, and consequently the British marine, by reducing Halifax and Quebec." A detailed plan of attack was enclosed, noting, among other advantages, the securing of the fisheries and the "accession of two states to the union." As for the naval war, Gérard's objections and Morris' assurances notwithstanding, Franklin was instructed

> to suggest the fatal consequences which would follow to the common enemy, if, by confining the war to the European and Asiatic seas, the coasts of America could be so freed from the British fleet as to furnish a safe asylum to the frigates and privateers of the allied nations and their prizes.[25]

[24] Gérard to Comte de Vergennes, October 20, 1778, Gérard, *Despatches and Instructions*, 340–45.
[25] *JCC*, XII, 1040–41; Samuel Flagg Bemis, *The Diplomacy of the American Revolution*, 61–62 and n.

Most important of all, Franklin was to press for loans or subsidies, the greatest need of the struggling republic. An appended paper, "Observations on the Finances of America,"[26] emphasized that such financial aid was the only hope of supporting the dangerously inflated paper currency—taxation and private borrowing at home had proved unfeasible.

The ambitious plan for an invasion of Canada shortly received a serious dampener from Washington. On November 11, he wrote the Congress that the expedition was impractical from a military point of view. The letter was referred to a committee headed by Morris. "You know more of the Subject than all of us together,"[27] Morris wrote Washington; nevertheless, while ostensibly accepting Washington's objections, as spokesman for the committee he again recommended that preparations go forward for joint American and French action in the expected event that the British "evacuate the Posts which they now hold within these United States."[28] Washington, not satisfied, thereupon requested a personal consultation at Philadelphia. He met with a five-man committee, including Morris, and the result was that on January 1, 1779, the Canadian scheme was permanently laid to rest.[29]

Franklin's instructions did not contain a complete statement of American foreign policy. The subject was too controversial to be decided without a thorough airing of conflicting views. The basic question was whether the American states should trim their war aims to suit France or refuse to yield to a foreign power any of the freedoms for which they were desperately fighting. The resolution of this problem called forth all the animosities, resentments, and frustrations which had accumulated in the fumbling and inefficient efforts to present a united front against the com-

[26] JCC, XII, 1048–52.
[27] October 26, 1778, LMCC, III, 464.
[28] JCC, XII, 1190.
[29] Ibid., 1227, 1230; Burnett, Continental Congress, 371–72. On Lafayette as the author of the Canadian plan, see Gottschalk, Lafayette Joins the American Army, 288–313.

mon enemy. In the Congress hitherto hidden differences emerged into the full light of day.

Morris, who was now exerting considerable influence in the formulation of foreign policy, took the position that America had no choice but to accept the obligations imposed by the French alliance. France would not actively enter the struggle as a mere tool of American ambitions. Furthermore, Morris did not himself wish to extend American boundaries, for reasons he had already expressed to Gérard.

The contest began, on the surface, over personalities. Silas Deane, one of the three American commissioners who had negotiated the treaty of alliance with France, had returned to America on the same vessel which brought Gérard. Congress had recalled him from his post because he had made lavish promises to French officers of commissions in the American army. Other, more serious, charges had also awaited him: he had been accused of engaging in private commercial ventures and misappropriating public funds. His difficulties stemmed from accusations made by the third commissioner, Arthur Lee of Virginia. Their dispute centered on the question of whether supplies furnished to the United States by the financier Caron de Beaumarchais before the signing of the treaty of alliance had constituted an American debt to Beaumarchais as an individual, as Deane affirmed, or a gift from France, as Lee contended. It had been generally understood that Beaumarchais was acting for the king of France, but to admit it publicly would be to impugn France's good faith as a neutral at the time of the transaction. On the other hand, to interpret the aid as a debt owed to a private person, rather than as assistance from a foreign government, would inflict a heavy financial burden on the United States.

Shortly after his arrival in Philadelphia, Deane appeared before the Congress to defend his record. It was immediately apparent that the Congress was deeply and bitterly divided on the issue. The next day, August 16, Morris wrote to John Jay: "Your Friend

Deane who hath rendered the most essential Services stands as one accused. The Storm increases and I think some of the tall trees must be torn up by the Roots."[30] The investigation continued for many months, and as the debates increased and overflowed into the press, the delegates ranged themselves into pro-Deane and pro-Lee camps. The president of Congress, Henry Laurens, could not restrain his pro-Lee partisanship and took the drastic step of resigning his chair in protest against a trend in the proceedings favorable to Deane. He was replaced by John Jay, an outspoken Deane supporter.[31]

The Deane and Lee factions were, in fact, embryos of national political parties. At close hand they appeared to be only groups of shortsighted politicians engaged in recriminations to the detriment of the general welfare. To men of the eighteenth century, the word party had the ugly connotation of a faction promoting selfish interests. Responsible popular government was then in its infancy, in England as well as in the United States, and it was not until later that freely organized parties matured and came to be recognized as acceptable and effective agents for the expression of the popular will.

The Deane and Lee factions foreshadowed the party lines that were to develop in the United States. Complex motives drew men to one standard or the other. Social and economic interests tended to influence the wealthy, aristocratic forces to align themselves with Deane, and the less affluent, democratic elements with Lee. Local conditions and personal attachments or antipathies often overrode those interests, however. Probably the greatest determinant was ingrown mental attitudes. Men of a cosmopolitan cast of mind, alive to the emerging position of the United States in the world of nations, supported Deane and his contention that France should not be discountenanced by a public declaration of financial aid provided before the signing of the alliance. Men of

[30] John Jay Papers.
[31] Burnett, *Continental Congress*, 364–66.

a parochial mind, confident of American self-sufficiency and suspicious of foreign entanglements, backed Lee and his contention that America should save money by proclaiming the debt to Beaumarchais as the gift of the French government that it really was.[32]

In the press Deane's chief antagonist was Thomas Paine, the radical pamphleteer and at the time secretary to the committee on foreign affairs of Congress. An article in several installments, written under his pen name "Common Sense," appeared during the opening week of 1779 in the *Pennsylvania Packet*. In it Paine asserted that official papers in his office conclusively proved that the supplies furnished by Beaumarchais were a free gift from the French government. The rash article transformed the issue from a congressional quarrel to an international incident. The French minister immediately called upon the Congress to repudiate Paine's statement.

Morris had early taken a position in the forefront of those who supported Deane, and in this stance he had the backing of Governor Clinton of New York.[33] Clinton was usually on the side of the radicals, but the New York radicals were never warm to their New England counterparts, who in this case were Lee's foremost advocates. When the Congress took up Gérard's protest, on January 7, 1779, Morris pressed for dismissal of Paine from his po-

[32] Herbert James Henderson, Jr., agreeing that factional differences were based on foreign policy issues, attributes them in considerable measure to the intellectual conflict between New England puritanism and enlightenment thinking. "Political Factions in the Continental Congress, 1774–1783," 10, 113, 234. Edmund S. Morgan maintains that parties were derived from personality differences centered in the "Puritan Ethic." The Calvinist mind supported men who exemplified "moral austerity," such as Samuel Adams, Richard Henry Lee, and Henry Laurens, against those who symbolized "luxury, extravagance, and avarice," such as Silas Deane, Robert Morris, and John Hancock; and the antagonisms were reciprocated. "The Puritan Ethic and the American Revolution," *William and Mary Quarterly*, Vol. XXIV (January, 1967), 26–33.

[33] Clinton to Morris, February 2, 1779, *PPGC*, IV, 536. For a suggestion that Morris was the leader of the Deane faction and wanted to remove Franklin in order to create a diplomatic vacancy for himself, see H. James Henderson, "Congressional Factionalism and the Attempt to Recall Benjamin Franklin," *William and Mary Quarterly*, Vol. XXVII (April, 1970), 253–67.

sition as secretary to the committee on foreign affairs, on the grounds that he had abused his trust, that repudiation of the secretary was inseparable from repudiation of his allegations, and that he never was fit for the position. In a speech on the floor of the Congress, Morris declared:

> It gave me great Pain . . . to hear in the Debates of Yesterday and this Morning the Word Party made use of. . . . There is indeed in this House a chosen Band of Patriots, who have a proper Respect for each others Opinions, a proper Sense of each other's Feelings, and whose Bosoms glow with equal Ardor in the common Cause, but no *Party*.

There was no issue here, he said, of the personal rights of this "mere Adventurer from England, without Fortune, without Family or Connections, ignorant even of Grammar."[34] Congress had employed him without specifying his tenure and could dismiss him at will.

Six days later, after much heated debate, the Congress agreed unanimously to a resolution proposed by Morris that the president assure Gérard, "in the clearest and most explicit Manner," of its complete disavowal of Paine's publications. The resolution further declared that France had given no supplies of any kind to the United States before the alliance.[35] Two days afterward, in response to another communication from Gérard, the Congress unanimously adopted a resolution penned by Morris, which declared that the United States would not conclude a truce or treaty with Britain without the consent of France. On January 16, Paine was formally dismissed from his position.[36]

The Deane forces had thus won the first round. But the issue had not yet been joined over the central question of whether or not France should have a voice in the terms of a peace treaty.

[34] Gouverneur Morris, "Speech Made in Congress ab: Mr. Payne—Taken down Afterwd. from Memory to Obviate Misrepresentation," Gouverneur Morris Collection.
[35] *JCC*, XIII, 55.
[36] *Ibid.*, 63, 75–76.

What France desired, and would insist upon before granting any loan, was assurances that the Americans would confine the object of the war to independence and would not involve their ally in a protracted struggle for territorial expansion. With this end in view, on February 15, 1779, Gérard politely but firmly requested the Congress to prepare a comprehensive statement of war aims as speedily as possible. The message was given added weight by the news that Spain was considering entering into the Franco-American alliance.[37]

The Congress appointed Morris chairman of a committee of five to explore the question, and he drew up a report which reached the floor on February 23. The opinion of the committee, he wrote, was that Spain was prepared to ally herself with the United States and that this alliance would force Britain to treat for peace under Spanish mediation. As a preliminary to any negotiation, Britain must be required to recognize the absolute independence and sovereignty of the United States. Beyond that, certain conditions must be insisted upon as an ultimatum, and others should be reserved as possible concessions in the give-and-take of diplomacy. The category of ultimatum included acknowledgment of American territorial boundaries between Canada and Nova Scotia and the Floridas, and between the Atlantic and the Mississippi; total evacuation of British land and sea forces; free navigation of the Mississippi as far as the southern limits of the United States; and free access to a port at the mouth of the Mississippi. Points to be yielded included cession of claims to Nova Scotia, in return for an equal share in the Newfoundland fisheries or acquisition of the Bermuda Islands; prohibition of the East Indies trade and the slave trade; renunciation of territorial expansion beyond the peace-treaty limits; transfer of the Floridas to Spain; and a reciprocal guarantee of all American possessions. Finally, with regard to the expected alliance with Spain, she should be asked for a subsidy to raise an American force of

[37] *Ibid.*, 184–85; Burnett, *Continental Congress*, 430–31.

six thousand infantry troops for the conquest of the Floridas, those territories to be given to Spain with the proviso that free navigation of the Mississippi was reserved for the United States.[38]

The manner in which Morris' report was received in the Congress quickly disclosed the new direction the controversy would take. Most of the points in the draft won substantial approval in brief time, but the sections dealing with the Newfoundland fishing rights and the free navigation of the Mississippi met with intense opposition. The divisions in the Congress on these points were chiefly geographical. The New England states stood solidly for a specific guarantee of fishing rights. The southern states demanded free navigation and commerce on the Mississippi.

The debates over the fisheries dragged on for six months. Morris took the position that, while these rights should be pressed for, they should not be insisted upon as a provision of the treaty, lest the war be prolonged over them. The *Journals* of the Congress show that he led the fight against the New Englanders.[39] In spite of a congressional rule of secrecy, the dispute spread outside the Congress. "Our pretended private business," said Morris, is "known and talked of in every one of the States."[40] A letter signed "Americanus" was published in the *Pennsylvania Gazette* of June 23, maintaining that America had no legal claim on the fisheries and would delay the peace by demanding them. The similarity of the name "Americanus" to Morris' pseudonym, "An American," brought charges in private and in print that he was the author of the letter;[41] as a result he was forced to issue a denial, signed

[38] *JCC*, XIII, 194–95.

[39] *Ibid.*, 349–52, 371, 372; *ibid.*, XIV, 563–66, 581, 750–52; Gouverneur Morris, Resolution Before Congress Concerning Treaty with Great Britain [draft], 1779, Gouverneur Morris Collection; Gouverneur Morris, Instructions to Minister for Peace [drafts], August 14, 1779, *ibid.*; Gouverneur Morris, Proposed Motion [March 22(?), 1779], *LMCC*, IV, 112–13.

[40] Henry Laurens, Notes of Proceedings, June 23, 1779, *ibid.*, 276.

[41] Josiah Bartlett to William Whipple, June 24, 1779, *ibid.*, 359n.; "Common Sense" (Thomas Paine), in *Pennsylvania Gazette*, June 30, 1779; "Tiberius Gracchus" [probably Timothy Matlack, secretary of the Pennsylvania Council], *LMCC*, IV, 98n., in *Pennsylvania Gazette*, June 30, 1779.

"Cato," in the *Pennsylvania Evening Post* of July 9.[42] Within the Congress, Morris and his friends labored to find a solution acceptable to the New Englanders and unobjectionable to France. After several tries Morris produced a report, delivered and approved on August 14, which contained the compromise that, while cession of Canada and Nova Scotia and guarantee of the right to the fisheries was "of the utmost importance," yet "a desire of terminating the war hath induced us not to make the acquisition of these objects an ultimatum on the present occasion."[43] At the same time, no treaty of commerce was to be signed without an agreement on the fisheries.

The question of the navigation of the Mississippi was taken up separately, and was not settled until September 17. Morris was absent from the Congress when it was resolved that, in the event of an alliance with Spain, the United States would agree to her conquest of the Floridas, in return for free American navigation of the Mississippi.[44] The resolution subsequently proved unimportant, for Spain never concluded an alliance.

The deep-rooted antagonisms exposed by the disputes over Deane and the fisheries inflamed the long-standing jurisdictional conflict between the government of Pennsylvania and the Congress. On April 15 the Congress received a letter from Joseph Reed, now president of Pennsylvania, enclosing a report of a joint committee of the state's council and assembly, which listed a train of alleged congressional infringements on the rights of Pennsylvania. In those allegations Morris' name figured prominently. The report

[42] For the manuscript of this letter, see Fragment against Thomas Paine, reply to attack on Robert Morris, signed "Cato" [1779], Gouverneur Morris Collection. "Common Sense" replied that he had never believed Gouverneur Morris to be the author of the "Americanus" article. *Pennsylvania Gazette*, July 21, 1779.

[43] [Gouverneur Morris], Instructions to Minister for peace Conference with Great Britain [draft], August 14, 1779, Gouverneur Morris Collection; *JCC*, XIV, 959–60; William C. Stinchcomte, *The American Revolution and the French Alliance*, 66–72.

[44] *Ibid.*, XV, 1084.

resurrected the old charge that Morris and Harvie had obstructed the enforcement of a Pennsylvania law fixing the exchange rate of specie and paper currency, in the affair of the British officers' tavern bill at Lancaster on January 24, 1778. It also recalled the incident at Valley Forge, when Morris refused to surrender to Reed the abusive letter from Deputy Quartermaster General Robert Lettis Hooper, Jr. To those charges it added a more recent complaint that Morris had appeared before the Pennsylvania assembly as attorney for one of the contestants in a disputed election, "to the great dissatisfaction of the inhabitants of Pennsylvania, who suppose the delegates of the United States sent here to attend the affairs of the common Union, not to advocate the measures of any party."[45]

Morris saw an advance copy of the report and on April 9 wrote a long reply to Reed. The affair of the British officers at Lancaster, he said, involved the national honor, since the British were on an international mission and were "not subject to the municipal Laws of the separate States so long as they demeaned themselves consistently with the Terms they had either tacitly or expressly agreed to." Regarding his part in the contested election, he could see no impropriety in continuing legal practice while serving as a delegate. Reed, then also a delegate, had done the same thing. "Was it an Insult to your Legislature that a Lawyer, being then also a Delegate, should appear before them in a contested Election?" As for Hooper's letter: "Sir I refused to deliver that Letter, because I think it wrong to turn to a man's Disadvantage private Communications." To prove that he had not condoned Hooper's actions, Morris reminded Reed that he had "cheerfully cooperated with you and Doctor Witherspoon in collecting Evidence against this very Hooper," as a member of an investigating committee of Congress.

Having answered the official charges, Morris went on to deal with the public and private abuse then being heaped upon him.

[45] April 14, 1779, *ibid.*, XIII, 453n.

Plainly considering Reed the chief instigator of the attacks, he wrote:

> It is in your Power to prevent me from harboring the slightest Intentions to do you an Injury. It is also in your Power to compel me to take Measures for my Defense. I shall expect that you will vindicate me from such Aspersions as you know to be groundless.[46]

The "aspersions" were that Morris had declared an intention to delay a case of Pennsylvania against General Benedict Arnold (who had not yet been exposed as a traitor), that he supported Deane from motives of personal gain, and that he had published an article unfriendly to Pennsylvania. The first two accusations Morris refuted without difficulty. The last referred to his letter, signed "An American," in the *Pennsylvania Packet* of February 27, 1779. He pointed out that the letter which had been written at Reed's own urging, had merely attempted to minimize appearances of national disunion.[47]

Morris' letter brought an unrelenting reply from Reed; but after a further exchange of notes the two men discussed their differences in a meeting at the State House, and Reed offered apologies sufficient to satisfy Morris.[48]

Reed's apologies did not speak for Morris' other enemies. There were always those who resented his air of superiority and feared his oratorical and organizing powers. Joseph Bartlett of New Hampshire said that he was "an eternal speaker, and for artifice a

[46] Manuscripts of Joseph Reed, VI. A large part of this letter is printed in *LMCC*, IV, 149–53.

[47] This letter, in attempting to minimize American difficulties, exposed Morris to the charge of acknowledging them. "Common Sense" and "T. G." in *Pennsylvania Packet*, March 2, 1779. Morris could hardly have expected gentle treatment, for in discussing "the late abusive writings" in his article, he had written, "Billingsgate language marks at most a Billingsgate education, and among those who know the real value of such performances, the reputation of a virtuous citizen will not suffer more from the scurrility of a news-paper, than from the nervous diction of an oyster-wench."

[48] Gouverneur Morris to Joseph Reed, July 9, 1779, Manuscripts of Joseph Reed, VI.

Duane, and for brass equal to any I am acquainted with."[49]
One charge of Reed's, that Morris "kept Company much with
Tories,"[50] was repeated throughout the war. Morris' record should
have made this slur unthinkable, but his Loyalist relatives and
former friends made him vulnerable. It was common knowledge
that his mother was a Loyalist. Yet even with her he had virtually no communication. The only two extant letters to her
during the war years are entirely personal in content. The first,
dated December 19, 1776, from Fishkill, is a message of consolation on the death of his sister Catherine. It reveals a deep religious conviction beneath his worldly exterior: "There is one
Comforter, who weighs our Minutes, and numbers out our Days.
It is He, who has inflicted upon us the Weight of public and
private Calamities, and He best knows when to remove the
Burthen."[51] The second letter, written at York on April 17, 1778,
is an attempt to cheer his mother under the clouds of war:

> I received great Pain from being informed that you are dis-
> tressed on my Account. . . . I would that it were in my Power to
> solace and comfort you in your declining Age. The Duty I owe
> to a tender Parent demands this of me, but a higher Duty has
> bound me to the Service of my fellow Creatures. . . . I know
> that for such Sentiments I am called a Rebel, and that such
> Sentiments are not fashionable among the Folks you see.[52]

Morris received no reply to these letters. Ironically, at the very
time that he was being accused of Loyalist associations, his mother's Morrisania estate was being despoiled by the British because
of her Patriot relatives. The British were quartering about fifty
horses there and cutting large areas of timber. She protested to
an official and was backed by William Smith, now chief justice
under the British. The answer was, "The King's Troops must be

---

[49] To William Whipple, June 20, 1778, *LMCC,* III, 310.
[50] Gouverneur Morris to Joseph Reed, July 9, 1779, Manuscripts of Joseph
Reed, VI.
[51] Gouverneur Morris Collection.
[52] *Ibid.*

supplied & I have the General's Order to cut on all Morrisania."
Smith stressed Mrs. Morris' loyalty, but the official replied, "She
could not commit Waste." When Smith reminded him that General Staats Long Morris was next in line to the estate, he returned,
"He will never pay the Legacies & it will come to Dick & gouverneur, Two Rebels." Finally, Smith appealed, "Is it right to destroy
the Property of the King's Friends?" "They will be paid for it,"
answered the official. "Will they?" asked Smith. "May be so,"
said the official, with a smile, "after the War is over."[53] Mrs.
Morris then sent a memorial to Sir Henry Clinton, the commander of the British forces, saying that without his intervention
she would be forced to abandon her estate and submit to wretchedness which her former rank and station rendered her ill qualified to bear.[54] Clinton's reply has not been found.

Morris' detractors also used the loyalism of his brother-in-law
Isaac Wilkins against him. Morris regretted Wilkins' decision to
side with the British but respected his motives.[55] Wilkins had
left America for England in 1775 and in that year had written a
letter to Morris. After being shunted about for more than three
years, the letter was found in the wreckage of a stranded ship on
the coast of New Jersey. The Patriot authorities impounded it
and never delivered it to Morris. It was opened, however, and
cited as "evidence" of his attachment to Loyalists. For all the talk,
the most damaging part of the letter was the innocuous passage:
"Go on and deserve well of your country. Endeavor to keep peace
and good order, and to moderate the madness of the people."[56]

In the Public Record Office in London is a memorial to Parliament written by John Vardill. In it Vardill states that he had
"furnished Government with much and valuable information by
an extensive correspondence with Congress Leaders," among

[53] Entry of February 10, 1779, William Smith Diary.
[54] April [no day], 1779, Historical Manuscripts Commission, *Report on American Manuscripts in the Royal Institution of Great Britain*, I, 425.
[55] Gouverneur Morris to Sarah Gouverneur Morris, December 19, 1776, Gouverneur Morris Collection.

whom was Morris. The list, however, also includes John Jay, Robert R. Livingston, and James Duane; and since Vardill was making out a case for financial payment for his services, his claim carries little weight.[57]

The one known private letter which Morris wrote during the war to any Loyalist other than a relative was the reply to a farewell note from his friend Peter Van Schaack, referred to earlier. It was impossible for Morris to turn his back upon the sweet-natured Van Schaack. In the letter Morris entreated his friend to harbor no resentment toward the Patriots:

> I am particularly afflicted, that you should be now obliged to relinquish your country, for opinions which are unfavorable to her rights. . . . It was always my opinion, that matters of conscience and faith, whether political or religious, are as much out of the province, as they are beyond the ken of human legislatures. In the question of punishment for acts, it hath been my constant axiom, that the object is example, and therefore the thing only justifiable from the necessity, and from the effect.[58]

Before any peace terms could be negotiated, the war had to be won. Winning the war was as much a matter of organization, finance, and supply as one of military strategy. Yet the currency had become inflated to a frightening level, and food and clothing were desperately wanting among the soldiers. Anyone willing to face the facts could see that these problems would vanish if the states would impose upon themselves the necessary taxes. "Taxation is the only Remedy," wrote Morris to Clinton.[59] But of all remedies that was the one the states were least likely to accept.

How, then, to raise money without taxation? When Morris returned to Congress from Valley Forge in 1778, after having wit-

---

[56] [No month or day], 1775, Sparks, *Morris*, I, 156.
[57] "Memorial of John Vardill . . . ," in Einstein, *Divided Loyalties*, 412.
[58] September 8, 1778, in Van Schaack, *Peter Van Schaack*, 131.
[59] September 2, 1778, PPGC, III, 724.

nessed the plight of the army at first hand, he applied himself to the well-nigh impossible task. The result was a bold and ingenious memoir, in which he made detailed recommendations for the reform of the entire financial and administrative system of the national government.[60] Only a loan, he recognized, could bring funds into the treasury immediately. For this loan, however, security must be advanced, and he proposed to set aside a portion of the public domain for that purpose. But the government of the Confederation owned no property in its own right. Morris would therefore have the government call upon the individual states to cede to Congress their claims to western lands in return for a proportionate reduction in their future quotas of the national debt. Out of part of this territory a new state would be formed, in which land grants would be made to army veterans, enemy deserters, and recipients of congressional gratuities. The remainder would be divided into districts with natural boundaries and used as security for national debts.

More fundamental reforms would be required to establish a secure financial footing on a long-term basis. To begin with, the currency must be stabilized. Morris would eliminate all state currencies: every state would turn over its existing issues to the federal government in return for certificates issued by Continental loan offices. Permanent sources of revenue must be created. One source would be a national tariff, the revenue from which would be used to set up a sinking fund for the payment of foreign debts; this proposal would necessitate elimination of all interstate restrictions on trade. Another source of income would be a per capita tax of one dollar, to be used to set up a sinking fund for internal debts. To supervise the new system there would be unified control under a single comptroller and a treasury board.

---

[60] [Gouverneur Morris], Proposal to Congress Concerning Management of Govt.—Finances, Army, Supplies, Etc., Gouverneur Morris Collection. This paper is undated, but Jared Sparks, who may have had information not now available, placed it as written "not many weeks after his return to Congress from Valley Forge." Sparks, *Morris*, I, 161.

Illustrations

Lewis Morris, grandfather of Gouverneur Morris

Painted in 1726 by John Watson. Courtesy of Brooklyn Museum Collection.

Lewis Morris, Jr., father of Gouverneur Morris

From a painting by Thomas McIlworth. Courtesy of the New-York Historical Society.

Morrisania

From a print of a painting from the collection of Livingston Rutherfurd, a descendant of Gouverneur Morris. Published in Livingston
Rutherfurd, *Family Records and Events, Compiled Principally from
the Original Manuscripts in the Rutherfurd Collection* (New York,
1894), 136.

William Smith

Miniature on ivory painted by Henry Stubble between 1785 and 1791.
Courtesy of the New-York Historical Society.

Catherine Livingston

Miniature, painter unknown. Courtesy of Mrs. Paul Hammond and the Frick Art Reference Library.

The State House in Philadelphia

Engraved by James Trenchard after a painting by Charles Willson Peale in 1778 and published in the *Columbian Magazine*, I (July, 1787), 512. Courtesy of the Historical Society of Pennsylvania.

Robert Morris

From a painting by Charles Willson Peale. Courtesy of the Pennsylvania Academy of the Fine Arts, Philadelphia.

"Zion Besieg'd and Attack'd"

Detail from a Pennsylvania cartoon of 1787. Courtesy of the Library
Company of Philadelphia.

George Washington

Bronze replica of a life-size statue by Jean-Antoine Houdon, the original of which is in the Virginia State Capitol at Richmond. Washington sat for the head at Mount Vernon in October, 1785. Gouverneur Morris posed for the body in Paris in June, 1789. Courtesy of Gorham Bronze Company, Providence, Rhode Island.

GEORGE WASHINGTON

Gouverneur Morris, 1789

Drawn in the spring of 1789 in Paris by Edmé Quénedy, with the aid
of a physiognotrace, which traced the profile from life, and engraved
by Gilles-Louis Chrétien. Published as frontispiece in Anne C. Morris,
ed., *Diary and Letters of Gouverneur Morris* (New York, 1888), I.

Adélaïde Marie Émilie, Comtesse de Flahaut

The child is three-month-old Charles de Flahaut, believed to have been fathered by Talleyrand. Painted by Adélaïde-Labille-Guiard in 1785 and published in Baron Roger Portalis, "Adélaïde Labille-Guiard (1749–1803)," *Gazette des Beaux-Arts, XXVI* (November, 1901), 360. Courtesy of the Bibliothèque Nationale, Paris.

Mrs. Gouverneur Morris (Anne Cary Randolph Morris), 1810

From a pastel by James Sharples. Courtesy of Angus J. Menzies and the Frick Art Reference Library.

Gouverneur Morris, 1810

From a pastel by James Sharples. Courtesy of Miss Ethel Turnbull and the Frick Art Reference Library.

Morris next reviewed the administrative organization of the government. At the outset, to alleviate the inherent weakness of the Congress as a multiheaded executive body, he proposed the appointment of a "Chief of States," or perhaps a committee of three, to exercise general authority, subject to approval of the parent body. Secondary executive boards, similar to those for war and treasury already in existence, would be set up for naval and commercial affairs. Most pressing of all, the chaotic army-supply system must be reorganized so as to co-ordinate under one body the purchasing and procurement functions of the various forces. Morris included a very detailed plan for the reform of the quartermaster, commissary, forage, and clothier general departments.

The striking feature of this paper was not only that it constituted a comprehensive design by a young man of twenty-six to promote essentially a centralized government—a plan ten years ahead of its time—but also that its author singlehandedly managed to carry all its provisions to the floor of the Congress for consideration. He aimed at nothing less than the complete enactment of his program.

Opportunities to bring forward his financial proposals came on July 30, 1778, when he was appointed to a committee to prepare a plan for the establishment of a new treasury board,[61] and again on August 27 of the same year, when he was appointed to another committee to "consider of the state of the money and finances of the United States."[62] He wrote the reports for both committees. The one on the treasury, enacted on September 26, provided for a board administered by a comptroller, auditor, and treasurer. "I have the pleasure to tell you," wrote Morris to Governor George Clinton the next day, "that at Length with infinite Pains and many Disappointments we have got an arrangement for our Treasury which promises the best Consequences."[63] The report on cur-

[61] JCC, XI, 731.
[62] Ibid., 843.
[63] September 27, 1778, LMCC, III, 428; JCC, XII, 921, 956–61.

rency and finance reached the floor on September 19.[64] To stabilize the currency, it proposed "that the Emissions of the several States be cried down as a Currency and loan office Certificates issued for the Amount." To pay the internal debt, the report called for a poll tax of half a dollar on every inhabitant. To pay the foreign debt, it called for a tariff of 2 per cent on all imports and the incorporation of all interstate commerce duties into a national sinking fund.

The report also advanced Morris' scheme for the cession of state western-land claims, those territories to be "erected into separate independent States, to be admitted into the Union, to have a Representation in Congress, and to have free Governments in which no Officers shall be appointed by Congress, other than such as are appointed through the other States."[65] Of that area, twenty to forty million acres were to be set aside as security for the negotiation of a loan in Europe. In the fall of 1777, Maryland had offered a similar proposal for the pooling of western lands and the creation of new states but had received no support. In reviving the idea, Morris suggested that the Congress appoint two committees to travel to the northern and southern state legislatures respectively and "negotiate" for the acceptance of the Articles of Confederation and of the reforms he had added. In a sense, Morris was also attempting to give backbone to the articles, which had not yet been ratified by all the states.

The Congress received Morris' plan with closely guarded secrecy. Sixty copies were ordered printed, and the printer was placed under oath not to divulge any of the contents or print additional copies and to deliver to the secretary of Congress, Charles Thomson, the proofs and unfinished sheets. The delegates debated the issues for more than a month, during much of which time Morris was absent. His presence could have made little difference, for the states were not yet prepared to accept strong central government.

[64] *Ibid.*, 928–33.
[65] *Ibid.*, 931.

His report never even came to a vote. It was rewritten by Elbridge Gerry of Massachusetts, minus the reforms Morris had asked for.[66]

A similar fate awaited his idea for an executive "Chief of States," or committee of Congress. In the Morris manuscripts at Columbia University is a draft of a resolution, dated sometime in 1779, for the appointment of such a committee, with the number of members to compose it left blank.[67] The official *Journals* of the Congress, however, contain no reference to the resolution.

Although Morris had little success in securing the formal enactment of his ambitious body of reforms, he could still make significant contributions to the efficiency of the army supply departments through administrative committee work. On November 10, 1778, he was appointed chairman of a committee to superintend the commissary and quartermaster departments. Matters had come to such a crisis that the committee was given blanket authority to "take such steps relating to the same as they shall think most [advantageous] for the public service."[68] Morris and the committee worked to inventory the resources of the different states, check engrossing, and even regulate the prices of army necessities. Inevitably these activities led to disputes with local authorities and also with the French consul.[69] Fortunately, there

[66] *Ibid.*, 1073–75.
[67] [Gouverneur Morris], Resolution Before Congress, 1779, Gouverneur Morris Collection.
[68] *JCC*, XII, 1114–15.
[69] Victor L. Johnson, *The Administration of the American Commissariat During the Revolutionary War*, 154–57; A Committee of Congress [Nathaniel Scudder, William Whipple, Gouverneur Morris] to the Several States, November 11, 1778, LMCC, III, 489–93; Gouverneur Morris to Mr. Risburg, June 5, 1779 [copy], Hollingsworth Manuscripts Correspondence, Historical Society of Pennsylvania; Matthew Smith to Gouverneur Morris, June 7, 1779, *Pennsylvania Archives*, 1st series, VII, 472; Kathryn Sullivan, *Maryland and France, 1774–1789*, 81; Gouverneur Morris and William Whipple to Caesar Rodney, January 19, 1779, George H. Ryden (ed.), *Letters to and from Caesar Rodney, 1756–1784*, 292; Gouverneur Morris, William Whipple, and Francis Lightfoot Lee to Jeremiah Wadsworth, February 17, 1779 [photostat]; Jeremiah Wadsworth Papers, Library of Congress; Gouverneur Morris–John Holker Correspondence, May–June, 1779, Franklin Collection, Yale University.

was only desultory military activity at the time, and the supply departments could expect relatively stable demands. Morris also served as chairman of the committee on the medical department and on the clothier general's department.[70] He reorganized the administration of both departments and supervised much of the day-to-day detail. In his capacity as chairman of various executive committees, the authority to conduct all business devolved upon him, with the perfunctory acquiescence of the other committee members. The assignment carried heavy responsibilities. Years later he wrote:

> Not to mention the attendance from 11 to 4 in the house, which was common to all, and the appointments to committees, of which I had a full share, I was at the same time Chairman, and of course did all the business, of the Standing Committees; viz., on the commissary's, quartermaster's, and medical Departments. You must not imagine that the members of these committees took any share or burden of the affairs. Necessity, preserving the democratic forms, assumed the monarchical substance of business. The Chairman received and answered all letters and other applications, took every step which he deemed essential, prepared reports, gave orders, and the like, and merely took the members of a committee into a chamber and for form's sake made the needful communications, and received their approbation which was given of course. [71]

In May, 1779, information reached Morris that his political enemies in the New York assembly were plotting to prevent his re-election to a third annual term in the Continental Congress. (He had lost his seat as assemblyman from Westchester in September, 1778, but had nevertheless been re-elected to a second

[70] William Shippen to Gouverneur Morris, June 17, 1778, Gouverneur Morris Collection; Morris to Shippen, June 17, 1779, *ibid.*; Morris to Jonathan Potts, September 17, 1778, Potts Papers, II, 487, Historical Society of Pennsylvania; Henry Laurens to Nicholas Cooke, January 3, 1778, LMCC, III, 11.

[71] To Thomas Truxton, December 14, 1809, Sparks, *Morris*, I, 217. The manuscript is in Gouverneur Morris Collection.

term in the Continental Congress on October 16.[72]) Governor George Clinton assured him that "Enmity like this, is an Evidence of your abilities, . . . and I have reason to believe will be attended with no Consequences to your Prejudice in the Minds of your Constituents."[73] Morris' friends, however, were not so sanguine. He had been away from his home state for a year and a half and under the pressure of hard work and ill health had not returned to mend fences. His enemies, it was said, charged him with neglecting New York State interests and devoting himself too much to national concerns.[74]

The only possible excuse for this accusation was his attitude toward the controversy between New York and Vermont. Both New York and New Hampshire had for long claimed colonial charter rights to the New Hampshire Grants, the original name for Vermont. New Hampshire had sold title to settlers in much of this land. New York had granted part of the same territory to speculators, who were determined to keep it. With the coming of the Revolution, the Vermont settlers had taken matters into their own hands and declared themselves a separate state, with the tacit consent of New Hampshire. Under the leadership of Ethan Allen and his Green Mountain Boys, they applied to the Congress for admission to the Confederation. New York, through its delegates in the Congress, bitterly opposed the application of the Vermonters. The Congress attempted to mediate the dispute but wanted to avoid taking sides. The issue dragged on for years and was not settled until 1783.

Morris dutifully worked with the other members of his delegation to press New York's claims to the territory in the Congress.

[72] John Jay to Gouverneur Morris, September 13, 1778 [copy], Sparks Manuscripts; LMCC, IV, lix.

[73] June 23, 1779, PPGC, V, 101. This letter appears to have been in reply to a letter of May 30, 1779, in which Morris refers to circulation of hostile reports about himself.

[74] John Jay to George Clinton, August 27, 1779, LMCC, IV, 690; Gouverneur Morris to George Clinton, February 20, 1779, PPGC, IV, 585; Sparks, Morris, I, 215.

He even blocked a move to promote Ethan Allen from lieutenant colonel to colonel.[75] But he believed in persuasion rather than force. To Clinton he wrote:

> These People appear to me to be determined on establishing Independence and I doubt whether they will be diverted from it by Force. This is a Remedy which cannot at present be exhibited nor will it at any Time be agreable to see Americans embruing their Hands in the Blood of each other.[76]

Candor at last compelled him to admit that he favored setting Vermont free: "It appears to me very doubtful whether Vermont, if independent, would not be more useful to New York, than as the Eastern District."[77]

He at first confidently expected to withstand the attacks upon him. "Be not uneasy for your Friend," he wrote his cousin Robert Morris, in New Jersey:

> I venture to assure you that he will rise from the Stroke and pity the Envy of his Foes. The Tales circulated among the People I can trace back to Men who having enlisted themselves under the Banners of Faction & being disappointed in their Views burn with deadly Hate and seek Revenge in low abuse and vilainous Insinuation.[78]

But his friends William Duer and Robert R. Livingston urged him to return to New York to defend himself, and on August 25, 1779, he obtained leave of absence from the Congress. He was away six weeks, but the trip was to no avail. The New York assembly at Poughkeepsie balloted for the delegates on October 1. The result was a tie between Morris and Ezra L'Hommedieu, an undistinguished member from Suffolk County. The election was decided by a joint vote of the assembly and the senate, where L'Hommedieu defeated Morris by one or two votes. "The Impru-

[75] Gouverneur Morris to George Clinton, PPGC, IV, 100; JCC, XII, 947.
[76] June 6, 1779, PPGC, III, 420.
[77] To George Clinton [undated], Sparks, Morris, I, 212.
[78] June 18, 1779, (Robert) Morris Papers, Box 4.

dence of some of Mr. Morris's friends in voting," wrote Clinton to John Jay, "occasioned the loss of his Election."[79] He gave no further explanation. Some hope remained that Morris would be named to the congressional seat shortly to be vacated by Jay, who had recently been appointed minister plenipotentiary to Spain, but the place fell to Philip Schuyler.[80]

Morris continued in Congress for another month, until about November 19, pending the arrival of his replacement. Henry Laurens complained that Morris' "dead preengaged Vote" had "established many an important point when he had no right to sit here," but admitted that after Morris' departure his absence "has nevertheless been much lamented."[81]

From his post in Spain, Jay exerted continuing pressure on Clinton to use his influence to ensure Morris' election to a later vacancy in Congress. On May 6, 1780, Jay wrote: "What has become of Morris? Dont let his Enemies in or out of the State run him down." And again, on June 20: "Where is Morris? Keep him up. It is a Pity that one so capable of serving his Country should be unemployed, but there are men who fear and envy his Talents and take ungenerous advantage of his Foibles." On April 6, 1781, Clinton wrote Jay that at the next meeting of the New York legislature Morris' election to Congress was "not improbable."[82] But Morris was not again to represent New York until 1799. In the meantime, he stayed on in Philadelphia.

[79] October 5, 1779, PPGC, V, 309. See also Sparks, Morris, I, 215; JCC, XIV, 993; ibid., XV, 1146; LMCC, IV, lvii, lix, 460 n.
[80] James Duane to George Clinton, October 30, 1779, PPGC, V, 337.
[81] Henry Laurens, Notes for Remarks [September 13(?), 1779], LMCC, IV, 418.
[82] PPGC, V, 685–86, 861; ibid., VI, 748.

CHAPTER VII

ORRIS HAD BEEN too much in the thick of the war effort simply to disappear into private life. A month after his departure from the Congress, he was nominated to the post of secretary to Benjamin Franklin in Paris. Opposition immediately arose from the pro-Lee group, led by James Lovell of Massachusetts, Henry Laurens, and Richard Henry Lee. Lovell, who did not want the job, permitted himself to be named only as a foil to Morris and then nominated Alexander Hamilton. Morris was receptive to the appointment, as he obliquely indicated in a letter to his cousin Robert Morris of New Jersey: "It is a Thing which I probably shall not get which I wish I may not get and which nevertheless from a concatenation of little Circumstances I could not refuse. Thank God there are ambitious Men in the World who will spare Me."[1] The choice among the field of candidates was delayed for several months. In the meantime, Morris worked at his law practice.

He also devoted considerable effort to a series of articles which appeared over the signature "An American" in the March and April issues of the *Pennsylvania Packet*. Their chief purpose was to awaken the public to the financial plight of the government. They failed to achieve the desired effect, but they expressed an

[1] February 20, 1780, (Robert) Morris Papers, Box 4. On the contest over the nomination, see James Lovell to Henry Laurens, December 15, 1779, and December 17, 1779, *LMCC*, IV, 538–39; Nathaniel Peabody to Henry Laurens, December 17, 1779, *ibid.*, 539–40; James Lovell to Richard Henry Lee, December 18, 1779, *ibid.*, 540–41; James Lovell to Samuel Adams, December 21, 1779, *ibid.*, 546–47; John Laurens to Alexander Hamilton, December 18, 1779, in Alexander Hamilton, *The Papers of Alexander Hamilton* (ed. by Harold C. Syrett and Jacob E. Cooke), II, 230–31; Alexander Hamilton to John Laurens, *ibid.*, 254–55.

approach which Morris was to attempt to implement in an official capacity in little more than a year.

The essays began with a broad review of economic principles and of the currency and finance of the Revolution. They argued against inflation and strongly advocated the doctrine of laissez faire, including defense of monopolies against government price-fixing proposals. They concluded with a proposed solution to the nation's difficulties, founded, said Morris, "in the nature of man, not on ideal notions of excellence." Loan-office certificates should be funded at their original specie value and exchanged for ten-year, nontaxable and nontransferable (except with "certain legal formalities") bonds, paying 5 per cent semiannual interest in specie. Bills of credit should also be exchanged for these bonds at the rate of forty to one (Morris said he would have preferred twenty to one), and the old bills should be burned in their former owners' presence. The total national debt, which Morris estimated at fifteen million dollars, should be "sunk in five equal annual payments after the war, or redeemed with specie, at the expiration of that term."[2] The income for these expenditures must come from taxes levied in specie.

On May 14, 1780, Morris prepared to set out for a week or ten days in the country. He had his phaeton, drawn by a famous pair of spanking grays, brought to his door. Then, in his usual, daredevil way, he allowed the horses to stand untethered while he climbed to his seat and shouted commands to them. Suddenly they started and threw him to the ground. His left leg caught in one of the turning wheels and the ankle joint was dislocated and the bones badly broken.[3]

[2] "Letter on the Currency, no. 1 1780" and "Letter on the Currency; No. 2 Plan for the Currency and Taxation," Gouverneur Morris Collection; "An American," in *Pennsylvania Packet*, March 4, 11, 23, and April 11, 1780 [quoted].
[3] Gen. John Cochran, "Reminiscences and Anecdotes," *American Historical Register and Monthly Gazette of the Patriotic-Hereditary Societies of the U.S.A.*, I, 436. Cochran states that he heard the story from his grandfather, Dr. John Cochran, surgeon general and director of military hospitals during the Revolution

His personal physician and friend, Dr. Samuel Jones, was out of town, and several other well-known practitioners were called to attend him. Upon consultation they recommended immediate amputation of the leg. He received the news calmly. After accepting the necessity, he asked: "Gentlemen, I see around me the eminent men of your profession, all acknowledged competent to the performance of the operation. You have already secured renown, the capital by which you live. Now the removal of my leg cannot add to your celebrity; is there not one among you younger in your calling who might perform the act, and secure the *èclat* for his benefit?"[4] Dr. James Hutchenson, a young man of Morris' own age and a surgeon in the Continental Army, was pointed out, and Morris agreed. The leg was removed below the knee. When Dr. Jones returned to Philadelphia, he was not satisfied about the necessity for the amputation. Surgeons afterward commonly cited the case as an example of faulty diagnosis and haste.[5]

Morris bore his misfortune with "becoming fortitude," reported Robert R. Livingston. When his friends came to see him, they tried to cheer him up by congratulating him on the success of the operation and the beauty of the stump, which led him to ask, "Would it not be advantageous to remove the other limb? we might then have a brace." Condolences poured in from all sides. "I never knew an individual more sympathized with," wrote Mrs. Robert Morris to Kitty Livingston's sister, Mrs. John Jay. "If I am not mistaken," replied Mrs. Jay, "that misfortune will call

---

and an acquaintance of Morris and an eyewitness of the accident. See also William Bingham to John Jay, July 1, 1780, in Jay, *Correspondence and Public Papers*, I, 366; Sparks, *Morris*, I, 223–24. For the date of the accident, see William Clajon to Gouverneur Morris, May 22, 1780, Horatio Gates Papers, Box 14, No. 43, New-York Historical Society; Jacob Hiltzheimer, "Extracts from the Diary of Jacob Hiltzheimer of Philadelphia, 1768–1798," *Pennsylvania Magazine of History and Biography*, Vol. XVI (January, 1892), 101.

[4] John W. Francis to Henry B. Dawson, November 17, 1860, *The Historical Magazine*, Vol. III (April, 1868), 194. Francis, secretary of the New-York Historical Society, knew Morris in his later years.

[5] Sparks, *Morris*, I, 223.

forth latent virtues that will enhance his merit, and consequently increase the esteem of which he is already the object." There were also wagging tongues that used his reputation as a *bon vivant* to spread a story that reached John Jay in Madrid. "I have learned," wrote Jay to Morris, "that a certain married woman after much use of your legs had occasioned your losing one." The tale had it that Morris had broken his leg when jumping from a lady's window to escape discovery. "I suppose," Morris replied, "it was Deane who wrote to you from France abt. the loss of my Leg. His Acct. is facetious. Let it pass. The Leg is gone and there is an end of the Matter."[6]

During his convalescence he stayed in the home of a friend, George Plater, a congressman from Maryland. Plater's wife, Eliz abeth, nursed Morris with more than ordinary kindness. Several years older than Morris, she was beautiful and, according to a visitor from France, "typical of Philadelphia's charming women; her taste is as delicate as her health: an enthusiast to excess for all French fashions, she is only waiting for the end of this little revolution to effect a still greater one in the manners of her country."[7] On Morris' part her attentions aroused more than gratitude. When the Platers returned to their Maryland home, at "Sotterly," in St. Marys County, Morris corresponded with "Eliza" through her cousin's wife, Mrs. William Bennett (Joanna) Lloyd, of Annapolis. He sent her roses and told her of the nervous headaches

[6] Robert R. Livingston to George Clinton, May 18, 1780, PPGC, V, 717; Francis to Henry B. Dawson, November 17, 1860, The Historical Magazine, Vol. III (April, 1868), 194; Mrs. Robert Morris to Mrs. John Jay, July 12, 1781 [1780], in Jay, Correspondence and Public Papers, I, 375n.; Mrs. John Jay to Mrs. Robert Morris, September 1, 1780, in William F. Boogher (ed.), Miscellaneous Americana, a Collection of History, Biography, and Genealogy, 29; John Jay to Gouverneur Morris, November 5, 1780, as quoted in Monaghan, John Jay, 219; entry of August 30, 1791, "Diary of the Second Viscount Palmerston in France, July 6–August 31, 1791," in Viscount Palmerston, The Despatches of Earl Gower . . . and the Diary of Viscount Palmerston in France during July and August 1791 (ed. by Oscar Browning), 308; Gouverneur Morris to John Jay, May 7, 1781, Gouverneur Morris Collection.

[7] Marquis de Chastellux, Travels in North America in the Years 1780, 1781 and 1782 (tr. and ed. by Howard G. Rice, Jr.), I, 135.

afflicting him, an affliction she shared with him, and she implored him to leave his work and seek relaxation. Ten years later, on May 5, 1790, at a dinner party in London, he met Mrs. Lloyd, who in the interval had married Francis Lowe Beckford, of Baring Park, England, and learned from her that Eliza had died on November 23 of the previous year. "I get away as soon as possible," he wrote in his diary, "that I may not discover Emotions which I cannot conceal. Poor Eliza! My lovely friend; thou art then at Peace and I shall behold thee no more. Never, never, never."[8]

The accident and resulting surgery immobilized him for six months. He could no longer accept the post as secretary to Benjamin Franklin in Paris, and on July 17 he sent a letter to the president of the Congress, informing him that "many Reasons" compelled him to decline the appointment.[9] By November 25 he was sufficiently recovered for Robert R. Livingston to congratulate him on his "restoration to the beau monde," and he replied that it was, indeed, "like a resurrection from the grave."[10] He was fitted with a simple wooden leg, which became his hallmark for the rest of his life. He once experimented with a copper leg but found it too cumbersome. His last wooden leg, a thirty-nine-inch long oak peg with a leather-covered rest between two securing arms, can be seen today at the New-York Historical Society. He sometimes fell on muddy or icy ground and would curse his misfortune, and he always remembered that he had put on one white stocking inside-out on the day of the fatal accident. Yet he resumed his activities as jauntily as ever. He took walks with friends and went horseback riding (and later, at the age of fifty-one, would not hesitate to ride the rapids of the St. Lawrence River in Canada). He returned to his law practice, and was admitted to the bar of the

[8] Eliza Plater to Gouverneur Morris, February 25, 1782, Gouverneur Morris Collection; Marquis de Barbé-Marbois to Gouverneur Morris, February 2, 1784, Historical Society of Pennsylvania; entry of May 5, 1790, GMDFR, I, 486n., 504 and n. Mrs. Beckford's first husband was Richard Bennett Lloyd.

[9] Papers of the Continental Congress, XVI, Letters M, No. 78, fol. 73.

[10] Morris to Livingston [December, 1780], Robert R. Livingston Papers, New-York Historical Society.

Supreme Court of Pennsylvania. To judge from one legal fee of four thousand dollars, he prospered in his profession.[11]

Socially, he rebounded as gaily as ever. The French consul at Philadelphia, the Marquis de Barbé-Marbois, has left an eyewitness account of a party Morris attended at Chester, fifteen miles west of Philadelphia on the Delaware River. A small group left Philadelphia for dinner there on a Sunday. They had a jovial time and drank a considerable quantity of champagne, just received from France. Morris, "whom the champagne had apparently made pretty drunk," got into a little, one-passenger sulky for a drive, and Mrs. William Bingham, the beautiful and vivacious sixteen-year-old wife of a wealthy but unprepossessing merchant, squeezed in beside him. Her alarmed husband, too drunk to overtake her himself, sent the fastest runner in the company after them. But when the pursuer succeeded in stopping the carriage, she refused to get out. "Madam," he pleaded, "it is your husband's command." She only called and waved good-by and whipped up the horses to go on.[12]

Early in 1780, as Morris watched public affairs, now from the sidelines, he saw the first real hope of the creation of national executive departments. The treasury had been declared bankrupt, a rebellion of the army had been only barely averted, and inefficiency and corruption were widespread. In this crisis it was proposed to appoint ministers of permanent departments of finance, war, marine, and foreign affairs. While the debates were going on, Morris made notes of the qualities he thought necessary in these ministers. The minister of finance should be "not only a

[11] Morris was admitted on April 2, 1781. Sheriff's Deed Book B, Supreme Court, "List of Attorneys Admitted in the Supreme Court of the Commonwealth of Pennsylvania," Prothonotary's Office, Philadelphia City Hall; Swiggett, *The Extraordinary Mr. Morris*, 88.

[12] Barbé-Marbois, *Our Revolutionary Forefathers*, 167–68; Anna Rawle to Mrs. Rebecca Shoemaker, November 4, 1780, in William Brooke Rawle, "Laurel Hill and Some Colonial Dames Who Once Lived There," *Pennsylvania Magazine of History and Biography*, Vol. XXXV, No. 4 (1911), 398.

regular bred merchant, but one who has been long and deeply engaged in the profession . . . and he should enjoy general credit and reputation, both at home and abroad"—an obvious reference to his friend Robert Morris. The minister of war "should be taken from the army, and have acted at some time or other as a quartermaster general, if not as a commander of a separate department" —a pointed recommendation of General Nathanael Greene. The minister of foreign affairs should know law, history, and the French and Spanish languages, he should be "educated more in the world than in the closet, . . . and he should by no means be disagreeable to the Prince, with whom we are in alliance."[13] Since the Chevalier Anne-César de la Luzerne, who had replaced Gérard as the French minister, favored Robert R. Livingston,[14] it would appear that Morris had his friend in mind. The Congress approved the creation of these posts and did indeed name Robert Morris, Greene, and Livingston. Robert Morris and Livingston accepted, but Greene, despite Gouverneur's efforts at persuasion, declined in favor of his army position.

As soon as Robert Morris took office as superintendent of finance on May 14, 1781, he asked Gouverneur to serve as his assistant. The request was informal, because the Congress had not yet officially created the post, but Gouverneur agreed. When a salary of $1,850 was provided for on July 6, Robert wrote Gouverneur a formal offer of the official position of assistant to the superintendent of finance:

I trembled at the arduous task I had reluctantly undertaken aided by your Talents and abilities I feel better Courage, and dare indulge the fond hope that uniting our utmost exertions in the service of our Country we may be able to extricate it from the present embarrassments. . . . My entire conviction of the great and essential services which your genius, Talents and capacity enable you to render to your Country and of that aid, ease,

[13] Sparks, *Morris*, I, 229–30.
[14] Dangerfield, *Chancellor Robert R. Livingston*, 140.

and confidence you can and will administer to my own exertions and feelings never left me one moment to hesitate about the choice I should make.[15]

Gouverneur, in accepting, told Robert:

Your Industry, your Abilities, and above all your Integrity will extricate America from her Distresses; & consequently, Malice will blacken and Envy traduce you. I will freely share in this bitter Portion of Eminence.[16]

He took the oath of office on August 8 before Thomas McKean, president of the Congress.[17] The ensuing three and a half years during which the two Morrises held office together were marked by a singular record of complementary effectiveness and mutual understanding. "I could do nothing without [Gouverneur]," wrote Robert to John Jay, "and our quiet labours do but just keep the wheels in motion." Later he commented that Gouverneur "has more virtue than he shows, and more consistency, than anybody believes."[18]

But there were many in Philadelphia who were alienated by Gouverneur's proud and often heedless brilliance. "Mr. Gouverneur Morris is the Financier's assistant, and censorious people say his director,"[19] said Joseph Reed, Gouverneur's old antagonist of Valley Forge days. A Dutch visitor, Gijsbert Karel van Hogendorp, observed in April, 1784:

Gouverneur Morris is not comparable to Robert. He has talents and much knowledge, but he has not a bit of character. He is very callous, and prides himself on being so; but he is vain, and unaware of it. His oratory is powerful, but studied. An air

15 July 6, 1781, Gouverneur Morris Collection. See also entry of August 4, 1781, Robert Morris Diary in the Office of Finance, I, Library of Congress.
16 July 7, 1781, New York State Library, Albany.
17 Entry of August 8, 1781, Robert Morris Diary, I.
18 January 3, 1783, and November 4, 1783, Jay, *Correspondence and Public Papers*, III, 13, 95.
19 To Nathanael Greene, November 1, 1781, W. B. Reed, *Life and Correspondence of Joseph Reed*, II, 376.

of superiority which he affects, to which everyone around yields, would leave him easily, I think, if his equal in talents came forward to crush him. He is a lawyer by profession, he is a master of subtlety and irony. He does not allow conversation to flag. One easily detects in him a touch of pedantry, and a little solid learning which entirely lacks method; but his brilliant qualities cover all these defects.[20]

On balance, the fairest estimate of Gouverneur was probably that of a Frenchman, the Prince de Broglie, in 1782:

One of the men, who appeared to me to possess the most spirit and nerve amongst those whom I met at Philadelphia, was a Mr. Morris, generally called Governor. He is very well educated, speaks excellent French, is very sarcastic but generally liked. I fancy however that his superiority, which he has taken no pains to conceal, will prevent his ever occupying an important place.[21]

When Gouverneur pledged himself to share freely in Robert's exposure to public abuse, he was already embroiled in a virulent press war between Robert and his enemies. On May 23 two pieces appeared in the *Freeman's Journal,* one castigating Robert for leaving Philadelphia for Princeton at a time when Philadelphia was threatened with capture by the enemy and the other assailing Gouverneur for asking permission to visit his mother, who was ailing with dropsy, in British-occupied New York. Gouverneur had it on good authority that the author of both articles was Sir James Jay, brother of John Jay.[22] The letter about Gouverneur, signed "Many," charged that his proposed trip to New York

---

[20] Graaf Gijsbert Karl van Hogendorp, *Brieven en Gedenkschriften van Gijsbert Karel van Hogendorp, uitgegeven door zijn jongsten, thans eenigen Zoon* (ed. by F. Van Hogendorp), I, 349.

[21] Prince de Broglie, "Narrative of the Prince de Broglie [1782], Translated from an Unpublished MS," *Magazine of American History, with Notes and Queries,* Vol. I (tr. by E. W. Balch), (March, 1871), 234.

[22] Morris named the author as "Sir J—— J——." [To Robert Morris] May 22, 1781, New York State Library, Albany.

would endanger the security of confidential information in his possession.[23]

Gouverneur replied, in a letter published over his name on May 30, that his mother's health had improved, that the New York State council had not given him permission to visit her, and that he was no longer planning to do so. The explanation did not silence his detractors. The abuse mounted in a series of published letters which ran the gamut of personal slander and revived disputes going back to 1778. A writer who signed himself "Lucius" told Gouverneur that "your disposition and principles totally disqualify you for a seat in Congress; or for any other place where a uniform adherence to public virtue is necessary"; charged that he wanted to see his mother because "the old lady had some property to leave, and might make a disposition of it to your disadvantage"; quoted Gouverneur as having written Benedict Arnold that he had helped jettison the proposed American expedition to Canada in 1778; and accused him of leaving his post in Congress in 1779 in order to electioneer in New York for reappointment. "A Citizen" revived the charges in connection with the Deane affair of 1779; accused him of engaging in trade and befriending Tories; and paid him the gratuitous compliment of calling him "an ingenious orator, who possesses an exuberant fertility of invention, and is capable of decorating the product of imagination with all the ornaments of language."[24]

Gouverneur scornfully answered that "if members of Congress are subjected to the enquiry of every idler who thinks proper to question the motives of their conduct," they would be degraded and have no time for business. An unsigned article defended his opposition to the Canadian expedition on the ground that it

[23] Letter of May 23, 1781, in *Freeman's Journal*, May 30, 1781. On Morris' request for passage to New York, see William S. Livingston to George Clinton, March 12, 1781, PPGC, VI, 682; Swiggett, *The Extraordinary Mr. Morris*, 83.
[24] "Lucius" to Gouverneur Morris, *Freeman's Journal*, June 6 and July 4, 1781; "A Citizen," *ibid.*, June 6 and June 27, 1781.

had been ill-considered and that Conway had been chosen as second-in-command at a time when he should have been dismissed for insubordination.[25]

All this, together with a heavy burden of official duties, the one-legged Gouverneur buoyantly endured. "If you see the Doctor," he told Robert, "tell him that Fatiguing from four in the Morning till eight in the Evening & sleeping only from eleven till three agrees with me much better than all the Prescriptions in all the phisical Books in all the Languages of all the World."[26]

The finance office opened for business in a house belonging to one William West on Front Street. In June, 1782, it was moved to a store rented from Jacob Barge at the corner of Market and Fifth streets.[27] To that office came the most prominent political and military men of the revolutionary government. The superintendent of finance was easily the pivotal figure of the government, and soon a semiofficial cabinet formed under his leadership. The members consisted of the two Morrises, Secretary of War Benjamin Lincoln, Secretary of Foreign Affairs Robert R. Livingston, Commander in Chief George Washington, and Secretary of Congress Charles Thomson. They met by agreement every Monday morning. "Finance, my Friend," wrote Gouverneur to John Jay, "the whole of what remains in the American Revolution grounds there."[28]

The task confronting the Morrises was the revival of public credit from virtual collapse. The general economic condition of

[25] Letter by Gouverneur Morris, June 14, 1781, *ibid.*, June 20, 1781; unsigned article, "Extracts from Journals of Congress, & Letters to Explain a Peace signed LUCIUS in *Freeman's Journal* of July 4, 1781," *ibid.*, July 18, 1781. "Lucius" published an open letter to Morris, dated July 21, *ibid.*, July 25, 1781, charging that Morris was the author of the unsigned article.

[26] To Robert Morris, June 4, 1781 [draft], Gouverneur Morris Collection.

[27] Entry of June 11, 1782, Robert Morris Diary, II.

[28] March 31, 1781 [draft], Gouverneur Morris Collection. On Robert Morris' political power, see Merrill Jensen, *The New Nation: A History of the United States During the Confederation, 1781–1789*, 55–60, 366; E. James Ferguson, *The Power of the Purse: A History of American Public Finance, 1776–1790*, 119–21.

the country in 1781 was good, but under the Articles of Confederation the Congress lacked the power to levy direct taxes on this wealth. The methods used to finance the Revolution were, in descending order of importance, bills of credit (paper money), domestic loans (government bonds), requisitions upon the states, and foreign loans. By the spring of 1781 all these resources had been exhausted. Paper money, the major source, had depreciated to a point where the cost of printing it was greater than its value. Domestic loans also suffered acutely from depreciation. The states were themselves in too great difficulties to honor requisitions. France had halted its loans to its ally. In the crisis the army was nearly naked and on the verge of starvation.[29]

The first remedy which the superintendent of finance proposed was the establishment of a national bank, to be called the Bank of North America. The recommendation, which was drafted by Gouverneur, was sent to Congress on May 17, 1781. "The first Bank, in this Country," Gouverneur later wrote, "was planned by your humble Servant."[30] The idea had been under discussion for some time. Alexander Hamilton had sent a similar, detailed proposal to Robert Morris shortly before. Gouverneur was also familiar with Sir James Steuart's *Inquiry into the Principles of Political Oeconomy*, the foremost work of the day on banking and mercantilism.[31] The final plan provided for an institution with a capital of $400,000 in shares of $400, to be paid in gold or silver. The bank was to have power to issue bank notes, which were to be honored by the government in payment of duties and taxes.

[29] Ver Steeg, *Robert Morris*, 43–57.

[30] Entry of May 17, 1781, Robert Morris Diary, I; Gouverneur Morris to Moss Kent, March 15, 1816, Private Correspondence, Papers of Gouverneur Morris, Library of Congress.

[31] Alexander Hamilton to Robert Morris, April 30, 1781, Hamilton, *Papers*, II, 604–35. Robert replied that "finding many points of it to Coincide with my own Opinions on the Subject, it naturally Strengthened that Confidence which every man ought to possess to a certain degree in his own judgment." May 26, 1781, *ibid.*, 645. Gouverneur Morris to President of the Bank, June 18, 1781 [draft], Gouverneur Morris Collection; Fritz Redlich, *The Molding of American Banking: Men and Ideas, 1781–1784*, I, 5–7; E. A. J. Johnson, *Predecessors of Adam Smith: The Growth of British Economic Thought*, 211.

The superintendent of finance was to have access to the records of the bank at all times. Congress approved the plan on May 26, 1781.

Robert Morris' purpose in creating the bank was to secure private resources to bolster public credit and cement the interest of private business to public finance. Stock subscriptions, however, were slow in coming. Fortunately, John Laurens, Henry Laurens' son, arrived in a French frigate at Boston with a loan from the French treasury of 2,500,000 livres in silver ($254,000), which was transported to Philadelphia by sixteen ox teams. The loan enabled Robert to subscribe $254,000 for government shares of bank stock. On December 31, 1781, Congress officially incorporated the bank. The next day Gouverneur purchased one share of stock at $400. The bank opened its doors to the public on January 7, 1782, in a building on the north side of Chestnut Street, west of Third. At first it was a struggle to keep enough silver in the bank to secure public confidence. Among the devices used was an endless chain of containers, filled with silver coin, which traveled from the vaults to the cashier's cage in full view of visitors.[32] Cornwallis' army had surrendered at Yorktown on October 19, 1781, several months before the bank had begun operations. The war continued in name, however, for almost two years. The bank helped to spur the renewal of peacetime commerce and provided short-term loans to the government. For a brief time it held a monopoly of banking in America. Barely two years later, however, it was fighting for survival against the challenge of agrarian enemies in the Pennsylvania legislature.

The second remedy for the national financial crisis was the use of the famous "Morris notes," a paper issue released by the Office of Finance and signed by Robert Morris himself, who thus pledged his own credit in support of the public debt. The notes were in

---

[32] "An Alphabetical List of the First Subscribers to the Bank of North America," Records of the Bank of North America, Historical Society of Pennsylvania; Ferguson, *Power of the Purse*, 136–38; Eleanor Young, *Forgotten Patriot: Robert Morris*, 122.

twenty-, fifty-, and eighty-dollar denominations and were payable to the bearer at sight. They were circulated widely, supplied needed public funds, and served as a medium of exchange.

The third remedy was a proposal for the establishment of a national mint. A national coinage would bolster national credit, facilitate commerce, and free the United States from dependence upon supplies of foreign coin. Gouverneur prepared the recommendation in the form of a report, which was submitted to Congress on January 18, 1782, in Robert's name. The report was the result of careful preparation. Gouverneur began by studying all the coins currently in circulation. He again consulted Steuart's *Political Oeconomy*. He became convinced that the national system must be a decimal one, with a small minimum unit for very small purchases, and must be exchangeable for the currency of the states without fractional remainders. In order to begin with a coin which was widely familiar and stable in value, he chose the Spanish silver dollar. He subdivided it into the maximum fractional unit which could be exchangeable in some even multiple for any state currency except the hopelessly confused one of South Carolina. It turned out to be 1/1,440 dollar, or a quarter of a grain of pure silver. He named this basic unit the quarter and developed the following decimal hierarchy of coins from it:

	Units
Crown	10,000
Dollar	1,000
Bill	100
Penny	10
Quarter	1

The congressional committee of the states discussed the report in a long session with both Morrises and unanimously voted acceptance on February 16, 1782. Complete acceptance by Congress itself, however, was delayed for some years. In 1784 a new committee under Thomas Jefferson was appointed to consider the coinage. He agreed that the decimal system should be introduced but rejected the basic unit of the quarter as too small. He preferred the dollar as the basic unit, subdivided only one hundred times. Gouverneur objected that this division disregarded the element of interchangeability, which was essential if the national coinage was to supplant the state systems. He altered his plan to specify a larger interchangeable basic unit, this time not an even fraction of the dollar.[33] Jefferson's plan, however, was adopted in August, 1786.

The fourth financial remedy was the introduction of a new contracting system for supplying the Continental armies. The new system required contractors to deliver their provisions directly to the soldiers who used them, so that no government funds would be paid for spoiled, damaged, destroyed, or nontransportable supplies. Gouverneur was very much involved in these arrangements, for which his congressional experience as chairman of the quartermaster, commissary, clothier general, and medical committees had amply prepared him. The new system supplied the troops more effectively than before, though it did not always work smoothly.[34]

It is probably no exaggeration to say that these measures, and the vigor and efficiency with which they were administered, averted financial catastrophe for the Confederation.

About a month and a half after Yorktown, on December 6, 1781, Sir Henry Clinton, the British commander in New York, proposed that commissioners from both sides meet to discuss exchange of prisoners and arrangements for the expenses of maintaining them. Washington, who had already been discussing similar plans with Robert Morris, accepted Clinton's proposal and

[33] Entries of January 18 and February 17, 1782, Robert Morris Diary, I; Papers of the Continental Congress, III, No. 137, 397A; Gouverneur Morris to Mr. Helmsley, April 30, 1785 [copy], Thomas Jefferson Papers, IX, Library of Congress. (The letter to Helmsley is datelined Philadelphia. Either the date or the place is incorrect, since Morris was in Virginia in April, 1785. Sparks, *Morris*, I, 277–79.)
[34] Ver Steeg, *Robert Morris*, 41–52; Ferguson, *Power of the Purse*, 131–33.

named Brigadier General Henry Knox as his military representative and Gouverneur as Robert's financial representative. They were instructed by two resolutions of Congress to explore the possibility of exchanging Henry Laurens, recently captured by the British while on his way to negotiate a treaty with Holland, for Cornwallis and also to obtain information about the British Board of Directors of the Associated Loyalists. The Americans were to meet the British—Major General William Dalrymple, Clinton's quartermaster general, and Andrew Elliot, superintendent general of the police of New York—at Elizabethtown, New Jersey, on March 28, 1782.[35]

The American representatives left Philadelphia on March 12 and arrived at Elizabethtown at noon on March 16. The next morning they received a letter from Washington, informing them that Clinton had requested a postponement of the negotiations until April 10. After a further exchange of notes Clinton agreed on a meeting date of March 28. In the meantime, the two Americans left Elizabethtown to wait in Morris County. They returned on March 28, but, "the Wind being hard at West," the British commissioners did not arrive by sea from New York until March 30, and the first meeting was held on Sunday, March 31.[36]

It quickly became apparent that the differences between the two sides were too great to permit ready resolution. The British, furthermore, were not even empowered to negotiate an over-all agreement on prisoners. They wanted the return of their soldiers, including Burgoyne's 4,880 troops, which according to the Convention of Saratoga were to have been shipped to England but had not been permitted to depart. Knox and Morris were willing to

[35] Entry of December 5, 1781, Robert Morris Diary, I; JCC, XXI, 1150–51, 1181.
[36] Henry Knox and Gouverneur Morris to George Washington, March 16, 22, and 29, 1782, Papers of George Washington; Henry Knox and Gouverneur Morris to Sir Henry Clinton, March 21, 1782, ibid.; Sir Henry Clinton to George Washington, March 23, 1782, ibid.; George Washington to President of Congress, April 30, 1782 [copy], enclosing complete record of all official correspondence of Washington, Clinton, and Knox and Morris relating to the negotiations, ibid.

exchange British soldiers for captured American civilians, but not for captured seamen. They offered to accept £200,000 for all past prisoner-maintenance obligations. The British refused the offer, preferring to pay for redcoats' maintenance with money to be used to purchase supplies in American territory, where the scarce hard cash would yield maximum returns. Knox and Morris offered to accept £50,000 for current prisoner expenditures, but Dalrymple and Elliot refused. Since no general agreement seemed feasible, the Americans did not even introduce the question of exchanging Cornwallis for Laurens.

Morris' old mentor, Chief Justice William Smith, followed the proceedings from his home in New York City. On April 5 he noted in his diary that he had learned from General Robertson that Dalrymple and Elliot were not empowered to negotiate the exchange of Laurens for Cornwallis and that Knox and Morris had refused any further discussions until this issue was made viable. On April 11 he received a letter from a Tory in Elizabethtown (almost certainly Henry Van Schaack, Peter's brother) reporting that Dalrymple had engaged in treasonable talk with Morris. He repeated this information to Elliot, who apparently took it up frankly with Knox and Morris, who in turn acquitted Dalrymple.[37]

As a matter of fact, it does appear that Morris gained some information from Dalrymple. In a letter to Robert Morris, written on the first day of the negotiations, he said that he had had "some very free conversation" with Dalrymple.[38] In a private letter to Washington, Knox and Morris supplied information on conditions inside the British lines. It is possible that some of this information came from Dalrymple. The Loyalist army corps, they wrote, were apprehensive of being sent off to service in the West Indies. The inhabitants of New York, disgusted with British con-

[37] Entries of April 5, 11 and 13, 1782, William Smith Diary. Smith named his source as "Mr. Van Scaak at Eliza Town." It was most likely Henry Van Schaack, who sometimes met his wife and other Kinderhook, New York, friends at Elizabeth Town in 1782. Van Schaack, *Memoirs of the Life of Henry Van Schaack*, 88. Washington warned Knox to protect Morris against an unnamed traitor. March 30, 1782, Washington, *Writings*, XXIV, 94.

[38] March 31, 1782, Gouverneur Morris Collection.

duct of the war and concerned lest the British leave them high and dry, were smuggling private funds to American-held territory for safekeeping. The guarantee of a pardon to these people, said Knox and Morris, would encourage them to abandon the British. There was bitter enmity between the British army and the board of directors appointed by the British ministry to promote the welfare and exchange of captured Loyalists. An American prisoner, Captain Joshua Huddy of the New Jersey line, had been hanged while in British custody, and the board had charged that the army had murdered him without Clinton's knowledge. Knox and Morris suggested that the American execution of a British officer in retaliation would inflame the hatred.[39]

With American passions exacerbated by the news of Huddy's hanging, and with the failure of the commissioners to agree on any basic terms, the negotiations reached an impasse. The representatives of both sides parted on April 20, and Knox and Morris retired to the nearby town of Basking Ridge, probably to the home of Morris' brother-in-law Samuel Ogden, to frame their report to Washington. On April 26, Morris was back at his desk in the Office of Finance.[40]

The capstone of Robert Morris' financial program was a comprehensive plan for funding the public debt. Gouverneur drafted this proposal, which was submitted to Congress on July 29, 1782, as the "Report on Public Credit." It has been described by Clarence L. Ver Steeg, historian of Revolutionary War finance, as "the most important single state paper on public credit ever written prior to Hamilton's First Report on Public Credit. Indeed, its sweep, boldness, and scope might well have provided Washington's Secretary of the Treasury with a model."[41] Its origin can be traced to

[39] Knox and Morris to Washington, April 21, 1782, enclosed in Washington to President of Congress, April 30, 1782, Papers of George Washington.
[40] Entry of April 26, 1782, Robert Morris Diary, II.
[41] Ver Steeg, Robert Morris, 124.

Gouverneur's "An American" letters on finance in the *Pennsylvania Packet* in 1780.

The plan was for the national government to assume, at face value, the total Revolutionary War debt, estimated at twenty-five to twenty-seven million dollars. In exchange for previous government-debt certificates a new loan would be issued, bearing 6 per cent interest. The purpose of this proposal, as of the other parts of the program, was to tie public to private credit on a national basis. The anticipated benefits were release of tied-up resources of creditors, foreign investment in the funded debt, and the emergence of hoarded funds. The sources of revenue proposed were a 5 per cent ad valorem duty on imports, a land tax of one dollar for every hundred acres, a poll tax of one dollar on all freemen and all male slaves between the ages of sixteen and sixty, and an excise tax of an eighth of a dollar a gallon on alcoholic beverages. Each of these sources, it was estimated, would yield half a million dollars yearly, thus paying, in their total, the six per cent annual interest of two million dollars on the entire debt.[42]

On this major issue the "nationalists" formed ranks against the "antinationalists" in a two-month-long battle in Congress. The two Morrises considered the program the determining factor of financial policy. The opposition was so strong, however, that the only hope of success lay in external pressures on Congress. If all classes of creditors would combine to demand payment of the public debt, Congress might be persuaded. Robert wrote:

> It is with pleasure that I see this numerous, meritorious and oppressed body of men, who are creditors of the Public, beginning to assert themselves for the obtaining of justice. I hope they may succeed, not only because I wish well to a righteous pursuit, but because this success will be the great groundwork of a credit which will carry us safely through the present just, important and necessary war, which will combine us closely together on the conclusion of a peace, which will always give to

42 JCC, XXII, 429-46.

the Supreme Representative of America a means of acting for the General Defense on sudden emergencies and which will of consequence procure the third of those great objects for which we contend—*Peace, Liberty, and Safety.*[43]

Gouverneur believed that there was a promising sign in what he saw as an awakening of the people to the inadequacies of the Confederation. To capitalize on this opportunity for invigorated government, he wished to see the war prolonged and the peace delayed, until a fibered financial structure could be erected. In a cogent letter to Greene on December 24, 1781, he wrote:

> Conviction goes but very slowly to the popular Mind but it goes. The Advantages of Union and Decision in carrying on a War.... The Waste and Expence and In Efficacy of disjointed Efforts over the Face of an immense Region   The Incompetency of determining what is best for the whole thro thirteen different Communities whose Rulers are yet ignorant what is best for the single one which they govern. . . . These must at last induce the People of America (if the war continues) to entrust proper Powers to the American Sovereign as they have already compelled that Sovereign reluctantly to relinquish the Administration & entrust to their Ministers the Care of this immense Republic—I say *if the War continues* for if it does not I have no Hope or Expectation that the Government will acquire Force *and I will go farther I have no Hope that our Union can subsist except in the Form of an absolute Monarchy* and this does not seem to consist with *the Taste and Temper of the People.*[44]

At that moment the most pressing of the public creditors was the army. Washington's forces, in their winter encampment in the wooded hills behind Newburgh, had become desperate for lack of pay, food, and supplies. On January 1, 1783, three of their officers, Major General Alexander McDougall and Colonels Mat-

---

[43] *Ibid.*, 435.
[44] To Nathanael Greene, December 24, 1781, Nathanael Greene Papers, William L. Clements Library, University of Michigan.

thias Ogden of the New Jersey line and John Brooks of the Massachusetts line, arrived in Philadelphia to petition Congress for redress of the army's grievances. Gouverneur welcomed this development as the needed impetus to force Congress to enact financial reform. That same day he exultantly wrote to Jay of his high hopes:

The Army have Swords in their Hands. . . . I will add however that I am glad to see Things in their present Train. Depend on it good will arise from the Situation to which we are hastening. And this you may rely on that my Efforts will not be wanting. I pledge myself to you on the present occasion, and altho I think it probable that much Convulsion will ensue Yet it must terminate in giving to Government that Power without which Government is but a Name. Government in America is not possessed of it but the People are well prepared. Wearied with the War, their Acquiescence may be depended on with absolute Certainty and you and I my Friend know by Experience that when a few Men of Sense and Spirit get together and declare that they are the Authority such few as are of a different Opinion may easily be convinced of their Mistake by that powerful Argument the Halter. . . . On the Wisdom of the present Moment depends more than is easily imagined and when I look round for the Actors— — — Let us change the Subject.[45]

It seems clear that he also spoke for Robert Morris, who could not so freely avow such sentiments.

The army officers presented their petition to Congress on January 6. "The uneasiness of the soldiers for want of pay is great and dangerous," they warned; "further experiments on their patience may have fatal effects."[46] The next evening the congressional committee reviewing the memorial conferred with Robert

[45] To John Jay, January 1, 1783, Gouverneur Morris Collection. See also Gouverneur Morris to Matthew Ridley, August 6, 1782, and January 1, 1783, Ridley Papers, Massachusetts Historical Society.

[46] Quoted in George Bancroft, *History of the United States of America from the Discovery of the Continent*, VI, 59.

Morris on the availability of funds to grant the officers' request. Morris flatly declared that he had no funds or any possibility of obtaining them unless some firm measures were adopted. Presented with this bleak picture, the committee met with the officers on the evening of the thirteenth. The officers bluntly stated that an immediate installment of pay would have to be issued if a mutiny was to be averted. McDougall vehemently declared that the army was "verging to that state, which, we are told, will make a wise man mad."[47] In its report to Congress the committee recommended some conciliatory payment to the army as soon as possible but could only agree with Robert Morris that the real answer depended on providing general revenues for the funding of the national debt. The report, drafted by Morris' ally, Alexander Hamilton, also recommended that the army be given no priority over other creditors.

Robert Morris concluded that this was the decisive moment to apply the ultimate pressure at his command. On January 24, the day the committee's report was scheduled to reach the floor, he submitted a letter of resignation, declaring that he would vacate his office by May 31 unless "permanent provision for the public debts of every kind" was made by that date.[48] Publication of the letter would, he hoped, arouse the army and other creditors and force Congress into action. Congress, however, to prevent this crisis, committed the letter to secrecy. The committee report was debated for two months, with no conclusive solution to the restoration of public credit. Morris was requested to remain in office until payment of the army could be completed, since that payment depended on use of the "Morris notes." On February 5, on the precarious credit of bills drawn on loans still under negotiation from Holland and France, he issued one month's pay to the

[47] James Madison, *Papers* (ed. by H. D. Gilpin), I, 257.
[48] Robert Morris to President of Congress, January 24, 1783, in *Pennsylvania Gazette*, March 5, 1873. Congress later granted a formal request by Robert Morris, dated February 26, 1783, to make his resignation public.

officers in notes and one month's pay to the soldiers in installments of half a dollar a week—a total of $253,232.86.[49]

Gouverneur now privately resorted to direct appeals to the army for action. On February 7, he wrote a straightforward letter to Knox of the northern army and on February 13 wrote one to Greene of the southern army. Efforts to obtain compensation from the separate states were futile, he warned them. The army must unite with the nation's other creditors and compel justice. "During the war they find you useful and after a peace they will wish to get rid of you and then they will see you starve rather than pay you a six-penny tax," he told Knox. The two field commanders rejected this appeal to force. "As the present constitution is so defective," replied Knox, "why do not you great men call the people together and tell them so. That is, to have a convention of the States to form a better constitution? This appears to us, who have a superficial view only, to be the most efficacious remedy." Greene wanted no part of mutiny or its consequences: "When soldiers advance without authority, who can halt them? We have many Clodiuses and Catilines in America, who may give a different direction to this business, than either you or I expect."[50]

The discontented army, however, found its own leaders. Incited by the anonymous circulars which have since become known as the "Newburgh Addresses," a budding officers' mutiny was narrowly averted by Washington, who discovered it in time to dissuade the participants in a dramatic appeal at a meeting in camp on March 15. The addresses had been written by Major John Armstrong, aide-de-camp to Gates, though some people suspected Gouverneur of being the author.[51] A minor mutiny did occur in

[49] Bancroft, History of the United States, VI, 62, 62n.; Madison, Papers, I, 252, 275.

[50] Morris to Knox, February 7, 1783, as quoted in Louis C. Hatch, The Administration of the American Revolutionary Army, 164; Morris to Greene, February 15, 1783, Sparks, Morris, I, 250–51; Knox to Morris, February 21, 1783, Gouverneur Morris Collection; Greene to Morris, April 3, 1783, Sparks, Morris, I, 251–52.

[51] Ibid., 252–53; Richard H. Kohn, "The Inside History of the Newburgh Conspiracy: America and the Coup d'État," William and Mary Quarterly, Vol. XXVII (April, 1970), 187–213.

Philadelphia, where a motley array of about three hundred raw recruits of the Pennsylvania line surrounded Congress and the Pennsylvania council (both of which were meeting in the State House) to demand their pay. Gouverneur and others attempted to pacify them, but when the Pennsylvania state authorities refused to call out the militia to restore order, Congress adjourned to Princeton, and the Morrises followed. When a rumor spread that Washington was sending troops to suppress the uprising, the insurgents submitted to the president of Pennsylvania.[52]

The crisis prompted the Congress to placate the army officers by commuting their pensions of half pay for life to a lump sum of five years' full pay. This and the other remaining war debts were made national, rather than state, obligations. Although the Morrises and their adherents had failed to obtain passage of a national program of taxation, they had at least succeeded in establishing a formal national debt which sooner or later would make it necessary for the national government to be strengthened in order to discharge it.[53]

On March 23 news arrived that a provisional treaty had been signed with Britain. On April 11, Congress announced receipt of the official treaty and proclaimed the cessation of hostilities. The final peace treaty was signed in Paris on September 3, 1783.

Thus the war ended without consummation of the funding program. There is some doubt whether it would have succeeded at that time, for commerce had declined and revenue might have been insufficient to meet the interest on the funded debt.[54] The ground had been prepared, however, to condition men's minds for national unification at a later date.

[52] Bancroft, *History of the United States*, VI, 97; entry of September 2, 1783, Robert Morris Diary, III.

[53] Ferguson, *Power of the Purse*, 164, 145; Jackson Turner Main, *The Antifederalists: Critics of the Constitution*, 86, 106–107.

[54] Ver Steeg, *Robert Morris*, 195.

Unofficial and Private

CHAPTER VIII

ORRIS, who had been deeply involved in the divisions of family and friends which the war had wrought, hoped earnestly that the return of peace would quietly close the old wounds. "My own heart, worn by the succession of objects which have invaded it, looks back with more than female fondness towards the connections of earlier days," he wrote to Peter Van Schaack, who had reopened their correspondence from England. Van Schaack asked, "If you should happen to go to Kinderhook, let me beg it as a particular favor, that you will see my dear boy," and in his reply Morris promised to do so. Returning to a favorite theme, he added, "I would open wide the doors of that temple which we have reared to liberty; and in consecrating an asylum to the persecuted of mankind, I would not exclude those who first drew the vital air, and first saw the light in America."[1]

On May 31, 1783, Morris set out from Philadelphia for his first visit to Morrisania in seven years. He found his mother still ailing. His Loyalist brother-in-law Isaac Wilkins was preparing to move with Isabella and their eight children to Nova Scotia. The Morrisania estate had suffered severely under British occupation. A Loyalist regiment had camped there for two years in a settlement of 70 huts and had cultivated the land and cut firewood. An inventory showed that the British had removed 45 head of cattle and 94 sheep and had deforested 470 acres of timberland. Morris

---

[1] Morris to Van Schaack, October 1, 1783, in Van Schaack, *Peter Van Schaack,* 372; Van Schaack to Morris, March 15, 1784, *ibid.,* 373; Morris to Van Schaack, June 18, 1784, *ibid.,* 374. Drafts of Morris' letters, and the received letter of Van Schaack are in the Gouverneur Morris Manuscripts, Parke-Bernet sale lot 102.

helped his mother present claims for these damages to the British. The total, £8,000, was assigned to General Staats Long Morris for collection in England. (He obtained £1,341 for the timber.)[2]

Gouverneur had intended to move permanently to New York, but his business obligations kept him in Philadelphia. He continued for a time as assistant to Robert Morris, who remained in office long after his announced intention to resign. He also became closely associated with Robert in the latter's comprehensive private business activities. Although he continued to practice law, his business interests were becoming his main concern. "Whether I shall go *extensively* into the Practice of the Law must depend on circumstances," he wrote Robert R. Livingston on September 8, 1784.[3] He was well aware that if he was to maintain himself in the social position in which he had been reared he must build his own fortune. In a bold effort to obtain working capital for widespread land speculation in New York, New Jersey, Pennsylvania, Delaware, and Maryland, Gouverneur and Robert entered into an agreement with John Vaughan on March 20, 1783, commissioning him to sail to Europe to borrow between $100,000 and $400,000 at no more than 5 per cent interest, Vaughan's share to be one half and the Morrises to receive one quarter each. Four days later the Morrises signed an agreement with Daniel Parker, a Massachusetts merchant, for joint investments in ships, naval stores, and American produce. Parker had a 50 per cent partnership with James La Caze, of Philadelphia, who was the agent for a concern in Cádiz. The Morrises were to have one quarter each of Parker's portion.[4]

[2] Entry of May 31, 1783, Robert Morris Diary, III; Gouverneur Morris to Sir Guy Carleton, June 11, 1783, Historical Manuscripts Commission, *Report on American Manuscripts in the Royal Institution of Great Britain*, IV, 143–44; Sparks, *Morris*, I, 265; *Morris et al. v. Morris*, 1785, Packet 68; Isaac Wilkins to Gouverneur Morris, July 26, 1783, and June 3, 1784, Gouverneur Morris Manuscripts, Parke-Bernet sale lot 107; Samuel Ogden to Gouverneur Morris, December 25, 1786, *ibid.*, Parke-Bernet sale lot 49.

[3] Robert R. Livingston Papers, New-York Historical Society.

[4] Robert Morris, Gouverneur Morris, and John Vaughan agreement, Gouver-

On June 10, 1784, he entered into a partnership with William Constable, Robert Morris, and, later, John Rucker, in the New York City merchant firm of William Constable and Company. Each partner was to purchase stock at £5,000 Pennsylvania specie, to be paid for as the need arose. Robert Morris paid £10,666 13s. 4d. for Gouverneur and himself, the added amount presumably constituting accumulated interest. Gouverneur's debt to Robert would be paid from future profits. Constable was the leading partner, with a guaranteed yearly income of £750 and an allowance of £400 for operating expenses. The other partners would receive yearly dividends of £750 only if the profits warranted them. Constable was to engage in no other business, and the company, which was to continue for seven years, would dissolve in the event of his death.[5] He conducted the business in his house at 39 Great Dock Street (now Pearl Street). Sleeping quarters were available there for Robert and Gouverneur whenever they went to New York.[6]

In Philadelphia, Gouverneur lived on Market Street, between Second and Third streets.[7] He rapidly evolved into a full-time businessman. In July and August, 1784, he purchased a total of 800 acres in Northumberland County, Pennsylvania. He also bought 2,000 acres in that state's Vincent Township of Chester County, according to an agreement he signed on September 6,

---

neur Morris Manuscripts, Parke-Bernet sale lot 84; Robert Morris, Gouverneur Morris and Daniel Parker agreement, *ibid.*, Parke-Bernet sale lot 83.

[5] Constable, William & Co., Articles of Co-partnership, June 10, 1784, New-York Historical Society, and copy of the same document, dated May 10, 1784, in Gouverneur Morris Manuscripts, Parke-Bernet sale lot 82; William Constable to Alexander Ellice, May 23, 1789, William Constable Letter Book 1782–1790, Constable-Pierrepont Papers, New York Public Library; Constable Rucker & Co. Accounts, 1786–1800, Journal No. 1, 1787, New-York Historical Society; William A. Davis, "William Constable, New York Merchant and Land Speculator, 1772–1803" (Ph.D. dissertation), 63–65.

[6] R. Burnham Moffat, *Pierrepont Genealogies*, 183, citing a memorandum by Mrs. Hezekiah Beer Pierrepont, the former Anna Maria Constable, daughter of William Constable; Noah Webster (ed.), *New York Directory for 1786*, 121, 193; David Franks (ed.), *The New-York Directory*, 24.

[7] Francis White, *Philadelphia Directory*, 50.

1785, with Philip Livingston and Robert Morris for a pooled venture. On April 20, 1785, he and Robert Morris jointly filed a petition with the New York legislature, "in their names and in the names of their associates," for the purchase of a 100,000-acre tract of land bordering the St. Lawrence River, southwest of the St. Regis River. The Petition was not granted because the territory had not yet been opened for public sale. On July 10, 1787, however, the St. Lawrence tract, which has since come to be known as "The Ten Towns," was sold by the state at an advertised auction in New York City. Alexander Macomb, a New York speculator, made the purchase for himself and a group of associates, including the two Morrises and Samuel Ogden. Gouverneur's portion was 60,641 acres, an entire township. In payment he sent Macomb a bond for £3,500 at 6 per cent, backed by Robert Morris. Another of his investments was a share of stock in a company formed on February 9, 1787, to finance John Fitch in the building of a steamboat.[8]

His law practice reflected his business sympathies. He drew up most of the petitions and briefs which the merchants presented to the Pennsylvania legislature in their lobbying for favorable legislation.[9] Probably his most important client was the Bank of North America, which he had helped to found. A serious threat

[8] William Henry Egle (ed.), "Warrantees of Land in the County of Northumberland, 1772–1892," *Pennsylvania Archives*, 3d series, XXV, 235, 237; Philip Livingston, Robert Morris, and Gouverneur Morris agreement, September 6, 1785, Gouverneur Morris Manuscripts, Parke-Bernet sale lot 39; [New York State], *Calendar of N. Y. Colonial Manuscripts Indorsed Land Papers*, 658; Gouverneur Morris to [?], November 1, 1787, Gouverneur Morris Collection; entry of October 1, 1788, Ledger, 1788–1804, Papers of Gouverneur Morris, Library of Congress; Franklin B. Hough, *A History of St. Lawrence and Franklin Counties, New York, from the Earliest Period to the Present Day*, 236–38, 241; William Ogden Wheeler (comp.) and Lawrence Van Alstyne and Charles Burr Ogden (eds.), *The Ogden Family in America, Elizabethtown Branch, and Their English Ancestry*, 104; Samuel Ogden to Gouverneur Morris, October 20, 1785, July 3, 1787, and July 26, 1787, Gouverneur Morris Manuscripts, Parke-Bernet sale lot 49; indenture between John Fitch and stock company formed to finance the building of the steamboat, February 9, 1787, American Philosophical Society. On Gouverneur Morris' ideas of the personal qualities necessary in a businessman, see his letter to Charles Croxall, October 18, 1784, Library of Congress.

[9] Sparks, *Morris*, I, 271.

to the bank's existence arose early in 1784, when a group of Phil-adelphia merchants who had not been able to obtain any of the bank's stock applied to the Pennsylvania assembly for a charter to form a competing Pennsylvania bank. On March 2, Morris and James Wilson, acting as counsel for the Bank of North America, appeared before a committee of the assembly to present the argu-ments against creation of a new bank. Morris maintained that one bank could risk a greater circulation of paper than two, because there was less exposure to a run on one than on either of two banks and because excessive "fictitious credit" could be created by playing one bank against another. Also, a single bank would more readily attract foreign investment and better provide finan-cial assistance to the government. The advocates of a new bank almost won, but the Bank of North America offered to issue more stock for purchase by the dissatisfied merchants. This concession was made because stock in the new bank was already being sold and the purchasers were paying for it with Bank of North America notes, which, when redeemed, were depleting the specie of the established bank. This move had the desired effect of killing the bill for a new bank.[10]

A much more serious attack on the bank, this one with a broad popular base, opened on April 4, 1785, when a bill to repeal the bank's charter was introduced in the agrarian-dominated Pennsyl-vania legislature. In the public eye the Bank of North America rep-resented the rising commercial class. At first the bank was refused a hearing, but in August the assembly decided to grant it. Morris, speaking for the bank, delivered a long address. He replied to charges that the bank encouraged speculation, discriminated against farmers by its policy of granting only short-term loans, and promoted export of specie because of foreign-stock purchases. Chiefly he had to contend with the public image of the bank as a corporate, monopolistic, and privileged-class institution. The root

[10] Notes of James Wilson, "Before a Committee of the Assembly, 2d. March, 1784," James Wilson Papers, Historical Society of Pennsylvania; Bray Hammond, *Banks and Politics in America from the Revolution to the Civil War*, 52.

of his argument was that the bank was a free and voluntary association which could be privately reconstituted if necessary. Once the charter had been granted to this association, its revocation would be a "violation of private property." "May not all charters be at once laid low, by a general law declaring the existence of corporations to be incompatible with the public welfare?" he asked. If the charter was repealed, he concluded, it would be necessary to call upon the courts to assume the enlarged power of declaring the act unconstitutional. "Such power in judges is dangerous; but unless it somewhere exists, the time employed in framing a bill of rights and form of government was merely thrown away."[11]

At first the efforts of Morris and the other bank spokesmen failed to convince the legislature. The charter was repealed on September 13, 1785. New state elections, however, returned a more friendly representation, among whom Robert Morris now sat as senator and Benjamin Franklin served as president. The issue was reopened and tensely debated in the assembly. In the press Thomas Paine was the leading champion of the bank. For the opposition an elaborate cartoon poster, drawn early in 1787, depicted Robert and Gouverneur leading a charge of the "Bankers Corps" against the "Mechanics" and the "Confederation," entrenched on a rock-ribbed fortification and flying a banner of "Franklin & Liberty." Robert was shown sitting on a charger as he directed the assault, while Gouverneur, undeterred by his wooden leg, led the attackers up the steep fortress wall with the cry, "Follow me up Boys I will be Governor [the cartoon's way of identifying him]. This Constitution is too democratic the People are not Virtuous enough to enjoy so much Liberty we are the Gentlemans party & will keep down those Plebians."[12] In the next

[11] Gouverneur Morris, "An Address on the Bank of North America," in Sparks, *Morris*, III, 438–40.

[12] Cartoon, "Zion Besieg'd & Attack'd," Library Company of Philadelphia. This is the only surviving cartoon on Pennsylvania politics from the period 1776–1790. Brunhouse, *Counter-Revolution in Pennsylvania*, 289.

election the supporters of the bank increased in strength, and a new charter was issued to the bank in March, 1787.[13]

As another encouragement of commerce, Morris attempted to promote American trade with the French West Indies. Since the British refused all foreigners access to their West Indian ports, Morris believed that there was little profit in negotiating any early commercial treaty with them.[14] In the hope of persuading France to lift restrictions on American trade, he wrote two long papers on the subject to the Chevalier François Jean de Chastellux in 1783 and 1784. These efforts helped persuade the French government to issue the *arrêt* of August 30, 1784, which temporarily relaxed restrictions in the seven Caribbean ports.[15] It was the newly opened China trade, however, which most attracted speculative merchants seeking large profits. Morris' business partners invested heavily in Asiatic voyages, and he hoped that the trade would stop the drain of American specie to Europe.[16]

Morris continued to be popular in Philadelphia society. One of his best friends was Chastellux, who had been major general and chief of staff to Rochambeau in the latter's army in America during the Revolution. They met at dinner at La Luzerne's home, where Chastellux was struck by the young American's "wit and vivacity."[17] Despite the fact that Chastellux was eighteen years older than Morris, a close relationship developed between the two men, and Chastellux later wrote from Paris: "It is not my fault if destiny has placed Gouverneur Morris in America, and me in

[13] Hammond, *Banks and Politics in America*, 54–63.
[14] Gouverneur Morris to [Roger] Sherman, January 13, 1784 [photostat], Letters to Jeremiah Evarts, Library of Congress.
[15] Gouverneur Morris to Marquis de Chastellux, June 17 and 24, 1784 [French translation], Affaires Étrangères Mémoires et Documents, États-Unis, II, 120–23, Library of Congress; Marquis de Chastellux to Gouverneur Morris, December 8, 1784, in Sparks, *Morris*, I, 271; Charles Callan Tansill, *The United States and Santo Domingo, 1798–1873: A Chapter in Caribbean Diplomacy*, 4–5.
[16] Gouverneur Morris to Charles Thomson, December 30, 1783, Papers of Charles Thomson, Library of Congress.
[17] Chastellux, *Travels in North America*, I, 131.

Europe. I have known him, I have loved him; I shall always love him. And my heart will always be drawn towards him."[18]

On September 25, 1783, in reply to a letter from Robert R. Livingston asking Morris how his amorous affairs were going, he protested that he was too busy to report anything: "Of the last [gallantry] I know Nothing having long been so secluded from the polite Circle unless upon public and formal Occasions that I am out of the Way of Intelligence."[19] There was gaiety at formal parties, however, as we learn from Peggy Chew, a bridesmaid at the wedding of the Marquis François de Barbé-Marbois to Elizabeth Moore in June, 1784. Three days of celebration followed the ceremony. Peggy wrote of the company at the bridesmaids' table: "Govr Morris kept us in a continual smile (I dare not say laughter for the world, but you may admit it in the back room)."[20]

But not all who met Morris accepted his uninhibited ways. Although he was a friend of Washington, it took a painful experience to teach him that he was not to overstep the bounds of propriety in their relationship. He made a wager with Alexander Hamilton, for supper and wine for himself and a dozen friends, that he would take a liberty with Washington at a forthcoming dinner. Present at the dinner were Hamilton, Dr. John Morgan, and Generals Washington, Lafayette, Knox, Greene, Steuben, and Wayne. Morris, sitting next to Washington, suddenly leaned back in his chair and clapped him on the back. "Wasn't it so, my old boy?" he exclaimed. But Washington gravely remained sitting, without a word or a change of feature. A strained silence settled on the company, and soon they awkwardly separated for

[18] To Gouverneur Morris, January 18, 1788 [copy], Sparks Manuscripts, MSS Historical, X. See also Marquis de Chastellux to Gouverneur Morris, October 11, 1784 [copy], *ibid.*; Marquis de Chastellux to Gouverneur Morris, January 16, 1787, Etting Papers, European Authors, Historical Society of Pennsylvania. Chastellux became a marquis upon his older brother's death in 1786.

[19] Robert R. Livingston Papers, New-York Historical Society.

[20] Peggy Chew [to a girl friend], June 23, 1784, in Elizabeth Read, "The Chews of Pennsylvania," *Magazine of American History*, Vol. IV (March, 1880), 202.

the evening.[21] Later, at the supper, Morris told Hamilton, "I have won the bet but paid dearly for it, and nothing could induce me to repeat it."[22]

A similar incident involved Baron von Steuben, the German inspector general of Washington's army. Steuben was very conscious of his military and social rank and the respect due him. At a dinner at headquarters, with Morris at his right side, he was expounding animatedly on the subject under discussion when Morris slapped him heartily on the back, exclaiming, with an oath, "Well done, General, well done!" Steuben took the intimacy as an insult and immediately rose from the table. "Confound the fellow with his old wooden leg, he will govern the whole country," he fumed, and stamped out.[23]

On January 25, 1785, Morris set out on a business trip to Virginia, which gave him an opportunity to visit Washington at Mount Vernon. His mission was to attend to Robert Morris' tobacco shipments and to help him collect a debt from Congressman Carter Braxton. "You will act for me therein as you would for yourself," Robert instructed him.[24] In Williamsburg, on April 5, Gouverneur received a letter from Robert R. Livingston, offering him a governmental appointment, possibly to the New York–Massachusetts Boundary Commission, on which Livingston, Jay, and Duane were serving. Morris replied that he could not accept,

[21] Cochran, "Reminiscences and Anecdotes," *American Historical Register . . . ,* I, 434.

[22] John Fine to Martin Van Buren, April 30, 1857, in Martin Van Buren, *Inquiry into the Origin and Cause of Political Parties in the United States,* 106. Van Buren states that Judge John Fine, of Ogdensburgh, New York, heard this anecdote in May, 1852, from Jacob Burnet, a former United States senator, who had heard it from Alexander Hamilton. For a slightly different version of this incident by Susan Eckhard, who was a daughter of James Read of Philadelphia and states that she heard it from Gouverneur Morris himself, see her letter to William Thompson Read [undated], in William Thompson Read, *Life and Correspondence of George Read, Signer of the Declaration of Independence,* 441 n.

[23] Quoted in Francis Bowen, *Life of Baron Steuben,* in Jared Sparks (ed.), *The Library of American Biography,* IX, 11.

[24] Robert Morris to Tench Tilghman, January 25, 1785, Robert Morris Papers, 1785–1795, New York Public Library; Robert Morris to Gouverneur Morris, April 13, 1785, Gouverneur Morris Collection.

on the ground that the Braxton lawsuit was "a tedious disagreeable Business which I cannot foresee the End of."[25] The case did reach a conclusion at the end of June, when an out-of-court settlement was agreed upon by both parties. Morris stopped off to see Washington at Mount Vernon on July 5. He stayed as a house guest until the morning of July 7, and Washington accompanied him on his way as far as Alexandria. He was back in Philadelphia by the middle of July.[26]

Early in May, 1784, Isaac Wilkins had forwarded to Morris a letter, dated April 10, from his half brother Richard Morris to his mother.[27] The letter requested an inventory of the Lewis Morris estate to determine whether Mrs. Morris had administered her trust equitably. Gouverneur was disturbed. An inventory of the estate's bonds had been made, but in the dislocations resulting from the war it had been mislaid. If the distrustful Richard pressed his demand immoderately, the old family disagreements would be reopened. On May 12, Gouverneur wrote Richard an eloquent plea for patience and reconciliation:

> I cannot see from whence your extreme Urgency on this Subject proceeds   Still less can I conjecture why you have (as I hear is the Case) held out the Idea of a Bill in Chancery. . . . There has been rather too much of it [disagreement] since my Father's Death and I did hope that now at least a Reflection on the Ties of Consanguinity would have prevailed among us rather than the bitter Remembrance of past Animosities. Let them not, I pray you, be revived. I do not expect that you will ever entertain for my Mother any Affection. Perhaps I myself may be viewed with equal Indifference; but let it rest there. If Love

[25] April 5, 1785, Duane Papers, Box 6, New-York Historical Society. On the New York–Massachusetts Boundary Commission, see Dangerfield, *Robert R. Livingston*, 204.

[26] George Washington, *Washington after the Revolution, 1784–1799* (ed. by William S. Baker) 28, 29; Sparks, *Morris*, I, 272.

[27] Gouverneur Morris to Sarah Gouverneur Morris, May 12, 1784, Gouverneur Morris Collection.

cannot exist, still there can be no Necessity for Hatred. It is at best but a bad Passion, and between near Connections rather ungraceful. Believe me Brother we shall serve ourselves quite as well and all our Friends infinitely better by joining to Support each other.[28]

Richard remained unmoved. On behalf of his absent brother, Staats Long Morris, his sister Mary Lawrence and himself, he filed a suit in chancery against Sarah Morris in December, 1785, demanding an accounting of the estate. The estate's papers were submitted for audit, and a deposition was taken from Francis Lewis regarding the arrangements entered into after Lewis Morris' death in 1762.[29]

The following month, on Sunday, January 15, 1786, Sarah Morris died. She was seventy-one years old. Gouverneur canceled a business trip to Baltimore and hastened to New York for the funeral.[30]

Richard Morris was appointed executor of the estate. In accordance with Lewis Morris' will, he advertised that all the family slaves would be sold on April 12. He filed a suit against Gouverneur Morris and Samuel Ogden, to replace that against Sarah Morris. They answered on April 15, but not to Richard's satisfaction.[31]

Word of Sarah Morris' death was meanwhile dispatched to Lieutenant General Staats Long Morris in England, at his country seat in the little village of Enfield, about ten miles from London. He was at that time serving as member of Parliament for

28 Gouverneur Morris to Richard Morris, May 12, 1784 [draft], *ibid.*

29 *Morris et al.* v. *Morris*, 1785, Packet 68.

30 Webster, *New York Directory for 1786*, 95; Robert Morris to Tench Tilghman & Co., January 19, 1786, Robert Morris Papers, New York Public Library; Gouverneur Morris to Thomas Nelson, March 10, 1786 [draft], Gouverneur Morris Collection.

31 Webster, *New York Directory for 1786*, 121; *Morris et al.* v. *Morris et al.*, April 15, 1786, Packet 71, New York State Court of Appeals.

Elgin burghs.[32] Upon receipt of the news, he decided to make a trip to America to sell Morrisania and his other American possessions. He arrived in New York on September 17, 1786. Gouverneur's sister Euphemia Ogden wrote him that Staats wanted to sell Morrisania to a member of the family and also "to make *peace* in the family—he is at present at the Chief Justics [Richard Morris'] where if its possible his mind will be poysoned by him poor man he is to be pitied."[33]

If the estate was to be purchased by one of Staats's brothers, the choice was between Richard and Gouverneur, for Lewis had long before received his share of the patrimony and was apparently contented. For reasons not known Richard was not interested in buying it, and Gouverneur thus became the prospective purchaser. He was on friendly terms with Staats, and it appeared that a reasonable arrangement could be agreed upon if Gouverneur would undertake to pay, in addition to the sale price, Staats's obligations, comprising £2,100 to Richard and £700 to each of the late Lewis Morris' four daughters and cancel Staats's debt to Gouverneur himself (Gouverneur's share of the estate). Pending this settlement, Gouverneur, Samuel Ogden, William Constable, and Jacob Carlyle, described as merchants, posted a bond for £10,000 to Richard Morris, to be redeemed when the lawsuit over the estate was concluded in chancery.[34]

The dispute continued for four months. Gouverneur, losing patience, wrote to his friend Richard Harison on March 21, 1787:

---

[32] On Staats Long Morris' residence in England, see Peter Ogden to Gouverneur Morris, January 7, 1784, Gouverneur Morris Collection; Mary Dorothy George, *Catalogue of Political and Personal Satires Preserved in the Department of Prints and Drawings in the British Museum, 1771–1783*, V, 522.

[33] Euphemia Ogden to Gouverneur Morris, September 18, 1786, Gouverneur Morris Collection.

[34] Samuel Ogden to Gouverneur Morris, December 25, 1787, Gouverneur Morris Manuscripts, Parke-Bernet sale lot 49; *In re Morris, Richard*, Chancery, November 18, 1786, File No. BM M–2547, Office of the County Clerk, New York City Hall of Records.

"I am not so attached to that Purchase as to walk towards it on bad Ground. My Title to the Premises devised must be perfect and if all others act with the same good Faith that I do there can be no Difficulty about the Matter."[35] Agreement on the sale of the property was at last reached on April 4. On that day Gouverneur, Staats, and Richard met and signed three documents. One was a transfer of the estate from Staats to Gouverneur. A second was a mortgage granted by Gouverneur to Staats for £3,000 at 5 per cent interest, payable on April 1, 1792. The third was a mortgage by Gouverneur to Richard for £2,100, payable on January 4, 1788.[36] In effect, Gouverneur was paying £10,000, the sum of the £3,000 payment to Staats and the estate's inheritance obligations of £2,000 to himself, £2,100 to Richard, and the £700 to each of the four heiresses. He was able to undertake this indebtedness because of the mortgages his brothers had agreed to, the £2,100 he could write off as the estate's debt to himself, and the willingness of the heiresses to defer payment of their inheritances.[37] In additional transactions with Staats, he also bought lands in New Jersey for deferred payments—a tract on the Raritan River at Morristown in Morris County for £3,000 and others in Sussex and Somerset counties for £4,000. These were for the purpose of resale.[38]

Thus Gouverneur became the owner of the nearly 1,400-acre

[35] Richard Harison Papers, Personal Correspondence, Box 1, New-York Historical Society.

[36] Samuel Ogden to Gouverneur Morris, January 21, 1786, Gouverneur Morris Manuscripts, Parke-Bernet sale lot 49; Certified Copies Westchester County Mortgages, Liber 1, pp. 236, 237, Register's Office, Bronx County Courthouse, Bronx, New York; Record of Mortgages D, p. 22, Division of Land Records, Westchester County Office Building, White Plains, New York.

[37] State of Account Between Mrs. Lawrence and Gouvr. Morris, January 14, 1789, Franklin Collection, Yale University Library; entry of September 23, 1789, Ledger, 1788–1804, Papers of Gouverneur Morris.

[38] Entries of September 23 and October 1, 1788, ibid.; GMRFR, I, xiii; Liber F 3, p. 28, East Jersey Records, Trenton, as cited in Rev. Rufus S. Green, "City, Village and Township Histories. Morristown," in 1739, *History of Morris County, New Jersey, with Illustrations, and Biographical Sketches of Prominent Citizens and Pioneers*, 109; indenture of sale of land in Sussex and Somerset counties, Gouverneur Morris Manuscripts, Parke-Bernet sale lot 48.

estate without the immediate transfer of any money.[39] Part of the debt he could expect to pay when he received his £2,500 inheritance from his mother's personal estate.[40] (She also left him "One large Damask table Cloth.") With that money he could discharge the short-term mortgage to Richard. If he wished to continue as the lord of Morrisania, he would somehow have to find the means of earning the remaining £7,500 on his own.

[39] For the acreage of the Morrisania manor, see "A Map of Land in Morrisania in the Town and County of Westchester Belonging to the Honorable Gouverneur Morris," surveyed by William S. Randel and John Randel, Jr., in 1816, Bronx County Courthouse.

[40] Will of Sarah Morris, June 9, 1783, Liber 23, pp. 323–25, Surrogate's Office, New York City Hall of Records.

Framing the Constitution

O N DECEMBER 30, 1786, the General Assembly of Pennsylvania elected Gouverneur Morris one of seven delegates to the national Constitutional Convention, to be held in May, 1787, in Philadelphia. As a New Yorker and a partisan conservative, he received only a bare majority of 33 votes out of 63. Four radical candidates were unable to poll a majority. The elected delegates and their votes were Robert Morris, 63; George Clymer, 63; Thomas Mifflin, 63; Jared Ingersoll, 61; Thomas FitzSimons, 37; James Wilson, 35; Gouverneur Morris, 33. Benjamin Franklin had been omitted through a misunderstanding about his availability. That omission was rectified by his election by unanimous vote on March 28, 1787.[1]

Gouverneur had asked not to be named as a delegate, on the grounds that he needed to put his Morrisania estate on a secure footing and to superintend his business ventures. His interest in politics had remained strong, and in 1786 he had joined with Benjamin Franklin, George Washington, James Wilson, Robert Morris, Thomas Paine, and Benjamin Rush to form the Society for Political Inquiries.[2] But he had wished to remain an observer. His election had taken place without his knowledge, while he was away at Trenton. Ten days later he wrote to Henry Knox:

---

[1] DIFUAS, 63–65; Charles Warren, *The Making of the Constitution*, 517n., 808; Brunhouse, *Counter-Revolution in Pennsylvania*, 290.

[2] T. I. Wharton, "A Memoir of William Rawle, LL.D.," Historical Society of Pennsylvania *Memoirs*, IV, 57; Charles Biddle, *Autobiography of Charles Biddle, Vice-President of the Supreme Executive Council of Pennsylvania, 1745–1821,* 223.

Had the Object been any other than it is I would have declined. The Appointment was the most unexpected Thing that ever happened to me for I have not only declared in general my unwillingness to accept of any Thing under this State but in this particular Instance objected to being named but it was done while I was at Trenton.[3]

Recognition of the need for a stronger national government was a portentous shift of public opinion. The national temper during the Revolution had been jealously averse to surrender of state autonomy, despite the urgent requirements of the Patriot armies. Now the condition of the government and the economy under the Articles of Confederation had convinced the great majority that reform was necessary. There was a widespread belief that times were bad in 1786 and that they had helped bring about such disturbances as Shays's Rebellion in Massachusetts. Although historical opinion is still divided about whether the national economy was in fact depressed or was in the process of recovering from a postwar downturn,[4] the people themselves had no doubts. They saw only an increase in paper money, severe farmer indebtedness, state levies on interstate commerce, inordinately high taxes, and English commercial restrictiveness. The immediate hardships were blamed on the defects of the Articles of Confederation. Matching this disenchantment was a universal confidence in the results which were expected from the convention. The newspapers devoted liberal space to it, and it was striking that virtually no attacks were made on the integrity or intentions of the delegates for a full six months' period before they met.[5] In 1802, in the United States Senate, Morris was to declare:

Never, in the flow of time was there a moment so propitious,

[3] January 9, 1787, Henry Knox Papers, Massachusetts Historical Society.
[4] Jensen, *The New Nation*, 218, 220–27; Curtis P. Nettels, *The Emergence of a National Economy, 1775–1815*, 60–64; Gordon C. Bjork, "The Weaning of the American Economy: Independence, Market Changes, and Economic Development," and Albert Fishlow, "Discussion," *Journal of Economic History*, Vol. XXIV, (December, 1964), 540–566.
[5] Warren, *Making of the Constitution*, 94–95.

as that in which the Convention assembled. The States had been convinced, by melancholy experience, how inadequate they were to the management of our national concerns. The passions of the people were lulled to sleep; State pride slumbered; the Constitution was promulgated; and then it awoke, and opposition was formed; but it was in vain. The people of America bound the States down by this compact.[6]

Viewed from the perspective of nearly two hundred years, the fifty-five delegates appear fully as distinguished as they did to their contemporaries. If their previous careers had not already marked them out, their contributions to the debates certainly did so. In their later careers two (George Washington and James Madison) became presidents of the United States; one (Elbridge Gerry) became vice-president; two (John Rutledge and Oliver Ellsworth) became chief justices of the Supreme Court; three (John Blair, James Wilson, and William Paterson) became associate justices of the Supreme Court; one (Alexander Hamilton) became secretary of the treasury; one (Edmund Randolph) became attorney general and secretary of state; ten (including Morris) were elected to the United States Senate; eight were elected to the House of Representatives in the First Congress of 1789; and four (including Morris) became ministers to foreign countries.[7]

The delegates were chiefly large landowners, businessmen, and professional men, and some were holders of government securities. For that reason, according to the view made popular by Charles A. Beard in *An Economic Interpretation of the Constitution,*[8] they were not representative of the rank and file of the people. They magnified the threat of the real and pretended evils of the Articles of Confederation and created a strong, centralized government for the purpose of protecting and enhancing property (principally the personal property of mercantile men) against the

---

[6] Gouverneur Morris in the United States Senate, January 8, 1802, Farrand, *Records,* III, 391.

[7] Warren, *Making of the Constitution,* 69.

[8] Charles A. Beard, *An Economic Interpretation of the Constitution,* 149–51.

encroachment of the small farmers. That analysis has recently been challenged by historians who maintain that fewer of the delegates possessed significant amounts of securities or other personalty than Beard asserted; that the votes of the delegates on specific issues showed little correlation with their personal interests; that most of the adult, white, male population in the country were landholders and shared the basic respect for property,[9] and that the real contest was between "extreme particularists of the [George] Clinton stripe and continental nationalists of varying shades and degrees."[10] Some intellectual historians maintain that men of all persuasions in the eighteenth century believed in the fixed depravity of human nature and the consequent necessity of "balanced" or "counterpoised" government,[11] while other interpreters view the convention as a battleground for a struggle between concepts of aristocracy and democracy.[12]

There were divisions among the delegates themselves. The lines tended to be drawn along large- versus small-state differences, sectional antagonisms, and varying degrees of willingness to hazard local political freedom in the hands of distant, centralized government. At short range the large- and small-state differences presented the greatest problem, and sometimes East-West relationships loomed troublesomely. But in the long view the most deep-seated and far-reaching of the divisions was that between the northern and southern states. Wedged between them was the great issue of slavery. According to the census of 1790, the first national census, the number of slaves in the states of Maryland,

[9] Forrest McDonald, *We the People: The Economic Origins of the Constitution*, 89–92, 106; Robert E. Brown, *Charles Beard and the Constitution: A Critical Analysis of "An Economic Interpretation of the Constitution,"* 61–72.

[10] Richard B. Morris, "The Confederation Period and the American Historian," *William and Mary Quarterly*, Vol. XIII (April, 1956), 151.

[11] On "counterpoised" government see Arthur O. Lovejoy, *Reflections on Human Nature*, 57–61; Richard Hofstadter, *The American Political Tradition and the Men Who Made It*, 7–10; Leonard Woods Labaree, *Conservatism in Early American History*, 131.

[12] On aristocracy versus democracy see Bernard Bailyn, *The Ideological Origins of the American Revolution*, 301; Gordon S. Wood, *The Creation of the American Republic, 1776–1787*, 18–24, 37–40, 413–25, 475, 513–16.

Virginia, North Carolina, South Carolina, and Georgia totaled 632,804, out of an aggregate of 699,374 in the entire country.[13] The hard core of slavery was to be found in North and South Carolina and Georgia. James Madison clearly perceived the magnitude of the issue when he said on the floor of the convention:

> The States were divided into different interests not by their difference of size, but by other circumstances; the most material of which resulted partly from climate, but principally from the effects of their having or not having slaves. These two causes concurred in forming the great division of interests in the U. States. It did not lie between the large & small States: it lay between the Northern & Southern.[14]

To Morris the convention represented the hope of realizing the centralized American union he had been working for throughout the Revolution and the years following. Few other public figures had pursued such an early, vigorous, and consistent course. In his personal economic interests he was a large landowner and a businessman deeply committed to commercial ventures and a holder of one four-hundred-dollar share of stock in the Bank of North America. In the main his concern was commercial, and he was a strong advocate of a governmental laissez-faire policy toward trade. It is worth noting, however, that as a debtor and a land speculator he could have profited greatly from increased inflation. Through upbringing, temperament, and conviction he looked upon government as the protector of property and the defender of liberty of conscience, expression, and the person. Although he distrusted popular government, he opposed monarchy in the United States because, as he had written to Greene in 1781, "this does not seem to consist with *the Taste and Temper of the Peo-*

[13] Statistics from United States census of 1790, as cited in Samuel Eliot Morison and Henry Steele Commager, *The Growth of the American Republic*, I, 244n. Charles Cotesworth Pinckney, in a speech in the South Carolina House of Representatives in January, 1788, stated that the convention used slave-population figures, which totaled 520,000 for these states. Farrand, *Records*, III, 253.

[14] *Ibid.*, I, 486.

ple."[15] The form of government, he believed, must depend upon established institutions and the political maturity of the people. That idea was implicit in his thinking from the beginning. It was a fundamental tenet of Steuart's *Inquiry into the Principles of Political Oeconomy*, which Morris had read at least as early as 1781.[16] He was an uncompromising opponent of slavery, having known it in his own family and learned to detest it. No delegate was to prove more firm in attacking it.

At thirty-five he was the youngest of the Pennsylvania delegates, but he became a major figure of the convention, surpassed only by Madison and Wilson. Brilliant, eloquent, never hesitant to speak his mind, he took the floor 173 times, more often than any other member.[17] A delegate from Georgia, Major William Pierce, a Savannah merchant and veteran artillery officer, left this vivid impression of him:

Mr. Gouverneur Morris is one of those Genius's in whom every species of talents combine to render him conspicuous and flourishing in public debate:—He winds through all the mazes of rhetoric, and throws around him such a glare that he charms, captivates, and leads away the senses of all who hear him. With an infinite stretch of fancy he brings to view things when he is engaged in deep argumentation, that render all the labor of reasoning easy and pleasing. But with all these powers he is fickle and inconstant,—never pursuing one train of thinking,— nor ever regular. He has gone through a very extensive course of reading, and is acquainted with all the sciences. No Man has more wit,—nor can any one engage the attention more than Mr. Morris. He was bred to the Law, but I am told he disliked the profession, and turned Merchant. He is engaged in some

[15] To Nathanael Greene, December 24, 1781, Nathanael Greene Papers.

[16] Gouverneur Morris to President of the Bank, June 18, 1781 [draft], Gouverneur Morris Collection; Sir James Steuart, *An Inquiry into the Principles of Political Oeconomy* (ed. by Andrew S. Skinner), I, 16–17, 20–26.

[17] "Constitutional Convention, 1787," *Historical Magazine*, Vol. V (January, 1861), 18.

great mercantile matters with his namesake Mr. Robert Morris.[18]

Morris' outspokenness brought him resentment as well as prominence. Wilson, weary of Morris' insistence on private property as the cornerstone of government, replied that he "could not agree that property was the sole or the primary object of Governt. & society. The cultivation and improvement of the human mind was the most noble object."[19] Madison bitingly referred to Morris on the floor as "a member who on all occasions, had inculcated so strongly, the political depravity of men, and the necessity of checking one vice and interest by opposing them to another vice & interest." But many years later Madison softened and gave Morris credit for willingness to change his mind:

> It is but due to Mr. Morris to remark, that to the brilliancy of his genius, he added, what is too rare, a candid surrender of his opinions, when the lights of discussion satisfied him, that they had been too hastily formed, and a readiness to aid in making the best of measures in which he had been overruled.[20]

On May 14, 1787, the day appointed for the first meeting of the convention, only enough delegates were present to form quorums for Virginia and Pennsylvania. It took twelve days for the requisite number to arrive. While waiting, the delegates gathered each morning and informally discussed the direction which the convention should take. In those talks Morris tried to promote a movement to allot greater representation to the large states, and he was supported by Robert Morris and others of the Pennsylvania delegation. Virginia, however, refused to go along, on the ground that it would be more effective to persuade the small states to surrender their equality voluntarily than to remove it arbitrarily from them.[21]

18 DIFUAS, 101–102.　　　　　19 Ibid., 373.
20 Ibid., 358; James Madison to Jared Sparks, April 8, 1831, Sparks, Morris, I, 286.
21 DIFUAS, 111 n.

On May 25, when delegates from seven states at last appeared to form a quorum, Robert Morris, on behalf of the Pennsylvania delegation, rose to nominate Washington as president of the convention. Washington was elected unanimously and conducted to the chair by Robert Morris and John Rutledge of South Carolina.

The first significant item of business was the adoption of rules for the conduct of the meetings. Each state was to have one vote, seven states were to constitute a quorum, and votes were to be decided by a majority of states present. Thus the equality of state representation which Morris had opposed was adopted, but the denial of a veto made the plan workable. A second momentous rule was the injunction of secrecy on the proceedings, effectively shutting the door of the State House on the whole country for the ensuing three and a half months. In 1830, Madison expressed the belief that no constitution would ever have been adopted if the debates had been made public, but Thomas Jefferson decried "so abominable a precedent as that of tying up the tongues of their members."[22]

Governor Edmund Randolph, on behalf of Virginia, the state which had taken the initiative in advocating the convention, introduced a series of fifteen resolutions for the reform of the Confederation. The resolutions, which became known as the Virginia Plan, constituted a bold departure from the Articles of Confederation. They called for a bicameral national legislature, the first house to be elected by the people and the second house by the members of the first; an executive to be chosen by the legislature for a fixed term, not specified, and to be ineligible for re-election; and a council of revision, consisting of the executive and a number of national judges, which would have a veto power over legislation. The national legislature could declare state laws unconstitutional and could act directly upon people, rather than through the states.

So drastic a plan, declared Alexander Hamilton of New York,

[22] To John Adams, August 30, 1787, Farrand, *Records*, III, 76.

required that the convention first settle the basic question of whether the United States was to have one government or separate state governments connected by treaties.[23] If it was to have one government, then the first of the Virginia resolutions, which proposed that the Articles of Confederation merely be "corrected and enlarged," was too weak. The next day Morris took up the cue and suggested to Randolph, who approvingly so moved, that three stronger resolutions be substituted:

> 1. that a Union of the States merely federal will not accomplish the objects proposed by the articles of Confederation, namely common defence, security of liberty, & genl. welfare.
> 2. that no treaty or treaties among the whole or part of the States, as individual Sovereignties, would be sufficient.
> 3. that a *national* Government ought to be established consisting of a *supreme* Legislature, Executive & Judiciary.[24]

There was an interval of silence, as the delegates pondered the import of these harsh resolutions. Then, in the discussion, Charles Cotesworth Pinckney of South Carolina objected that the purpose of the delegates was revision of the Confederation and that if the first resolution was adopted their business was at an end. This argument persuaded the delegates to drop both the first and the second resolutions and to concentrate on the third.[25] There the debate centered on the terms *national* and *supreme*. Morris declared that the government must have compulsory powers. "A federal agreement which each party may violate at pleasure cannot answer the purpose. . . . We had better take a supreme government now, than a despot twenty years hence—for come he must."[26] After an unsuccessful attempt by George Read of Delaware to restrict the convention to a revision of the Articles of Confederation, the resolution was passed. Connecticut voted against it, and New York was divided.

23 *DIFUAS*, 926.
24 *Ibid.*, 120
25 *Ibid.*, 749.
26 *Ibid.*, 929.

The convention then took up the second of Randolph's resolutions, which stated that representation in the legislature should be proportional to either population or state contributions of revenue to the national government. For this proposal Madison, with Randolph's consent, substituted a resolution emphasizing the general principle that equality of state representation must not prevail. Read then reminded the convention that the Delaware delegates were instructed to leave the group if this proposal carried. Morris immediately replied that, regrettable as the secession would be, the principle was indispensable.[27] The dispute reached an impasse, and the only recourse was to postpone it until the specific provision came up for consideration.

The next day, May 31, Morris took a one-month leave from the convention to attend to the affairs of his Morrisania estate. He had hired an overseer and a large force of laborers, and he needed to lay out the work for them. He wished to make extensive building changes, and there was tree and crop planting to be done.[28]

He returned to the convention on July 2. The delegates were still threshing out the question of state versus proportional representation. On that day a motion that each state be allowed one vote in the Senate came to a tie vote. "We are now," said Roger Sherman of Connecticut, "at a full stop."[29] Morris took the floor to press for a house appointed for life, without pay, by the executive. His object was to create an aristocratic, wealthy body which would balance the popularly elected first house. The doctrine of

[27] *Ibid.*, 123.
[28] Sparks, *Morris*, I, 282.
[29] *DIFUAS*, 318. The following story was told to Jared Sparks by David B. Ogden, Gouverneur Morris' nephew: When Morris returned to the convention, he went to Robert Morris' house, where Washington was staying, and learned that everyone was despondent in the belief that the convention was about to dissolve in failure and that Hamilton was preparing to leave. At the request of those present, Gouverneur went to see Hamilton the next morning and, after a long discussion, persuaded him to remain. Then, at the convention, he made a long and effective conciliatory speech. Conversation between Jarad Sparks and David B. Ogden, March 14, 1831, Letters, Sparks Manuscripts; Jared Sparks to James Madison, March 30, 1831, Sparks, *Morris*, I, 283–84. James Madison, however, could not verify it. Madison to Sparks, April 8, 1831, *ibid.*, 285–86.

human selfishness and class antagonism, he said, applied equally to the motivations of rich and poor:

> The Rich will strive to establish their dominion & enslave the rest. They always did. They always will. The proper security agst. them is to form them into a separate interest. The two forces will then controul each other. Let the rich mix with the poor and in a Commercial Country, they will establish an oligarchy. Take away commerce and the democracy will triumph.[30]

This brash plan received no support. Instead, a committee brought in a compromise which entailed representation of one for every forty thousand inhabitants in the first branch and equal representation of states in the second. All money bills were to originate in the first house. Morris vehemently opposed this solution as both too subservient to the states and too democratic. He came to the convention, he said, as a "Representative of America" and even "in some degree as a Representative of the whole human race." He warned:

> This Country must be united. If persuasion does not unite it, the sword will. . . . The scenes of horror attending civil commotion cannot be described, and the conclusion of them will be worse than the term of their continuance. The stronger party will then make traytors of the weaker; and the Gallows & Halter will finish the work of the sword.[31]

Equality of the states in the Senate, he said, would encourage individual states to disregard acts with which they disagreed, thus undermining the national government.

As for the popularly elected house, he wanted property as well as population to be the basis of representation, for "property was the main object of Society."[32] Provision also ought to be made to prevent the maritime states from being outvoted by the western states, which, if uncontrolled, would involve the rest in wars: "The

30 *DIFUAS*, 319-20.
31 *Ibid.*, 326–27.
32 *Ibid.*, 330.

Busy haunts of men not the remote wilderness, was the proper school of political Talents. If the Western people get the power into their hands they will ruin the Atlantic interests. The Back members are almost always averse to the best measures."[33] Rutledge supported this position with a motion to apportion representation according to state contribution to the national revenue, but it was voted down, with only South Carolina in favor.[34] Instead, the convention adopted representation by population with apportionment according to a census to be taken every ten years.

When it was proposed that slaves be counted in the ratio of five to three freemen, a compromise for which precedent already existed, Morris mounted his supreme effort of opposition. Either the slaves were to be considered as inhabitants or as wealth, he said. If inhabitants, they would be counted with the rest; if wealth, why count them, but no other wealth?[35] He noted the point already made by Rufus King of Massachusetts and by Madison that the real division in the convention was not between the large and small states but between the northern and southern states. If the South triumphed, he warned, it would precipitate a war with Spain for the Mississippi:

> A distinction had been set up & urged, between the Nn. & Southn. States. . . . If it be real, instead of attempting to blend incompatible things, let us at once take a friendly leave of each other. . . . If the Southn. States get the power into their hands, and be joined as they will by the interior Country, they will inevitably bring on a war with Spain for the Mississippi. . . . The interior Country having no property nor interest exposed on the sea, will be little affected by such a war.[36]

It was a prophetic warning. Substitute Britain for Spain and Canada for the Mississippi, and the speech is a prediction of the War of 1812.

[33] *Ibid.*, 357.
[34] *Ibid.*, 331.
[35] *Ibid.*, 355.
[36] *Ibid.*, 371–72.

Morris called up his greatest reserve of indignation for the institution of slavery itself. His speech on August 8, as reported by Madison, reveals a fervent conviction ordinarily not visible beneath his suave brilliance:

> He never would concur in upholding domestic slavery. It was a nefarious institution. It was the curse of heaven in the States where it prevailed. Compare the free regions of the Middle States, where a rich & noble cultivation marks the prosperity & happiness of the people, with the misery & poverty which overspread the barren wastes of Va. Maryd. & the other States having slaves. Travel thro' the whole Continent & you behold the prospect continually varying with the appearance and disappearance of slavery. The moment you leave the E. Sts. & enter N. York, the effects of the institution become visible, passing thro' the Jerseys & entering Pa. every criterion of superior improvement witnesses the change. Proceed southwdly & every step you take thro' the great region of slaves presents a desert increasing, with the increasing proportion of these wretched beings. The admission of slaves into the Representation when fairly explained comes to this: that the inhabitant of Georgia and S.C. who goes to the Coast of Africa, and in defiance of the most sacred laws of humanity tears away his fellow creatures from their dearest connections & damns them to the most cruel bondages, shall have more votes in a Govt. instituted for the protection of the rights of mankind, than the Citizen of Pa. and N. Jersey who views with a laudable horror, so nefarious a practice. . . . He would sooner submit himself to a tax for paying for all the negroes in the U. States, than saddle posterity with such a Constitution.[37]

All of Morris' proposals on representation were voted down. Futile, too, was his opposition to granting to the popular house the sole right to introduce money bills.[38] The compromise which was evolving was certainly not his. It was therefore remarkable that he successfully moved on July 12, in a master stroke, that

[37] *Ibid.*, 497-98.

"direct taxation ought to be proportioned to representation."[39] This motion became a factor in persuading the larger states to accept the compromise plan. On July 16 the entire section, which was to become known as the Great Compromise, was adopted. Later Morris repudiated the provision on direct taxation, asserting that he had only meant it as "a bridge to assist us over a certain gulph; having passed the gulph the bridge may be removed."[40] It was too late—the provision was retained.

The large states looked upon the passage of the compromise as a very serious defeat. The next morning, before the convention reassembled, their delegates met to consider what action to take. The reactions were so disorganized that no conclusion could be reached, and small-state delegates who attended the meeting saw that no move that would upset the agreement need be feared. Nevertheless, when the day's formal session began, Morris was the first delegate on the floor, with a motion to reconsider the entire issue. It was not seconded, probably for fear of its disruptive consequences.[41] Thereafter, the compromise, although several times reviewed, was never in serious jeopardy.

It remained to spell out the organization and powers of Congress. Somewhat surprisingly, Morris opposed a provision of the Virginia Plan which would have given Congress authority to negative any state law which contravened the Constitution or treaties. He termed the power unnecessary and "terrible to the States."[42] The provision was defeated, despite the arguments of Madison. Morris supported the provision granting to the Senate confirmation power over appointments.[43] He and King jointly introduced the principle of voting per capita, rather than by state, in the Senate.[44] He unsuccessfully sought to substitute a freehold re-

[38] *Ibid.*, 503.
[39] *Ibid.*, 363.
[40] *Ibid.*, 448.
[41] *Ibid.*, 387–88.
[42] *Ibid.*, 390.
[43] *Ibid.*, 403.
[44] *Ibid.*, 439–40.

quirement for suffrage for the lower house, in place of the requirements of the separate states. This motion exposed him to the
old charge that he favored government by an aristocracy. He replied that aristocracy would more likely arise from the sale of the
votes of the propertyless poor to the unscrupulous rich—a prophecy that could soon become a reality as developing industry
produced a large working class. His speech, as reported by Madison, presents a cogent argument:

> He had long learned not to be the dupe of words. The sound
> of Aristocracy therefore had no effect on him. It was the thing,
> not the name, to which he was opposed, and one of his principle
> objections to the Constitution as it is now before us, is that it
> threatens this Country with an Aristocracy. The aristocracy
> will grow out of the House of Representatives. Give the votes
> to people who have no property, and they will sell them to the
> rich who will be able to buy them. We should not confine our
> attention to the present moment. The time is not distant when
> this Country will abound with mechanics & manufacturers who
> will receive their bread from their employers. Will such men
> be the secure & faithful Guardians of liberty? Will they be the
> impregnable barrier agst. aristocracy?—He was as little duped
> by the association of the words "taxation & Representation."
> The man who does not give his vote freely is not represented.
> It is the man who dictates the vote. . . . He did not conceive
> the difficulty of defining "freeholders" to be insuperable. Still
> less that the restriction could be unpopular. 9/10 of the people
> are at present freeholders and these will certainly be pleased
> with it. As to Merchts. & c. if they have wealth & value the
> right they can acquire it. If not they don't deserve it.[45]

Morris advocated giving Congress power to tax exports as well
as imports.[46] The South, fearing for its tobacco exports and apprehensive that it would be forced to pay permanent tribute to the
commercial North, strongly opposed the proposal. Morris moved
that the issue be referred to a committee, along with the questions

of importation of slaves and a navigation act. "These things," he said, "may form a bargain among the Northern & Southern States."[47] From the resulting committee report and extended debates over it emerged the compromise which prevented Congress from prohibiting importation of slaves before 1808, meanwhile allowing a duty on them not exceeding the average of other import duties. Navigation acts were to be enacted by majority vote. All export duties were banned. Morris withdrew his opposition to slave importation for the sake of union, rather than drive out South Carolina and Georgia.[48]

He opposed admission of new states to the Union on equal terms with the original ones. The usually urbane Madison, nettled by Morris' distrust of westerners, replied that "it must be imagined that he determined the human character by the points of the compass."[49] Morris, realizing that he could not convince the majority, obtained passage of a motion which simply stated that "new States may be admitted by the Legislature into this Union,"[50] with no elaboration other than prohibition of the formation of new states from old ones without the consent of the parent states. By couching the provision in general terms, he left the door open for Congress to exclude new states. In 1803 he wrote:

> In wording the third Section of the fourth Article, I went as far as circumstances would permit to establish the Exclusion. Candor obliges me to add my Belief that had it been more pointedly expresst a strong Opposition would have been made.[51]

[45] Ibid., 488–89.   [46] Ibid., 553, 554, 585.   [47] Ibid., 593.
[48] Ibid., 617. George Mason afterward charged that South Carolina and Georgia, in order to obtain New England support for importation of slaves for twenty years, agreed to the clause on navigation acts. George Mason's Account of Certain Proceedings in Convention [To Thomas Jefferson, September 30, 1792, as recorded by Jefferson], Farrand, Records, III, 367. See also Richard Barry, Mr. Rutledge of South Carolina, 329–34.
[49] DIFUAS, 358.
[50] Ibid., 639.
[51] To Henry W. Livingston, December 4, 1803, Private Correspondence, II, 149, Papers of Gouverneur Morris.

If he hoped that future Congresses would choose to deny equality to the new states, he was doomed to disappointment.

Unquestionably the most penetrating and enduring contribution which Morris made during the convention was in the deliberations on the formation of the executive. His whole career and the causes for which he had fought pointed toward this need in a national government. He had found the Continental Congress weak and the state legislatures subject to popular pressures and intrigue. To the extent that he distrusted the legislature, he wished to strengthen the executive, and he drew heavily upon his experience with the framing and subsequent functioning of the relatively strong office of the governor of New York.

The foundation of the presidential office had been laid by Wilson during Morris' absence in the early days of the convention. Wilson advocated a chief magistracy of one man, to be elected by the people at large for a short term with unlimited re-eligibility. He was to have an absolute veto in conjunction with a council of revision, modeled on that of New York. When the method of popular election received no support, he proposed an electoral college made up of electors from state districts.[52] The principle of the single executive won approval, but Wilson's other ideas were at first rejected.

Morris returned to the convention just as the subject was resumed. He immediately took up the fight for Wilson's plan, and for the remainder of the convention he was, as one authority describes him, the "floor leader" of the drive for an independent presidency.[53] Under his guidance Wilson's plan was expanded, modified until Wilson himself opposed it, and manipulated through the bargaining process by which it reached its final, accepted form.

[52] *DIFUAS,* 136
[53] Charles C. Thach, Jr., *The Creation of the Presidency, 1775–1789: A Study in Constitutional History,* 99.

On July 17, when the Virginia Plan of presidential election by the legislature was introduced, Morris moved to replace that proposal with popular election. He argued that election by the legislature would be the work of intrigue and faction, while election by the people would make faction impossible, because of the extent of the country, and would encourage the selection of distinguished, nationally eminent men. Only Pennsylvania, of ten states present, voted in favor of the motion. When, after several reconsiderations, the convention persisted in voting for election by the legislature, Morris moved on August 24 that the president be chosen "by Electors to be chosen by the People of the several States."[54] This proposal was defeated, five to six.

During Morris' absence in the early period of the convention, the president's term of office had been fixed at seven years, with ineligibility for re-election. When the subject was reopened on July 17, Morris opposed prohibition of a second term on the ground that it "tended to destroy the great motive to good behavior, the hope of being rewarded by a re-appointment. It was saying to him, make hay while the sun shines." Dr. James Mc-Clurg of Virginia then moved that the president serve during good behavior. Morris immediately seconded the motion with gusto: "This was the way to get a good Government," he exulted. He was "indifferent how the Executive should be chosen, provided he held his place by his tenure." When George Mason of Virginia charged that the move paved the way for monarchy, Morris replied that he was "as little a friend to monarchy as any gentleman. . . . the way to keep out monarchical Govt. was to establish such a Repub. Govt. as wd. make the people happy and prevent a desire of change." McClurg's motion was defeated.[55]

Giving up the idea of a president elected for life, Morris held out for re-eligibility and a short term, preferably two years, so as to make the president as responsible as possible to the electorate

[54] *DIFUAS*, 612.
[55] *Ibid.*, 396–99.

and correspondingly removed from the legislature. Additionally, he should not be impeachable, for that would reduce his effectiveness as a check on the legislature. After hearing the arguments of Wilson, Mason, Randolph, Franklin, and Madison in favor of impeachment, however, Morris changed his mind and supported impeachment for treachery and bribery.[56] He would arm the president with an absolute veto over Congress, to be overridden by a three-fourths vote. That provision was essential, he said, to guard against the propensity of unstable legislatures to issue paper money.[57] To provide the president with effective administrative aides, he proposed a "council of State," essentially a cabinet, to be chaired by the chief justice of the Supreme Court in the absence of the president and to consist of secretaries of domestic affairs, commerce and finance, foreign affairs, war, and marine and a secretary to the council to be known as secretary of state. They were to hold office during the president's pleasure and to be subject to impeachment.[58] All these provisions the convention debated, reconsidered, and postponed.

On August 31 the Committee of Eleven, composed of one member from each state, with Morris representing Pennsylvania and Madison representing Virginia, was elected to complete the postponed and unfinished portions of the Constitution. Prominent among them was the section on the presidency. The committee delivered a report on September 4. From the fact that Morris was the spokesman on the floor for the section on the presidency, it is clear that he was its author. The plan specified a presidential term of four years, with no prohibition against reelection. The method of election stipulated that each state choose, according to its own system of election, a group of electors equal to its combined numbers of senators and representatives in Congress. The electors were to meet and vote in their respective states for two candidates, one of whom was not to be an inhabitant of

[56] *Ibid.*, 421.
[57] *Ibid.*, 548–49.
[58] *Ibid.*, 573–74.

the voting state. The sealed votes were then to be transmitted to the Senate, where the presiding officer of that body was to open and count them. A majority of all the electors would elect the president. If no candidate received a majority the Senate was to choose by ballot one of the five highest on the list. The candidate with the second-highest vote was to be vice-president.[59] The proposal was an attempt at a compromise between popular election, which would favor the large states, and election by Congress, which would favor the small states. It was widely expected that, while Washington would be the overwhelming choice in the first election, the vote thereafter would be so scattered that the result would be that the large states would, in effect, nominate the candidates and the small states would elect the president in the Senate.

Randolph, Mason, Charles Pinckney, and Wilson quickly objected to giving the power of the eventual choice to the Senate rather than the entire Congress. Morris replied that the elections would probably be decided by the electors, since, because each of them had two votes, only a quarter of the total would constitute the required majority of the number of electors. Madison supported Morris by pointing out that the large states would have the concerted incentive of deciding the election by the electors, to prevent yielding the power to the small states in the Senate. Randolph nevertheless exclaimed, "We have in some revolutions of this plan made a bold stroke for Monarchy. We are now doing the same for an aristocracy." Mason declared that he "would prefer the government of Prussia to one which will put all power into the hands of seven or eight men, and fix an aristocracy worse than absolute monarchy." Just as the debate appeared to be reaching a deadlock, Hamilton helped clear the air by asserting that he "meant to support the plan to be recommended, as better than nothing." Shortly afterward, Hugh Williamson of North Carolina proposed election by both houses of Congress, voting by states. Sherman of Connecticut moved substitution of the House

59 *Ibid.*, 660.

of Representatives, voting by states. Mason approved, and without further debate the motion was carried by ten states, with only Delaware opposed.[60] Thus ended what Charles Warren, a student of the Constitution, called "the longest and hardest fought battle of the whole Convention." The method of electing the president was the feature of which the delegates were the most proud, and it was the one which later escaped with the least public criticism.[61]

As for the president's powers, the Committee of Eleven had recommended that he be authorized to make treaties and nominate and appoint ambassadors and Supreme Court justices, with the advice and consent of the Senate, a two-thirds vote being required for the approval of treaties. In spite of Morris' earlier espousal of a "council of State," the report restricted itself to the statement that the president could require opinions in writing from the heads of the executive departments. All these proposals aroused opposition. Wilson wanted the House of Representatives as well as the Senate to approve treaties. Madison thought that treaties should be ratified by two thirds of the Senate, without any approval by the president. Morris answered that "no peace ought to be made without the concurrence of the President, who was the general Guardian of the National Interests." The provision as reported was sustained. Mason proposed a privy council of six members to share the appointive power with the president in place of the Senate. The council was to be appointed by the Senate for six-year rotating terms and was to be composed of two members from New England, two from the Middle Atlantic states, and two from the South. This proposal was supported by Wilson, Franklin, Dickinson, and Madison. Morris, however, stood firm against those giants, with only King giving him strong support. "The question of a Council was considered in the Committee," said Morris, "where it was judged that the Prest. by per-

60 *Ibid.*, 670, 672, 675, 678.
61 Warren, *Making of the Constitution*, 630; Max Farrand, *Framing of the Constitution*, 175; Edward G. Bourne (ed.), *The Federalist*, II, No. 68, 35.
62 *DIFUAS*, 686–88.

suading his Council, to concur in his wrong measures, would acquire their protection for them." At the vote only Maryland, South Carolina, and Georgia sided with Mason. The provision for presidential authority to require written opinions from the department heads then passed overwhelmingly.[62]

The convention now revived and passed the section requiring money bills to originate in the House of Representatives. Morris had at first accepted this provision in committee as a concession to the large states to win them over to support of the plan for the executive but had afterward repudiated it as too restrictive.[63]

In considering the judiciary, Morris seconded Wilson in proposing that judges of the Supreme Court be appointed by the executive. When this motion was decisively voted down, he seconded a motion by Nathaniel Gorham of Massachusetts that the judges be nominated and appointed by the executive with the advice and consent of the Senate.[64] Although the convention did not spell out the authority of the Supreme Court to declare laws unconstitutional, Morris clearly took that authority for granted when he stated: "Legislative alterations not conformable to the federal compact, would clearly not be valid. The Judges would consider them as null & void."[65]

He continued in the convention the championship of civil liberties which he had begun in the New York State Constitutional Convention of 1777. He opposed a motion by Mason to empower Congress to enact sumptuary laws, on the ground that they "tended to create a landed Nobility, by fixing in the great-landholders and their posterity their present possessions."[66] He did not explain how these laws create a landed nobility, but he appears to have had the same goal in mind that he had when he unsuccessfully fought to outlaw quitrents in New York in 1777.

[63] *Ibid.,* 667, 692–93, 335, 337, 499, 503, 546.
[64] *Ibid.,* 400, 401, 403.
[65] *Ibid.,* 437.
[66] *Ibid.,* 574, 940.

At other times he spoke out against bills of attainder,[67] religious tests for public office,[68] and suspension of the writ of habeas corpus except under national threat of war.[69]

Finally, on the method of ratifying and amending the Constitution, Morris at first unsuccessfully favored one national convention.[70] Then he joined with Charles Pinckney in sponsoring the requirement of state conventions. This proposal, he said, would prevent the enemies of the plan from "giving it the go by."[71] The people would at first be disposed toward it but would reverse themselves under the influence of intriguing members of the state governments. Martin and Gerry sarcastically replied that the people would be against the Constitution for a different reason and would not approve it unless hurried into it. The motion was defeated, seven to four. Eight days later Madison moved the amending process now included in the Constitution, and it was quickly approved, with only Delaware opposed and New Hampshire divided. Rutledge obtained inclusion of a guarantee prohibiting amendments to curtail the slave trade until 1808.[72]

The deliberations of the convention were virtually completed. It remained to assemble the provisions as amended and agreed upon and to draft a complete document with suitable grace of wording and unity of tone. On September 8 a committee consisting of Dr. William Samuel Johnson of Connecticut, Hamilton, Gouverneur Morris, Madison, and King was elected for this purpose.[73] Although Johnson, a respected legal scholar and a small-states advocate, served as chairman, there can be no doubt that the work of the committee was done by Morris. Madison, who served with him on the committee and must have known,

[67] *Ibid.*, 596.
[68] *Ibid.*, 647.
[69] *Ibid.*, 627.
[70] *Ibid.*, 439.
[71] *Ibid.*, 652.
[72] *Ibid.*, 696.
[73] *Ibid.*, 694.

testified to Morris' contribution in a letter to Jared Sparks on April 8, 1831:

> The *finish* given to the style and arrangement of the Constitution fairly belongs to the pen of Mr Morris; the task having, probably, been handed over to him by the chairman of the Committee, himself a highly respected member, and with the ready concurrence of the others. A better choice could not have been made, as the performance of the task proved.[74]

Morris himself wrote of his work in a letter to Timothy Pickering on December 22, 1814: "That Instrument was written by the Fingers which write this Letter. Having rejected redundant and equivocal Terms I believed it to be as clear as our Language would permit."[75] According to Pickering, in a comment in 1828, Wilson was said to have claimed the authorship.[76] The only surviving support of that claim, however, is an unamplified statement by Abraham Baldwin, a delegate from Georgia, that "Messrs Morris & Wilson had the chief hand in the last Arrangt & Composition."[77]

Four days after the appointment of the committee, Dr. Johnson presented its report, accompanied by the draft of a letter of submittal to Congress in Morris' handwriting. It is a fascinating exercise to compare the report with the proceedings of the convention which had been referred to the committee.[78] We see the clear marks of Morris' gift for precision, vigor, and grace of expression. There is an elevating grandeur, an exhilarating tempo, and a rationality of sentence structure which represents the best of eighteenth-century literary style. The original twenty-three ar-

[74] Sparks, *Morris*, I, 284–85. John Adams was informed, on September 16, 1789, by Oliver Ellsworth, that the proceedings were committed "to Governeur Morris, Mr. Maddison and some others." John Adams, *Diary and Autobiography of John Adams* (ed. by L. H. Butterfield) III, 221.
[75] Personal Papers, Miscellaneous Letter M, Library of Congress.
[76] Warren, *Making of the Constitution*, 688.
[77] Entry of December 21, 1787, Stiles, *Literary Diary*, III, as cited in Farrand, *Records*, III, 170.
[78] *Ibid.*, II, 565–79, 590–603.

ticles were combined into seven. The Preamble was significantly changed from "We the People of the States of New-Hampshire . . ." to read "We the People of the United States," thus apparently making the Constitution a compact among the people, not the states. It has been maintained that the original wording, naming the individual states, could not be retained because no one could predict which of the nine states required to ratify the document would do so. The Committee of Detail, however, which drafted the original wording, knew that less than unanimous ratification was anticipated when it named all the states.[79] The exact reason why Morris and the Committee of Style decided to omit the listing of the states must remain a mystery, but Morris' decided nationalism provides a strong clue. Certain it is that the new version, in its further rewording, invoked the spirit of national unity on a moral plane compatible with that of the Declaration of Independence. The original wording read:

> We the People of the States of New-Hampshire, Massachusetts, Rhode-Island and Providence Plantations, Connecticut, New-York, New-Jersey, Pennsylvania, Delaware, Maryland, Virginia, North-Carolina, South-Carolina, and Georgia, do ordain, declare and establish the following Constitution for the Government of Ourselves and our Posterity.[80]

The revised wording read:

> We the People of the United States, in order to form a more perfect Union, establish Justice, insure domestic Tranquility, provide for the common defence, promote the general Welfare, and secure the Blessings of Liberty to ourselves and our Posterity, do ordain and establish this Constitution for the United States of America.[81]

Another, more obvious effort to inject centralized authority was

[79] Article XXI of the report of the Committee of Detail left a blank for the number of required states. *DIFUAS*, 481.
[80] Farrand, *Records*, II, 565.
[81] *Ibid.*, II, 569.

the insertion in Article I, Section 10, of a provision prohibiting the states from passing "laws altering or impairing the obligation of contracts." This provision had not appeared in the original article. Since only Morris among the committee members had opposed such a provision during the debates, the responsibility for the insertion of the clause devolves on Wilson, King, or Madison, with Wilson, who was a bank lawyer, the most likely probability.[82] In still another instance there is some evidence that Morris attempted to give special weight to the famous "general welfare" clause of Article I, Section 8, by making it an independent power of Congress. In the committee's report the clause was separated from the preceding clauses by a semicolon, thereby singling it out from the others:

> They [Congress] shall have power To lay and collect taxes, duties, imposts and excises; to pay the debts and provide for the common defence and general welfare of the United States.[83]

In the original version the clause had been separated from the others by only a comma.[84] In 1798, Albert Gallatin stated on the floor of the House of Representatives that he was "well informed" that the change in punctuation was a "trick," contrived by "one of the members who represented the State of Pennsylvania." The ruse, said Gallatin, was discovered by Sherman, who secured restoration of the original punctuation. [85]

Yet, on the whole, Morris was faithful to the intent of the enacted provisions. The convention took three days to review and collate the report. Most of the weary delegates heartily approved of the work. A number of miscellaneous, last-minute changes were proposed on the floor, in hopes of conciliating various groups. Among these was a move by Robert Morris, in one of his rare

[82] Forrest McDonald, *E Pluribus Unum: The Formation of the American Republic, 1776–1790*, 187n.
[83] Farrand, *Records*, II, 594.
[84] *Ibid.*, 569.
[85] Albert Gallatin in the House of Representatives, June 19, 1798, *ibid.*, III, 379; Farrand, *Framing of the Constitution*, 182–83.

remarks in the convention, to give Congress the specific power to establish a national bank. The proposal was defeated after Gouverneur opposed it on the ground that it would arouse the opponents of the bank and jeopardize ratification in Pennsylvania.[86] Another move was one by Gouverneur that "no State, without its consent shall be deprived of its equal suffrage in the Senate." This motion, an attempt to quiet the "circulating murmurs of the small States,"[87] was carried without debate or opposition.

On September 17 the delegates gathered for the final session to sign their names to the engrossed document. Franklin arose with a written speech, which Wilson read for him. It was a warm and eloquent plea for all to conquer their doubts and submerge their differences in support of the Constitution. In his effort to win over the dissenters, he made a motion, which had been drawn up by Morris, that the members sign the document under the statement, "Done in Convention by the unanimous consent of the States present the 17th. of Sepr. &c—In Witness whereof we have hereunto subscribed our names."[88] In that way all members could signify that their state delegations had approved the document even if they themselves had not.

Before the motion could be voted upon, Gorham asked whether or not it was too late to change representation in the House of Representatives from one for every forty thousand inhabitants to one for every thirty thousand. Here Washington rose to make his only contribution to the convention's discussions. It would give him "much satisfaction,"[89] he said, to see the proposal accepted. The delegates unanimously agreed.

[86] Thomas Jefferson's *Anas*, March 11, 1798, giving Baldwin's account of an incident in the House of Representatives, Farrand, *Records*, III, 375–76.

[87] *Ibid.*, II, 631.

[88] *DIFUAS*, 740. In spite of the rule of secrecy, Morris' authorship of this motion was known no more than three days later to one of Lafayette's officers then visiting Philadelphia. Gaston de Maussion to Madame de Maussion, September 20, 1787, in Princess Radziwill (tr.), *They Knew the Washingtons: Letters from a French Soldier with Lafayette and from His Family in Virginia*, 170.

[89] *DIFUAS*, 741.

Randolph then declared that he could not possibly change his mind and sign. Morris unavailingly attempted to persuade him to do so, pointing out that he himself had reservations but would accept the decision of the majority:

> Mr. Govr. Morris said that he too had objections, but considering the present plan as the best that was to be attained, he should take it with all its faults. The majority had determined in its favor and by that determination he should abide. The moment this plan goes forth all other considerations will be laid aside, and the great question will be, shall there be a national Government or not? and this must take place or a general anarchy will be the alternative.[90]

William Blount of North Carolina volunteered that he had not expected to sign but would now do so under the proposed form. Franklin's motion was carried, with ten states voting in favor and South Carolina divided. All members present but Randolph, Mason, and Gerry signed their names. The last name to appear on the engrossed document was that of "Gouvr. Morris" for Pennsylvania (readers unfamiliar with his handwriting usually mistake the signature for Gouv.).

That evening the delegates and the members of the Pennsylvania assembly, which had been meeting across the hall in the State House at the same time, joined for a dinner at the City Tavern. Afterward Washington retired "to meditate on the momentous work which had been executed."[91]

The next day, Washington, Robert Morris, and Gouverneur Morris dined at one o'clock for the last time at Robert's house. Then they rode together to Gray's Ferry,[92] on the Schuylkill. From there Washington continued to Mount Vernon, Robert returned

---

[90] *Ibid.*, 742. See also Gouverneur Morris to Walter Rutherfurd, December 3, 1789 [1787?], Livingston Rutherfurd, *Family Records and Events*, 136–37.

[91] Warren, *Making of the Constitution*, 720.

[92] Entry of September 18, 1787, Washington, *Washington after the Revolution*, 83.

home, and Gouverneur set out for Morrisania, to embark on a second career of fortune building, travel, and high diplomatic and political office—but never to match his moment of greatness as molder of the presidency and stylist of the Constitution.

The French Revolution
and the
Decline of American Aristocracy

CHAPTER X

ROM THE WESTERN shore of the Atlantic, where he had played a leading role in one revolution which was to change the destinies of men, Morris now turned to the eastern shore, where another was about to begin. On December 18, 1788, he boarded the ship *Henrietta* at Philadelphia and embarked on a cold and stormy voyage of forty days which brought him to the port of Le Havre, France, on January 27, 1789.

His purpose was to negotiate urgent business matters for Robert Morris and for William Constable and Company (Rucker had recently died). After the convention he had returned to full-time commercial and legal activities, among which had been a seven-month stay in Virginia, in company with Robert Morris, where the two men had tried to straighten out difficulties connected with Robert's contract for a monopoly on the sale of American tobacco to the French Farmers General. The journey had given him another opportunity to visit Washington at Mount Vernon and to observe the struggle in Richmond over ratification of the Constitution, but his chief concerns were private. When it appeared that the only hope of mollifying the French over arrears in the tobacco shipments lay in personal conversations, his business partners decided that he should go to France. Equally important would be the opportunity to unload huge blocks of land bought on speculation in the St. Lawrence country and in the Holland Purchase of the Genesee River valley in western New York State. Most ambitious of all was a daring plan formed by Gouverneur, Robert Morris, William Duer, William Constable, and Samuel Osgood to negotiate with France the purchase of the American debt to that country of thirty-four million dollars at a reduced price of approximately fifty cents on the dollar, in the expectation that the debt would be redeemed at a higher value by the United States. Approval of the project by the American government was to be obtained by Osgood, who was a member of the Board of Treasury. Failing that, it was hoped that Gouverneur would be named minister to Holland, where he could exert the needed influence. He was to co-ordinate his efforts with two European-based investment groups: an association of the American Andrew Craigie with Frenchmen Brissot de Warville and Stephen Clavière and a combination of the English-based American Daniel Parker and the Frenchman Le Couteulx de Cantaleu. If successful, the network would become an international banking house which would rival the Dutch syndicates in bidding for American loans and engaging in land and security speculations.[1]

In Paris, armed with letters of introduction from Washington, Franklin, and the Comte de Moustier, the French minister to the United States, Morris quickly made acquaintances in select circles. His brilliance and polish were the equal of the best in French salon society, and his unbeholden, outspoken manner was peculiarly and appealingly American—"the Simplicity of my Dress and Equipage," as he said, "my wooden Leg and Tone of

[1] Robert Morris to Mrs. Robert Morris, November 15, 1787, through April 26, 1788, Robert Morris Papers, Henry E. Huntington Library; entries of November 19, 21, 1787, and July 12, 15, 1788, George Washington, *The Diaries of George Washington, 1748–1799* (ed. by John C. Fitzpatrick), III, 269, 270, 387, 388; Robert Morris to Alexander Donald, November 30, 1788, Signers of the Declaration of Independence, I, 114, Pierpont Morgan Library; Robert Morris to Jeremiah Wadsworth, December 16, 1788, Jeremiah Wadsworth Papers, Box 139, Connecticut Historical Society; Andrew Craigie to Daniel Parker, October 29 and November 19, 1788, and Rufus King, memorandum, December 21, 1788, in Joseph Stancliffe Davis, *Essays in the Earlier History of American Corporations*, I, 167–69; Ferguson, *Power of the Purse*, 264–66.

republican Equality."[2] Nor, in a land where women's amorous adventures began after marriage, did his stock suffer from the reputation for gallantry which had preceded him across the ocean. Although his diary, which he began keeping soon after his arrival in Paris, and his letter books attest to his steady devotion to business (not to mention his capacity for rapid writing), he settled into a round of social visiting which became a daily pattern for the ten years he was to spend in Europe.

He saw much of Thomas Jefferson, America's envoy in Paris, who he found commanded "very much Respect . . . merited by good Sense and good Intentions" but with whom he differed "in our Systems of Politics." Jefferson recoiled from his countryman's cavalier conservatism and blushed to his temples at some of Morris' off-color expressions. Morris renewed his friendship with Lafayette, whom he found "very much below the Business he has undertaken" of leading a revolution. His friend Chastellux had died just before his arrival. Among his new acquaintances were Jacques Necker, the director-general of finance, "a very poor financier" who was "utterly ignorant also of Politics," and the Comte de Montmorin, minister of foreign affairs, whom Morris set down as one who "means well, very well. But he means it feebly." He also met Talleyrand, the clubfooted bishop of Autun, whom he rated a "sly, cool, cunning and ambitious Man."[3]

He had come to Paris convinced that "An Engaget. in which the Heart can take any Share is out of the Question," but within six months he was deeply involved in an affair with Adélaïde de Flahaut, the twenty-eight-year-old wife of the sixty-three-year-old Comte de Flahaut. According to a court portraitist, she had "a pretty figure" and "a charming face with the wittiest [brown]

[2] Entry of November 18, 1790, GMDFR, II, 64.

[3] Gouverneur Morris to Robert Morris, July 21, 1789, ibid., I, 159n.; Charles J. Ingersoll, Recollections, Historical, Political, Biographical, and Social, I, 453, citing remarks of William Short, Jefferson's secretary; entry of September 18, 1789, GMDFR, I, 223; Gouverneur Morris to George Washington, January 24, 1790, Papers of George Washington; entry of June 6, 1789, GMDFR, I, 108.

eyes in the world," and she had been conducting an affair with Talleyrand, by whom she had had a child. Her liaison with Morris lasted for three years of almost daily intimacies, sometimes in the presence of her female companion, who was nearsighted and could not understand endearances whispered in English. "How I pant to encircle the Nymph in my Arms,/ How glow with incessant Desire!" Morris wrote Adélaïde. She importuned him to help obtain an appointment for her husband as French minister to the United States so that she could be with Morris there; and, anticipating her aged husband's death, she proposed marriage, but Morris would not give of himself completely.[4]

Although he did not have other affairs during his years with Adélaïde, he charmed many fascinating women. He formed a lifelong friendship with Madame de Staël, Necker's daughter, a "woman of wonderful wit," at whose home the elegant world gathered twice weekly for supper and once for dinner. Had he been free, he thought, he could have stimulated her "Curiosity to the Experiment of what can be effected by the Native of a New World who has left one of his Legs behind him." He became the confidant of the blonde, wealthy Duchess d'Orléans, who poured into his ear tales of the inhumanities of her faithless, licentious husband. Perhaps the most beautiful of his Parisian friends was the Comtesse de Ségur, "a very sensible and indeed a very lovely Woman," who, however, was in love with her husband.[5]

In the conversations of these ladies, as, indeed, everywhere in Paris, Morris found that republicanism was "absolutely a moral Influenza." Bad harvests, industrial depression, and a severe winter had produced unemployment and bread riots. Peasant demands for tax relief and middle-class demands for social equality aggravated the unrest. And the financial aid which France had

[4] Vigée-Le Brun, *Souvenirs*, as quoted in *GMDFR*, I, 17n.; entries of August 7, 1791 and September 24, 1789, *ibid.*, II, 236, I, 228.
[5] Gouverneur Morris to George Washington, January 24, 1790, Papers of George Washington; entries of September 26, May 21, and November 7, 1789, *GMDFR*, I, 234, 85, 291.

extended to the Americans in their revolution was now precipitating bankruptcy at home. Yet, noted Morris, "the Materials for a Revolution in this Country are very indifferent." The nobility, "Hugging the dear Privileges of Centuries long elapsed," were inept and corrupt. The common people had "no Religion but their Priests, no Law but their Superiors, no Moral but their Interest." The king, "a small beer Character," was too unperceiving and weak-willed to take preventive steps. Lacking any experience in self-rule, the reformers wished to establish a government on the American model.

Morris recognized the need for reform and sympathized with the yearning of America's wartime friend and "natural ally" for liberty, but he warned that destruction of the old order before the people were educated to the responsibilities of a new one could only result in the triumph of despotism. "I have here the strangest Employment imaginable," he wrote. "A Republican and just as it were emerged from that Assembly which has formed one of the most republican of all republican Constitutions I preach incessantly Respect for the Prince Attention to the Rights of the Nobility, and Moderation." The advice was scarcely welcome to those thirsting for a new era. Lafayette bluntly accused him of injuring the cause of democracy, and he as bluntly replied that he was "opposed to the Democracy from Regard to Liberty."[6]

Disapprovingly, he watched as the States-General convened without the guidance of a concrete program of reform from the king, the Bastille fell, the aristocrats in the National Assembly renounced their privileges, the Declaration of the Rights of Man was proclaimed, a mob of women in Paris forced the royal family to move from Versailles to Paris, and the assembly seized the lands of the Catholic church. Horrified, he saw the decapitated

---

[6] Gouverneur Morris to Marquis de La Luzerne, March 8, 1789, *ibid.*, I, xli; Gouverneur Morris to George Washington, April 29, 1789, Papers of George Washington; Gouverneur Morris to William Carmichael, July 4 and February 25, 1789, Commercial Correspondence, Papers of Gouverneur Morris, I, 72–76, 23; entry of June 23, 1789, GMDFR, I, 121.

body of one of the king's ministers dragged through the streets with the head on a pike.

Morris would have had the king take the initiative and propose a mildly limited monarchy, rather than become the tool of misguided idealists such as Lafayette or opportunists such as Mirabeau ("Every Country has its John Wilkes").[7] If there was to be a constitution, it should be one giving the "King of the French" (meaning the king of all the French people) unrestricted appointive and removal powers, command of the armed forces, and control over diplomatic relations, including war and peacemaking (subject to approval of his appointed ministerial council). The legislature should consist of a hereditary senate of ninety members and a four-hundred-member national assembly, elected in rural districts on the basis of a property qualification and in the cities by males who had reached their majority and were married. All revenue laws should originate in the popular house and all laws, after passage by both houses, should be subject to the king's veto. The judicial system, which should guarantee trial by jury and freedom of religion, should be headed by an appellate court of judges appointed for life, whose decisions could be reviewed by the senate.[8] Morris communicated these views to members of the National Assembly, to Lafayette, Montmorin, Necker, and Talleyrand, and even to the king and queen, sometimes on request and sometimes on his own initiative. Soon he was in the uncommon position of a foreigner intimate with the councils and intrigues of the aristocracy.

On January 21, 1790, Morris received two letters from President Washington, requesting him to serve as an informal emissary to London to sound out the British government on its willingness to evacuate the Northwest forts in compliance with the provisions of the peace treaty of 1783, and pay for slaves which

[7] Entries of July 22 and October 4, 1789, *ibid.*, 158–59, 242.
[8] Gouverneur Morris, "Notes on the Form of a Constitution for France" [n.d.], (tr. from the French), Sparks, *Morris*, III, 481–500.

had been taken away by the British armies when they left America, in violation of the treaty. Morris was also to explore the possibility of negotiating a treaty of commerce.[9] Washington was using this unofficial approach to avoid a repetition of the rebuffs accorded earlier overtures by the Confederation government.

When he wrote to Morris, Washington was unaware that a crisis was developing between England and Spain. In July, 1789, the Spaniards had seized a British post and three ships at Nootka Sound, in Vancouver Island, off the western coast of North America. Morris learned about the incident through confidential sources, months in advance of its public disclosure, and at once grasped the possibilities inherent in the situation.[10] Spain was allied to France in the Family Compact of 1761. A war ranging Spain and France against Britain would serve the dual purpose of bolstering the French monarchy against the revolutionaries and disposing the British to cultivate American friendship, or at least neutrality. The day after he received Washington's letter, Morris went to Montmorin and told him about the part of his mission calling for the negotiation of a commercial treaty with Britain. He preferred, he said, a pact with France for trade with the West Indies, but French refusal to make such an agreement was driving America into the arms of Britain. When Montmorin replied that his government was too weak to decide on such an agreement, Morris seized the opening to recommend that France go to war as a means of reinvigorating the monarchy. The record of this remarkable conversation in his diary reads as follows:

> I communicate to him in the most perfect Confidence the Commission with which I am charged in Part. I tell him two very great Truths: that a free Commerce with the british Islands

[9] GMDFR, I, 462–64, 466–67.
[10] Entry of May 3, 1790, *ibid.*, 502; Gouverneur Morris to William Constable, May 6, 1790, *ibid.*, 509. Morris may have learned of the Spanish attack at Nootka Sound from William Carmichael, who claimed early knowledge of it, but no specific evidence to that effect has been found. Samuel Gwynn Coe, *The Mission of William Carmichael to Spain*, 84.

is the Object which will chiefly operate on us to give us the Desire of a Treaty of Commerce with Britain, and that I prefer much a close Connection with France. He tells me that their great Misfortune here is to have no fixed Plan nor Principle and at present no Chief. I tell him that they ought to go to war.[11]

Morris had a particular kind of war in mind. Three weeks later he told Lafayette that France should leave the ocean to the British, after first reinforcing the West Indies, and then invade Holland, England's ally, with the largest army that could be mustered. Lafayette, Morris knew, "burns with Desire to be at the Head of an Army in Flanders and drive the Stadtholder into a Ditch." A week later Morris told a French business acquaintance that France's interests called for seizure of Belgium as well, in order to keep "all Enemies at a most respectable Distance."[12]

Only a hint of this whole scheme was sent to Washington. The day after he received Washington's instructions, Morris replied with two letters, one official and one private. In the first he reported his discussion with Montmorin about the West Indies, and in the second he reported counseling the minister for war, but in neither letter did he explicitly reveal that he had disclosed his mission to England. Even at that, the letters miscarried, and by the time copies were sent and a reply could be returned, Morris' mission had been terminated.[13]

He arrived in London on March 27, having stopped along the way at Brussels, Antwerp, Amsterdam, and Rotterdam on business matters. Before going to the British Foreign Office he visited the French ambassador La Luzerne (now a marquis), his friend of Philadelphia days when La Luzerne had been minister to the United States, and confided in him that he had come to negotiate British compliance with the American peace treaty but said noth-

11 Entry of January 22, 1790, *ibid.*, 374–75.
12 Entries of February 15 and 21, 1790, *ibid.*, 412, 419; Gouverneur Morris to George Washington, January 22, 1790, Papers of George Washington.
13 *Ibid.*; Washington to Morris, December 17, 1790, Washington, *Writings*, XXXI, 173.

ing about a commercial treaty.[14] If La Luzerne had pooled his information with Montmorin, the French would have known the entire purpose of Morris' mission.

When Morris had his first interview with the Duke of Leeds, the foreign secretary in William Pitt's cabinet, he found that the British resisted surrendering the forts or paying for the removed slaves but might consider sending an ambassador to the United States. In subsequent written exchanges Leeds flatly insisted upon prior American payment of Loyalist debts and, while endorsing the general idea of a commercial treaty, showed no disposition to open negotiations. Morris pointedly warned him that Congress had considered enacting retaliatory tariffs. "I thought it best to heap Coals of Fire on their Heads and thereby either bring them into our Views or put them most eminently in the wrong," he wrote Washington. But Leeds would not be moved to a specific commitment for talks. Morris concluded that the British were awaiting developments in Europe and the results of the next parliamentary election.[15]

One new development turned out to be an announcement by Pitt on May 6 that he had sent an ultimatum to Spain, demanding restoration of the ships and crews seized at Nootka Sound, payment of indemnities, and recognition of British rights of settlement on the western coast of America. Now, Morris decided, was the time for the Franco-Spanish war with England he had been contemplating. The day after the public disclosure he wrote three significant letters, the first to Lafayette; the second to the Chevalier Jean de Ternant, who had been proposed as French minister to the United States; and the third to William Carmichael, American chargé d'affaires at Madrid and a close friend of Morris. The last two letters were enclosed in the one to Lafayette, who was to

---

[14] Entry of March 28, 1790, GMDFR, I, 461–62.

[15] Morris' correspondence with the Duke of Leeds and Washington is assembled in Sparks, Morris, II, 6–19. The manuscripts of Leeds's letters are in the Gouverneur Morris Manuscripts, Parke-Bernet sale lot 62. The quotation is from Morris to Washington, May 1, 1790, Papers of George Washington.

read and forward them, and the batch was sent through the French ambassador's confidential mail.[16] Together they comprised a bold plan for a concerted Franco-Spanish attack on Britain. Morris warned Lafayette:

> This Country is arming and I am convinced with a Determination to compel not only Spain but every other Power to subscribe to such terms as she may chuse to dictate. You will strive in vain to deprecate the Blow, therefore you must prepare to meet it. Or rather so to strike as may prevent it.

Since Britain lived by her commerce, France should first embargo her trade and then strike swiftly at all British commercial vessels, making a special point of capturing the sailors and never exchanging them. Then would follow an invasion of Belgium through Luxembourg, Brussels, and Antwerp. Emperor Leopold II of Austria, brother of Marie Antoinette, could be persuaded to cede to France his rights to the Austrian Netherlands, which had recently revolted, in return for French assistance in fighting Turkey. Prussia could be held at bay by strongly fortifying Liège. Next, a seaborne assault on Holland would be launched from Dunkirk against Amsterdam—John Paul Jones would provide the plan of attack. Interestingly, Morris anticipated help from popular, democratic forces in both the Low Countries. In the Austrian Netherlands he looked to the followers of General Jean-André van der Meersch, then in prison at Antwerp, who opposed the repressive regime of conservative counterrevolutionaries. In Holland he counted upon republican-minded Dutchmen who detested the House of Orange, which had been restored to power in 1787 after intervention by Prussia and Britain.[17]

[16] All three letters, dated May 7, 1790, are in Commercial Correspondence, Papers of Gouverneur Morris, II, 34–35. See also entry of May 7, 1790, *GMDFR*, I, 505–506; Gouverneur Morris to William Carmichael, July 13, 1790, Commercial Correspondence, II, 56.

[17] R. R. Palmer, *The Age of the Democratic Revolution: A Political History of Europe and America, 1760–1800*, 355, 335–40; Marquis de Lafayette, *Mémoires, Correspondence et Manuscrits due Général Lafayette*, (ed. by H. Fournier Aîné III, 45 n.; H. Pirenne, *Histoire de Belgique*, V, 527, 546, 568.

The letter to Ternant was written in similar vein, to enable Ternant to conduct his negotiations in America in full awareness of the projected European war.

The letter to Carmichael urged him to persuade the Spaniards to dispatch a squadron against Newfoundland and another against the British East Indies. Like the French, the Spaniards should direct a prime effort toward capturing the seamen, to drain Britain of her manpower.

As for Morris' home government, he sidestepped British interception of his official dispatches by asking his business friend William Constable to inform Washington of the crisis. Britain, he reported, was using the Nootka Sound incident to establish claims to the American west coast but was not strong enough financially to sustain a conflict. Spain, he believed, would never submit.[18] Until now, he had written not a word about the crisis, even though he had learned of it months before in Paris. For a man with his habitual ebullience it would have been difficult to report the event without a telltale analysis and speculations which would have revealed his secret war scheme. Perhaps it was simply better to say nothing, and even now to communicate the news indirectly and briefly.

On May 20 and 21, two weeks after the publication of Pitt's ultimatum to Spain, Morris had his second meeting with Leeds, and on the second day Pitt himself sat in on the talks. The prime minister proved no more amenable to surrender of the Northwest forts or to compensation for the slaves than Leeds, but he insisted that Britain was more agreeable to a commercial treaty than Morris had recognized. Morris answered with undiminished firmness that the return of the forts must precede all other agreements. "We do not think it worthwhile to go to war with you for these posts," he warned, "but *we know our rights, and*

---

[18] May 6, 1790, *GMDFR*, I, 509–10. Constable replied on June 23, 1790, that he had delivered the message that day. William Constable Letter Book, 1782–1790.

will avail ourselves of them, when time and circumstances may suit." If the British wished to negotiate a commercial treaty in earnest, they had only to transmit their intentions in writing. Regarding an exchange of ambassadors, the British must make the first appointment, he said, and the United States would probably follow suit. Morris came away convinced that Britain would consent to a trade treaty only as the price of American neutrality in the impending war with Spain.[19]

Whether or not his hard bargaining hit its mark, it was a fact that Britain began to consider surrender of the posts for fear the United States would seize them in the event of war. On May 29, Morris learned from John Inglis, a member of the British fur-trading firm of Phyn, Ellis and Inglis, that Lord Grenville, secretary of state for home affairs, had been inquiring about the value of the Northwest forts and was thinking of giving them up. On June 17 he heard that Grenville had almost decided to do so.[20] If the European crisis should worsen, America might very well gain the posts.

On the morning of June 21, Lafayette's aide-de-camp, Boinville, brought Morris the news he had been waiting for. The British, reported Boinville, had sent an overland express to India with instructions to commence hostilities. It looked as if the hour had arrived for the Franco-Spanish offensive. Morris handed Boinville a four-thousand-word memoir for Lafayette, developing his previous ideas on war strategy. He had been in frequent contact with Boinville, who had been shuttling back and forth between France and England for the past six weeks, and believed Lafayette sympathetic to his plans.

"There is no word perhaps in the dictionary, which will take the place of *Aristocrat* so readily as *Anglais*," Morris' memoir

[19] Entry of May 20, 1790, GMDFR, I, 518–22; Gouverneur Morris to George Washington, May 29, 1790, Papers of George Washington.
[20] Entries of May 29 and June 17, 1790, GMDFR, I, 530, 542–43; Gouverneur Morris to George Washington, May 29 and July 3, 1790, Papers of George Washington. See also A. L. Burt, *The United States, Great Britain, and British North America, from the Revolution to the Establishment of Peace After the War of 1812,* 111–13.

read. Some people talked of an alliance between France and England—one might as well talk of an alliance between Rome and Carthage. "The chance indeed is that Carthage must be destroyed." The Spaniards must seize Newfoundland, and the French, led in the field by Louis XVI, must invade Belgium and Holland. Then the French fleet must feint toward the French West Indies, thus drawing off the British navy, and turn suddenly to attack England herself, landing first at Plymouth and afterward at London and Brighton. All this concentration on European operations, Morris imperturbably noted, would probably result in the loss of the French colonies, but in return France would gain Flanders and the internal stability to establish a durable constitution. A chain reaction might even set in to create a new world order. Poland might be safeguarded, Greece liberated from Turkey, and India from Britain. The Black Sea might be opened to navigation, Egypt might win independence and the Barbary powers be restrained.[21]

But there was to be no war in 1790. The French National Assembly, preoccupied with the problems of the revolution, gave only lukewarm support to the Family Compact. In Madrid, Carmichael discouraged Spanish hopes that America would provide aid in return for free navigation of the Mississippi. He had rejected Morris' schemes and was, in fact, in close communication with the British minister to Spain, Alleyne Fitzherbert. Morris had disclosed his war plans to the Spanish minister in London, the Marqués del Campo, who, however, had not relayed them to the Conde de Floridablanca, the Spanish foreign minister. Instead, Floridablanca received from the British garbled reports of Morris' negotiations, purporting to show that the Americans desired a military alliance with England. Carmichael was only too happy to use the deception as an excuse to ignore Morris' urgent

[21] Entry of June 21, 1790, *GMDFR*, I, 547; Gouverneur Morris to George Washington, July 3, 1790, Papers of George Washington; Gouverneur Morris, "Plan of a Campaign for France," June, 1790, Sparks, *Morris*, II, 473–85. See also entry of October 30, 1790, *GMDFR*, II, 41.

letters, on the plea of the danger of aggravating Spanish suspicions. Floridablanca, seeing Spain isolated, signed a joint declaration with Fitzherbert on July 24, agreeing to restitution of the captured vessels and indemnification of injured parties but not yielding claims to Nootka Sound.[22]

Morris heard the disheartening news in London on August 6. He had a last, fruitless interview with Leeds on September 15. The British, he wrote Washington, "will not treat with us at present, unless they can see their way to an offensive and defensive Alliance, which we shall be in no hurry to contract." In the long run, only the establishment of America's financial credit and the threat of commercial retaliation at a critical juncture would force Britain to yield. Two and a half months later, after a trip to Europe, he had a conference with Leeds's undersecretary. By then Spain had signed the Nootka Sound Convention, conceding Britain's rights to settlement on the American west coast. Morris learned that Leeds was less tractable than before; on the one point on which he had previously given encouragement—the exchange of ambassadors—he no longer showed any interest. In any event, Washington had already decided on December 17 that further negotiations were useless. He and Jefferson wrote Morris, terminating his mission and commending him on his conduct of the negotiations.[23]

[22] Fitzherbert (later Lord St. Helens) told Lord Grenville that Carmichael was "very well meaning, and has been, upon many occasions, materially useful to us." February 28, 1792, Historical Manuscripts Commission, *Report on the Manuscripts of J. B. Fortescue, Esq., Preserved at Dropmore*, II, 257. William Carmichael to Thomas Jefferson, January 24, 1791, and David Humphreys to Jefferson, [January 13 or 15 or February 6 or 12], 1791, as quoted in Jefferson to George Washington, April 2, 1791, Thomas Jefferson, *The Writings of Thomas Jefferson* (ed. by Paul Leicester Ford), V, 315; Gouverneur Morris to William Carmichael, February 17, May 22, and July 13 and 14, 1791, Commercial Correspondence, Papers of Gouverneur Morris, II, 119, 141 and III, 56, 57; Morris to Carmichael, May 14, 1792, Private Correspondence, Papers of Gouverneur Morris, I, 111; William Ray Manning, "The Nootka Sound Controversy," American Historical Association *Annual Report* for 1904, 405–406.

[23] Entries of August 6, September 15, and December 17, 1790, GMDFR, I, 569–70, 598, II, 87. The relevant correspondence is in Sparks, *Morris*, II, 32–56, 130, and Washington, *Writings*, XXXI, 173. The quoted letter to Washington is dated September 18, 1790, Papers of George Washington.

Only afterward did Morris learn that critics in the United States had charged him with acting belligerently toward the British; revealing his mission to La Luzerne, who in turn had revealed it to the British; and siding with opposition leaders Edmund Burke and Charles James Fox against the Pitt ministry. He never knew that the charges had originated with Hamilton, now secretary of the treasury, who had initially urged Morris' appointment on Washington but now apparently sensed a pro-French bias in Morris' reports. Hamilton had been in regular contact with a British agent in New York, Major George Beckwith. He had planted these suspicions with Beckwith for transmittal to England and then had misrepresented Beckwith's messages to give Washington the impression that the British were officially displeased with Morris. He had also suggested to Beckwith that the negotiations be taken out of Morris' hands and transferred to the United States. When Robert Morris and Washington told Morris about the charges, he answered that the British would not tailor their decisions to an envoy's personality but would consult their own interests; that he had never divulged his negotiations about the Northwest forts to La Luzerne (who would not have revealed them anyway, for fear that France might be called on to support American claims); and that he had spoken only once to Fox and never to Burke. Washington, refusing to be swayed by a British undercover agent, supported Morris and resisted Hamilton's efforts for an American-British alliance.[24] Hamilton never knew how close to the mark he had been in his insinuations about Morris' anti-British tactics.

Morris' hard-line approach of threatening the British with retaliatory trade restrictions ultimately justified itself. As secretary of state, Jefferson supported and continued this policy. As the Democratic-Republican leader of the House of Representatives,

[24] Gouverneur Morris to Robert Morris [November 14, 1791], GMDFR, I, 615–17; George Washington to Gouverneur Morris, January 28, 1792, Washington, Writings, XXXI, 468–70; Julian Boyd, Number 7: Alexander Hamilton's Secret Attempts to Control American Foreign Policy, passim.

Madison introduced proposals for anti-British barriers in 1791 and 1794 which were only narrowly defeated. Without this weapon, the British would never have signed Jay's Treaty in which they agreed to evacuate the Northwest posts and pay for spoliations of American commerce—a final acknowledgment of American independence.[25]

To Morris the Nootka Sound controversy had been only one opportunity to bring about a war between France and Britain. Back in Paris, on May 1, 1791, he broached another plan to Montmorin, who had also continued to advocate a conflict. The new plan would also include an invasion of Holland and the Austrian Netherlands, but this time without a naval attack on Britain. Austria would be promised Silesia and, in exchange for the Low Countries, Bavaria. Poland would be lured with the promise of northern expansion to the Baltic; and the Order of Malta, with Constantinople. As for the French West Indies, Morris had "a different Plan for them which I do not communicate"—independence, and the opening of their ports to American commerce. For that project, he turned to the Baron de Cormeyré, one of the French commissioners to the islands and an American partisan. Cormeyré, spurred by the offer of a bribe, agreed to attempt to induce the Legislative Assembly (successor to the National Assembly under the French constitution of 1791) to authorize him and the other commissioners to draw up a proposal for colonial self-government and liberalized trade regulations. With these concessions as an opening wedge, the commissioners would then encourage the island assemblies to demand independence.

These schemes also proved futile. Montmorin resigned in Sep-

---

[25] Samuel Flagg Bemis, in his exhaustive study of Jay's Treaty and its preliminaries, sees no gain from the Morris mission to England. He gives Hamilton's conciliatory tactics the chief credit for opening diplomatic relations in 1791 and paving the way for the treaty in 1794. But the book can be read equally as the record of Britain's mounting concern about the threat of American commercial retaliation, as demanded by Jefferson and his followers. Samuel Flagg Bemis, *Jay's Treaty: A Study in Commerce and Diplomacy*, *passim*.

tember, 1791, taking with him any prospects a European war might have had. An insurrection of slaves and free blacks in St. Domingue in late 1791 halted the independence movement there. Morris, although an opponent of slavery, was not ready to sanction a slave revolt, particularly in the Caribbean, where the incendiary spirit might spread to the United States. His only remaining hope of cultivating pro-American sentiment now lay in channeling payment of part of the American debt to France to St. Domingue, a policy which he urged on William Short, the American chargé d'affaires in Paris, and which Jefferson and Washington independently adopted at home.[26]

To this point Morris' web of diplomacy had had a kind of grand consistency about it: the promotion of a Franco-British war which would remove the threat of British world domination and arrest the march of the French Revolution and from which America could extract evacuation of the Northwest posts and free trade with the French and British West Indies. But by the end of 1791, changes had taken place in France which forced him to reassess his aims. The new constitution, stripping the nobles of their power, had been signed by the king, and Montmorin had resigned. Prussia and Austria had issued the Declaration of Pillnitz, which advocated the restoration of absolute monarchy in France. The Girondists and Jacobins had seized on the king's veto of measures against the aristocratic *émigrés* and nonjuring priests to demand overthrow of the monarchy and creation of a republic. Most of the parties desired war with Austria, France's traditional ally against Britain, as the means of advancing their own fortunes. Talleyrand was sent to England to negotiate a guarantee of British neutrality in the coming conflict.

In Morris' eyes such an agreement would be a calamity. It

26 Entries of May 1, August 4, 20, September 3, October 31, November 1, 12, 13, 15, 16, 19, 21, 22, and 24, 1791, GMDFR, II, 175, 233, 241, 254, 298, 299, 305, 306, 307, 312, 313, 314; Gouverneur Morris to George Washington, September 30, 1791, *ibid.*, 277.

would eliminate the breathing spell which he believed could expose the weaknesses of the French constitution and restore the king's popularity. It would open the way for the exportation of revolutionary unrest throughout Europe. It could link Spain with Britain, in which event the United States would find itself "all at once surrounded by hostile Nations." Morris left Paris for London shortly after Talleyrand, and the newspapers in France and England charged that he went to undermine Talleyrand's mission. There is no proof of this charge, and Morris denied it, but he made no secret of his disapproval. He even quarreled with Adélaïde de Flahaut about it, their first difference over political affairs. The British, untempted by proffered concessions from Talleyrand which they could obtain for themselves, rejected them. Instead, they were encouraging the independence movement in St. Domingue and hoping for American support in exchange for mediation with the Indians on the American frontier; Morris hoped that the revolutionary contagion would spread to Jamaica, creating an independent government amenable to trade with the United States. Yet ultimately Talleyrand was successful. France declared war against Austria on April 20, 1792, and two weeks later Morris heard that Britain had informed Austria that she regarded her as the aggressor and would not honor their alliance.[27]

In the meantime Morris had been receiving reports that he was under consideration for appointment as Jefferson's successor to the post of minister plenipotentiary to France. Washington sent his name to the Senate, where the nomination was hotly debated. James Monroe labeled him a "monarchy man," and Roger Sherman called him "profane." Despite the opposition, however, Morris was confirmed on January 12 by a vote of sixteen to eleven. He received official word of the appointment from Jefferson on April 6. He also received a candid letter from Washing-

[27] Morris to Washington, February 4 and March 17, 1792, Papers of George Washington; entries of February 19, March 6, and April 23 and 24, 1792, GMDFR, II, 369, 376, 414–16.

ton, relaying the accusations which had been levied against him and warning him

> that the promptitude, with which your brilliant imagination is displayed, allows too little time for deliberation and correction; and is the primary cause of those sallies, which too often offend, and of that ridicule of characters, which begets enmity not easy to be forgotten, but which might easily be avoided, if it was under the control of more caution and prudence.

Morris contritely replied, "*I now promise you* that Circumspection of Conduct which has hitherto I acknowledge form'd no Part of my Character."[28]

The contrition was short-lived. Soon after his return to Paris, he was deep in a plan he had formulated for the flight of the king from the capital. On the morning of the departure, July 10, however, Louis XVI lost his nerve, and Morris commented that the scheme "Flash'd in the Pan." Two weeks later the distracted king, regretting having missed an opportunity to escape and fearful of a conspiracy against him by the Federals, a volunteer army, turned over to Morris the management of his affairs and the guardianship of his funds, amounting to 996,750 livres. As Morris told the story four years later, "a sort of royal army," to be paid out of the money entrusted to him, was organized to thwart the conspiracy. It was a last-minute, futile effort. The expected insurrection, spurred on by the Brunswick Manifesto, threatening Paris with destruction by the Prussians if the royal family was harmed, erupted on August 10. The leader of the royal forces, the Marquis de Mandat, was slain and his men slaughtered or overpowered. The Jacobins forced the Legislative Assembly to suspend the king from his functions. The monarchy was at an end.[29]

---

[28] Jefferson to Morris, January 23, 1792, *ibid.*, 396–97; Morris to Jefferson, April 6, 1792, *ibid.*, 399–400; *ibid.*, 387n.; Washington to Morris, January 28, 1792, Washington, *Writings*, XXXI, 469; Morris to Washington, April 6, 1792, Papers of George Washington.

[29] Entries of July 11 and 24 and August 2, 1792, GMDFR, II, 465, 472, 487; Gouverneur Morris to Thomas Jefferson, July 10, 1792, *ibid.*, 463; Gouverneur Morris to "Son Altesse Royale," December, 1796, Morris, *Diary and Letters*, I,

In the wake of the denouement refugees of the lost cause took sanctuary at Morris' house, at 488 rue de La Planche, Faubourg St.-Germain. Among them were Adélaïde de Flahaut and her son and the Comte d'Estaing (the unsuccessful commander of a French fleet in the American Revolution). Morris could not extend his diplomatic immunity to them, but neither could he bring himself to turn them out, although sheltering them might expose him to the attacks of the insurgents. Even the diplomats were leaving Paris and advising Morris to do likewise. He decided that his duty obligated him to remain, and he was the only envoy to retain his post during the Terror.

From then on, Morris' already bad relations with the French government rapidly worsened. On August 29 the minister of foreign affairs, Pierre-Hélène-Marie Le Brun, requested an advance American payment of $800,000 (the French exchange equivalent of 4 million livres) on the debt to France, for use in purchasing supplies for St. Domingue. Morris had previously agreed to honor a 6-million-livre payment of regular installments which had been negotiated with the old government, but he refused to treat with the new one until he received authorization from Philadelphia. Also, he preferred that payments for St. Domingue be made in America, where the supplies would be purchased and where the machinations of Parisian speculators could be avoided. To Washington he confided that his purpose was to permit the United States "to temporize and see how Things are likely to end, and in such Case, leaving me at large with the Right reserv'd to avow or disavow me." Le Brun's reply to Morris' disclaimer of authority to negotiate was so offensive that Morris requested his passport to England. The French press thereupon charged that he intended to obtain an Anglo-American alliance against France and seized upon his reference to his government as "my Court," in his letter

---

558; Georges Lefebvre, *The French Revolution from Its Origins to 1793* (tr. by Elizabeth Moss Evanson), 235–41.

to Le Brun, as evidence of his aristocratic proclivities. Le Brun, however, apologized, and Morris withdrew his request.[30]

The violence of August 10 was followed by a wave of massacres of accused royalist conspirators, and on January 21, 1793, Louis XVI was executed. On February 1, France declared war on England and Holland, who were joined five weeks later by Spain. Now it was France against Europe, and a clear call for revolution as a preliminary to French conquest. With the extremists in the saddle, Lafayette fled to Luxembourg, where the Austrians imprisoned him. He claimed American citizenship and protection. Morris, backed by Jefferson, could not recognize the claim, but advanced him 10,000 florins of American funds on his own security. He also lent 100,000 livres of his own money to Lafayette's wife, who had stayed behind in France, and saved her from execution when she was imprisoned. Another claimant of American citizenship was Thomas Paine, Morris' long-standing political enemy, who had accepted French citizenship and had served in the National Assembly, but was now also imprisoned in Paris. Morris left him in prison, and he was not released until the next minister, James Monroe, interceded for him.

Adélaïde de Flahaut escaped with her son to England and did not see Morris again for three years. At the age of sixty-six her husband had fought for the king at the Tuileries on August 10 and was afterward imprisoned. He escaped by bribing his jailer, but when his attorney was mistakenly seized for complicity in the break, Flahaut turned himself in to free the attorney and was eventually guillotined.[31] D'Estaing, who had ignobly testified against the queen at her trial, also met death on the guillotine.

Morris' relations with the new government were so strained that at the end of May, 1793, he moved to a twenty-acre country estate

[30] Morris to Washington, October 23, 1792, GMDFR, II, 566. See also Morris to William Short, August 20, 1792, *ibid.*, 506; Morris to Jefferson, October 23, 1792, *ibid.*, 564; Morris to Hamilton, December 24, 1792, Hamilton, *Papers*, XIII, 378, 3n.–6n.

[31] Baron André de Maricourt, *Madame de Souza et sa Famille: Les Marigny, Les Flahaut, August de Morny* (1761–1836), 142–44, 453–55.

at Seine-Port on the Seine, twenty-seven miles from Paris. There he was occupied chiefly with negotiations concerning violations of the rights of American neutral trade and French imprisonment of American sailors. The end of his mission came when the mounting French complaints about him culminated in a request for his recall in retaliation for Washington's rejection of Edmond Charles Genêt in the United States. Washington, still loyal to Morris, sent him his approbation and defended him against the attacks of his Democratic-Republican critics. Monroe arrived to replace him in August, 1794.[32]

At first Morris considered returning to America, but for reasons of both business and pleasure he decided to remain in Europe for what turned out to be another four and a half years. He left Seine-Port on October 14 and traveled through Switzerland and Germany for eight months. In June, 1795, he went to Britain for a year's stay.

In London, on June 27, he met Sir James Bland Burges, undersecretary for foreign affairs in the American department, and had a long conversation with him. Morris said that he heartily endorsed Jay's Treaty, which had recently been negotiated. Whatever his feelings had been at the time of his London mission in 1790, he was now convinced that England was America's best friend. The French Revolution menaced all of Europe, and the only way to bring it to an end was to restore the Bourbon monarchy in the person of the late king's younger brother, the Comte de Provence, the self-styled Louis XVIII. For this the assistance of Britain and Austria was indispensable, and in return the loyalty of Louis could be assured by an indemnity, secured by occupation of several French towns.

Burges' report of this discussion led to further talks with Lord Grenville, who had succeeded Leeds as secretary for foreign affairs,

---

[32] Albert Hall Bowman, "The Struggle for Neutrality: A History of the Diplomatic Relations Between the United States and France, 1790–1801" (Ph.D. dissertation), 122–37; Washington to Morris, June 19, 25, 1794, Washington, *Writings*, XXXIII, 409–10, 413–14.

and Pitt. The British were just then giving naval support to an invasion of France by a large group of *émigrés* at Quiberon Bay in Brittany, and so Grenville was agreeable to a Bourbon restoration. Morris showed him a draft of a manifesto he had written for Louis to arouse royalists to his cause, and Grenville approved it. Instead, however, Louis issued the uncompromisingly reactionary Declaration of Verona—a "wild Thundering Manifesto," Morris called it. On July 7, Morris learned that the expedition had been defeated.[33]

For the remainder of his stay in Europe he continued to send a stream of information and advice to Grenville from Switzerland, Dresden, Vienna, Brunswick, Hamburg, Frankfurt, Ratisbon, and Stuttgart, where he mingled in court circles. He saw Adélaïde de Flahaut occasionally, but she was now deep in an affair with José María de Souza, a Portuguese diplomat, whom she later married, and had little time for her old lover. Morris finally succeeded in obtaining Lafayette's release from prison at Olmütz.

In his commercial activities Morris had built up a fortune which would assure him a life of affluence. Speculations in securities, shipping, and above all in sales of his St. Lawrence lands and the lands of his business associates formed the bulk of his profits. In 1791 he also bought 250,000 acres in the Genesee River area of western New York. The grandiose scheme of organizing an international banking network to purchase the American debt to France failed. Morris had expanded it in Europe to include purchase of the Spanish debt and even the American domestic debt. When Dutch bankers refused to join the venture and undercut

[33] Entries of June 27, 29, and 30 and July 2, 11, 15, and 27, 1795, Gouverneur Morris Diary, V, Papers of Gouverneur Morris; Morris to Washington, December 19, 1795, Private Correspondence, *ibid.*, II, 6; J. B. Burges to Lord Grenville, June 28, 1795, Historical Mss. Comm., *Manuscripts of J. B. Fortescue . . . at Dropmore*, III, 87–89; Gouverneur Morris, "Draft of a Manifesto to Be Made by the King of France, Late Monsieur," July, 1795, (tr. from the French), Gouverneur Morris Manuscripts, Parke-Bernet sale lot 52, and Sparks, *Morris*, II, 529–31; Lord Grenville to Gouverneur Morris, July 10, 1795, Letters of English Statesmen, Dreer Collection, Historical Society of Pennsylvania.

him with a counterproposal of their own, the project collapsed. He had better luck in speculating in securities of the American states, based on advance news from Constable of Hamilton's intention to have the federal government assume state debts.[34]

After several changes of plans over the years, in 1798 he at last decided to return to the United States. On October 7 he left Hamburg aboard the *Ocean* and after a disagreeable voyage landed at New York on December 23. He had been abroad for ten years.

At Morrisania he began building a new mansion, in French style, on the foundation of the old manor house. He rode up to Albany to argue a heated legal case, in which Hamilton and Aaron Burr were opposing counsel.[35] He journeyed to the St. Lawrence River valley to appraise his northern lands. He went to see his friend Robert Morris, who had lost his fortune in land speculations and, reduced to penury, was confined in a Philadelphia debtors' prison.

His Federalist friends welcomed his return to the United States. Jay was governor of New York. Hamilton, a leading light of the party, urged Morris to re-enter politics. When one of the New York senators, James Watson, resigned his post in April, 1800, the Federalist legislature elected Morris to fill the remaining three years of the unexpired term. He defeated another candidate, Peter Gansevoort of Albany, by a vote of twenty-five to eleven in the senate and fifty-four to forty-eight in the assembly.[36]

[34] "In the Case of Robert Morris a Bankrupt. Extract from the Examination Before the Commissioners" [n.d.], Historical Society of Pennsylvania; Ferguson, *Power of the Purse*, 264–67, 270–71; Davis, *Essays in the Earlier History of American Corporations*, I, 170–73.

[35] *Le Gueu* v. *Gouverneur and Kemble*. James A. Hamilton, *Reminiscences of James A. Hamilton; or, Men and Events, at Home and Abroad, During Three Quarters of a Century*, 12.

[36] Jabez D. Hammond, *The History of Political Parties in the State of New-York, from the Ratification of the Federal Constitution to December, 1840*, I, 131, 134.

He took his seat in Philadelphia on May 3, only a week and a half before the adjournment of this Sixth, Federalist-dominated, Congress, which would reconvene in November in the new Capitol in Washington, D.C. He arrived in time to vote with the majority to defeat a bill allowing the importation of slaves into the Mississippi Territory. He supported an unsuccessful attempt to prosecute William Duane, editor of the *Philadelphia Aurora*, for attacks on the Senate—a departure from his early defense of freedom of the press.[37]

The move to Washington in November coincided with the shift of political power to Virginia and the Jeffersonians in the presidential election of 1800. Morris found that many Federalists were so galled by Jefferson's victory that they were prepared to vote for Burr when the tie vote in the electoral college gave the House of Representatives the final decision. He refused to sanction those tactics. "Since it was evidently the intention of our fellow Citizens to make Mr. Jefferson their President," he told Hamilton, who had no use for Burr, "it seems proper to fulfill that Intention." Jefferson swept in a Republican Congress with him: there were eighteen Republicans and fourteen Federalists in the new Senate, which convened in December, 1801. A harbinger of the new democratic mood was the adoption of a resolution by the Senate on January 5, 1802, admitting a stenographer to the floor so that the debates could be recorded and published. Now the whole country could sit in judgment on the proceedings. Morris at first supported the resolution but then voted against it when an amendment requiring the reporter to be bonded was defeated. "This is the beginning of Mischief," he noted in his diary that day. The Federalists were at the crossroads as a party. One of their number who arrived with the new Congress commented that the Federalists had "the weight of talent and property; but unless they are more attentive & industrious their talents

[37] *Annals of the Congress of the United States*, VI, 172, 183, 184.

& wealth will not save them from the ravages of demoralizing democracy."[38]

The first target of the victorious Republicans was the Judiciary Act of 1801, which had added sixteen circuit judges and seven district judges to the national court system. They proposed to repeal the act as the means of removing the Federalists whom President John Adams had named to the positions just before leaving office. Morris viewed the repeal as a body blow to the Constitution. It was probably a mistake, he privately admitted, to have filled the vacancies with "midnight" appointments, but to dismiss the judges, whose tenure the Constitution guaranteed for life, would clearly undermine the judiciary. "The amount of it is," he told the Senate, "you shall not take the man from the office, but you may take the office from the man." If the judiciary lost its independence, it could no longer fulfill its prime function of preventing "an invasion of the Constitution by unconstitutional laws" and an invasion of personal liberty by the executive. "We are here," he pleaded, "to save the people from their most dangerous enemy, *to save them from themselves.*"

The Republicans, still smarting under the courts' support of the Sedition Act of 1798 (which Morris had opposed), wanted none of that deliverance, nor, in their rebuttals, did they overlook his aristocratic condescension. They passed the repeal bill on February 3, 1802, by the hairbreadth margin of sixteen to fifteen, and the House followed a month later. Morris never became reconciled to the defeat. He tried to persuade Hamilton to sponsor a protest petition of New York lawyers. He even proposed the formation of committees of correspondence "from Baltimore to

[38] Morris to Hamilton, December 19, 1800, Private Correspondence, Papers of Gouverneur Morris, II, 98; Noble E. Cunningham, Jr., *The Jeffersonian Republicans in Power: Party Operations, 1801–1809,* 71; *Annals of Congress,* VII, 1st session, 22; entry of January 5, 1802, Gouverneur Morris Diary; William Plumer to Edward Livermore, December 21, 1802, as quoted in Lynn W. Turner, *William Plumer of New Hampshire, 1759–1850,* 103. Many younger Federalists attempted to reorganize the party so as to increase voter appeal. David Hackett Fischer, *The Revolution of American Conservatism: The Federalist Party in the Era of Jeffersonian Democracy, passim.*

Boston" and a "general Meeting of the Citizens of New York" to consider "what constitutional Measures can be adopted in the present Moment to secure the Independence of the State, and the national Compact of the Union, from the Dangers with which they are threatened."[39]

The next goal of the Republicans, as Morris saw it, was an attack on the executive. On May 3, 1802, the Senate considered a resolution passed by the House, proposing that candidates for the presidency and vice-presidency be separately designated in national elections, to prevent a repetition of the tie vote of 1800. Morris considered this resolution the final move of the slave-owning South to engulf the New England stronghold of Federalism. It would guarantee majorities in the electoral college and prevent the final choice by the House, where the small states could prevail. This time Morris won his case. "My Vote was in the Negative," he noted with satisfaction, "and had it been otherwise the Resolution would have passed."[40] It was only a temporary triumph; the Republicans had their way when the Twelfth Amendment to the Constitution was ratified on September 25, 1804.

When Morris went to Washington the foremost diplomatic issue under consideration was American ratification of the Convention of 1800, which ended the two-year undeclared war with France. Morris had been opposed to the French Directorate and was even more so to Napoleon Bonaparte, recently created first consul, whose rise he saw as the fulfillment of his prophecy that the revolution would end with a dictator. He was willing to accept the treaty merely as an end to hostilities but voted with a majority in the Senate to expunge Article II, which suspended

[39] Morris to Robert R. Livingston, February 20, 1801, Sparks, *Morris*, III, 153–54; "First Speech on the Judiciary Establishment," January 8, 1802, *ibid.*, 371, 369, 375. *Annals of Congress*, VII, 183. Morris to Alexander Hamilton, February 22, 1802, Private Correspondence, Papers of Gouverneur Morris, II, 119; Lowell H. Harrison, *John Breckinridge: Jeffersonian Republican*, 141–46.

[40] Morris to President of the Senate and Speaker of the Assembly of the State of New York, December 25, 1802, *ibid.*, 132. See also Morris to Lewis R. Morris, December 10, 1803, *ibid.*, 149–55, expressing Morris' fear of the New York-Virginia alliance.

the treaties of 1778 until settlement of American claims totaling twenty million dollars. He feared that the French might "buy many of our influential Citizens with their own Money, and, intriguing at the same Time with our desperate Demagogues, force us back into a Union derogatory both to our Honor and to our Interest."[41]

The Americans did not know that the French foreign minister, Talleyrand, had been eager to conclude the peace because he was negotiating with Spain (which had deserted England for France in 1796) for the retrocession of Louisiana and was fearful that the United States might join Britain in her war against France and seize the western territory from France's weak ally. When it was learned that the transfer had been arranged according to the secret provisions of the Treaty of San Ildefonso, and, in addition, that the Spanish intendant of Louisiana had closed the American deposit at New Orleans, popular wrath rose to a high pitch. Jefferson attempted to quiet the alarm of westerners by sending Monroe on a special mission to France to purchase New Orleans and East and West Florida. The Federalists, seeing what might be their last hope of a return to national power, issued an inflammatory appeal to the West. On February 14, 1803, James Ross of Pennsylvania, the only western Federalist in the Senate, introduced a group of resolutions authorizing the President to use United States land and naval forces and fifty thousand southern and western militia to seize a place of deposit on the island of New Orleans. No one expected Jefferson to exercise this authority, and thus he could be accused of having surrendered western interests.

Morris rose to defend the resolutions on February 24. He had just been defeated for re-election by the Republican majority in the New York legislature, and he believed the occasion to be

---

[41] Gouverneur Morris to Nicholas Low, February 8, 1801, Sparks, *Morris*, III, 152; *Annals of Congress*, VI, 769, 771; Gouverneur Morris to Alexander Hamilton, January 5 and 16, 1801, Private Correspondence, Papers of Gouverneur Morris, II, 100, 103–106.

"the last scene of my public life." His speech was the most partisan and illiberal of his career on record. Discarding his earlier convictions that America should profit from Europe's distress, he demanded war with France at the very time that she was least distracted by European conflict. Appealing to sectional interests and setting aside his detestation of slavery in the name of concern for law and order, he importuned the South to demand New Orleans as a base from which to suppress the slave insurrection in St. Domingue:

> That event will give to your slaves the conviction that it is impossible for them to become free. Men in their unhappy condition must be impelled by fear, and discouraged by despair. Yes—The impulsion of fear must be strengthened by the hand of despair!

Seizure of New Orleans would also forestall a French invasion of the South, with its attendant threat of Indian attacks and slave uprisings. "When the armies of France shall have reached your frontier," he warned, "the firing of the first musket will be a signal for general carnage and conflagration." But the Ross resolutions were defeated by a vote of fifteen to eleven.[42]

Unlike many of his Federalist friends, however, Morris was sincere in desiring the acquisition of Louisiana. When the purchase treaty was signed, after he had left office, he recognized it instantly for the bargain it was. "I am content," he said, "to pay my share of the fifteen millions, to deprive foreigners of all pretext for entering our interior country." He would have preferred not to have absorbed the inhabitants as American citizens, for he distrusted western egalitarianism, but now that the die was cast

---

[42] Morris lost his seat to Theodorus Bailey of Dutchess County. When the Federalists saw no hope of electing Morris, six of them switched votes to Bailey, in order to defeat John Woodworth, the Republican caucus designee. Hammond, *The History of Political Parties in . . . New-York*, I, 191–92. *Annals of Congress*, VII, 2d session, 185, 192, 255; Arthur Preston Whitaker, *The Mississippi Question, 1795–1803: A Study in Trade, Politics, and Diplomacy*, 200–17; Turner, *William Plumer*, 105–106.

he decided that they were "the natural and political allies of the northern and eastern states."[43]

His term in the Senate expired on March 3, 1803, and he returned to Morrisania. He kept busy with the management of his farm, business activities, and occasional journeys to New England and upstate New York. On July 12, 1804, he went to New York City to be with Hamilton, who lay mortally wounded from his duel with Burr. "The Scene is too powerful for me," he wrote, "so that I am obliged to walk in the Garden to take Breath. After having composed myself, I return and sit by his Side till he expires."[44] Afterward he had the sad task of pronouncing a funeral oration and taking up a subscription to pay his friend's debts.

On Christmas Day, 1809, he married his thirty-five-year-old housekeeper, Anne Cary Randolph, in a surprise ceremony at Morrisania. She was an orphaned daughter of Thomas Mann Randolph of Virginia and the sister of Thomas Mann Randolph, Jr., who had married Jefferson's daughter Martha and was to become governor of Virginia. Her stepmother rejected her, and after her father's death she went to live with her sister Judith, who had married a cousin, Richard Randolph. There "Nancy," as Anne was called, met with a tragedy which marred the rest of her life. Richard Randolph was brought to trial on a charge of having on September 30, 1792, destroyed a newborn child resulting from his adultery with his sister-in-law Nancy, an incestuous act according to the morality of the time. Defended by Patrick Henry and John Marshall, Richard was acquitted when the testimony of a Negro slave, who said that he had found the dead infant on a woodpile, was not admitted in court. Nancy's sister and the other Randolphs believed her to be the real guilty party, and when Richard died, she was cast out of the house, destitute,

[43] Morris to Jonathan Dayton, November 9, 1803, Sparks, *Morris*, III, 183; Morris to Jonathan Dayton, February 19, 1804, Private Correspondence, Papers of Gouverneur Morris, II, 164.
[44] Entry of July 12, 1804, Gouverneur Morris Diary.

to make her own way in a day when women had little prospect of earning their own living. Richard's younger brother, John Randolph of Roanoke, known to history for his vitriolic public tongue, pursued her with charges of having poisoned her brother-in-law, of intimacy with a Negro slave, and of advances to a guest at the home of friends.

Morris had first met Nancy, then a girl of twelve, during a visit to Virginia in 1786. He met her again in 1788. When he next saw her, in 1808, she was teaching at an academy in Stratford, Connecticut. Undeterred by her history, which she told him candidly, he offered her a position in his home. She could bring peace, he said, among quarreling servants who would accept supervision from a gentlewoman. Her coming would also still gossip that he had been conducting an affair with his last housekeeper, a handsome but common woman. Nancy went to live at Morrisania in April, 1809, and the two were married eight months later.

His relatives, the Ogdens, Wilkinses, and Merediths, faced with the loss of a rich inheritance, were outraged by the marriage. He replied:

> If I had married a rich Woman of seventy, the World might think it wiser than to take one of half that Age without a Farthing, and if the World were to live with my Wife I should certainly have consulted its Taste—but as that happens not to be the Case, I thought I might without offending others endeavor to suit myself, and look rather into the Head and Heart than into the Pocket.

When his son, Gouverneur, Jr., was born on February 9, 1813, his nephew Martin Wilkins suggested that the baby be named Cut-usoff, after Napoleon's Russian nemesis, General Mikhail Kutu-zov. After Morris' death his relatives even tried to challenge the boy's paternity. Yet Morris and his wife were happy together.[45]

[45] Entry of December 25, 1809, *ibid.*; William Cabell Bruce, *John Randolph of Roanoke, 1773–1833*, I, 106–29, II, 273–302; deposition of Lewis Morris, October 28, 1817, *Ann C. Morris v. David B. Ogden*, New York State Supreme

He had had his share of conquests, and now, with an appreciation of the practical requirements of marriage, he had selected a compatible woman of youth, good looks, loyalty, high birth, good education, and, if that much of her enemies' charges was true, lively sexuality.

The Senate was not, after all, the last scene of his public life. On March 13, 1810, the New York legislature appointed him chairman of a seven-man board of commissioners to explore alternate routes for the construction of a canal between the Hudson River and Lake Erie. He had thought of such a project as early as 1777 and had mentioned it to Morgan Lewis and Philip Schuyler at Fort Edward. In 1802 he had gone further and proposed consideration by Congress of a comprehensive, nationwide network of waterways "from the Waters of the Potomack to those of the Ohio from the Hudson to Lake Ontario from the Chesapeake to the Delaware and from the Delaware to the Hudson."

The members of Morris' canal board, which contained a majority of four Federalists, worked together harmoniously. In 1811, after exploring the terrain in person, they recommended a southern route to Lake Erie rather than to Lake Ontario. They also advocated the fanciful principle of an inclined plane, which was Morris' idea, hoping to turn to advantage Lake Erie's elevation of 565 feet above the Hudson. In December, 1811, the New York legislature sent Morris and a fellow board member, DeWitt Clinton, to Washington to lobby for federal funds. They found that both Congress and Madison doubted the constitutionality of federal internal improvements and appeared to resent the prospect

---

Court, New York Public Library; Swiggett, *The Extraordinary Mr. Morris*, 392–99; Mrs. Gouverneur Morris Papers [1818–1828], Print Department, Museum of the City of New York; Ann C. Morris to James Madison [n.d.], Papers of James Madison, Library of Congress, XCI; Morris to John Marshall, December 2 and 28, 1809, Morris to Gertrude Meredith, February 9, 1813, Private Correspondence, Papers of Gouverneur Morris, III, 74–75, 77–78; Morris to John Parish, July 6, 1816, *ibid.*, IV, 74.

of the growth of New York. They returned home to prepare a bold report recommending that New York go it alone, at a cost of five million dollars. At that point the outbreak of the War of 1812 suspended action. When the canal project was revived on April 17, 1816, Morris was not reappointed to the commission.[46]

The War of 1812 represented to Morris the realization of the worst fears which the Republican repeal of the Judiciary Act of 1801 had aroused in him. He had opposed the embargo as an absurd attempt to frighten England, in support of "a rash Opinion that foreign Sailors in our Merchant Ships are to be protected against the Power of their Sovereign," although, paradoxically, if a war broke out, it would be "ruinous to the Southern States." At first he hoped that war would be averted, and he thought the best policy for the Federalists was to remain inactive. But when the conflict appeared imminent, he suggested to DeWitt Clinton that a convention of both political parties north of the Potomac be called to propose overcoming southern domination of the nation by eliminating representation based on two-thirds of the slaves. When war did come, he declared it the work of "the inland States under the Pretext of protecting Commerce and Seamen but for the avowed Purpose of conquering Canada and with the obvious Intention of scattering Millions among their Constituents."[47]

He grimly refused to support the war. "If Peace be not immediately made with England," he wrote two weeks after hostilities commenced, "the Question on Negro Votes must divide this Union." Early in August, 1812, a "general committee" for a peace

---

[46] William W. Campbell, *The Life and Writings of DeWitt Clinton*, 27–28; Morris to Henry Lee, January 22, 1801, Private Correspondence, Papers of Gouverneur Morris, II, 111; Sparks, *Morris*, I, 496–504; Nathan Miller, *The Enterprise of a Free People: Aspects of Economic Development in New York State During the Canal Period, 1792–1838*, 21–39; Ronald E. Shaw, *Erie Water West: A History of the Erie Canal, 1792–1854*, 13–63.

[47] Morris to Lewis B. Sturges, February 12, 1814, Private Correspondence, Papers of Gouverneur Morris, III, 174; Morris to Simeon DeWitt, December 18, 1808, Historical Society of Pennsylvania; Morris to David B. Ogden, April 5, 1813, Private Correspondence, III, 156.

movement, consisting of Morris, John Jay, Rufus King, Richard Harison, Egbert Benson, Matthew Clarkson, and Richard Varick, held several meetings at Morrisania. The group formulated a series of antiwar resolutions, including a call for the creation of committees of correspondence in the states. Then a mass meeting of the self-styled "Friends of Liberty, Peace, and Commerce" was held in New York on August 18 at Washington Hall, at the corner of Broadway and Reade Street, where the resolutions were adopted. On August 29, Morris went so far as to publish an "Address to the People of the State of New York" in the *New-York Herald*, under his old, thinly disguised pseudonym "An American," advocating separation of the northern states from the Union. He spoke at a protest meeting at White Plains on September 4, and on September 15 he attended a three-day presidential nominating convention of the Federalist party at Kent's Tavern on Broad Street in New York. DeWitt Clinton, who had defected from the Republicans, won informal endorsement over Rufus King. Clinton went on to win the New York electoral vote, but lost the national count to Madison.[48]

Four more years of Madison in the presidency were to Morris a catastrophe. "I supposed him to be out of his Senses," he wrote, after reading Madison's inaugural address, "and have since been told that he never goes sober to Bed." He advocated that Congress refuse to pay the war loans of the Madison administration. They were, he asserted, another southern subterfuge to avoid imposition of a direct tax, which according to the Constitution would be apportioned to include three-fifths of the slaves. Comparing his

[48] Morris to Charles W. Hare, June 30, 1812, *ibid.*, 123; entries of August 1, 3, 4, 5, and 10 and September 15, 16, and 17, Gouverneur Morris Diary; Rufus King statement, "War with England Declared, June 18, 1812," in Charles R. King, *The Life and Correspondence of Rufus King*, V, 267–71; *New-York Herald*, August 19, 1812; Morris to Benjamin R. Morgan, August 20, 1812, Private Correspondence, Papers of Gouverneur Morris, III, 129–30; William Jay, *Life of John Jay* . . . I, 446–48; Dixon Ryan Fox, *The Decline of Aristocracy in the Politics of New York, 1801–1840* (ed. by Robert V. Remini), 168–72; Robert Ernst, *Rufus King: American Federalist*, 316–19.

stand on the war with that of the Quakers on all wars, he pronounced the conflict immoral and therefore unsupportable:

> Those who consider themselves as moral Agents, accountable to God, hold it impious to support an unjust War . . . . The Debt, therefore, now contracting by Messrs. Madison and Co. is void, being founded in moral Wrong of which the Lenders were well apprized.[49]

More than that, he had now unequivocally decided for secession. On May 15, 1813, he wrote to Harrison Gray Otis of Massachusetts proposing, in a suggestion anticipating what was to be the Hartford Convention, the calling of a meeting of states which were "the friends of peace and commerce," particularly the New England states. A year later he unsuccessfully tried to persuade his nephew David B. Ogden, a member of the New York legislature, to sponsor a state convention to initiate union with New England. When the Hartford Convention met in December, 1814, he thought its resolutions too timid.[50] The news of the signing of the Treaty of Ghent put an end to all hopes of the formation of a separate confederation.

He continued to deprecate the Madison administration in its postwar measures. He opposed the chartering of the Second Bank of the United States on the ground that its notes would be inflationary. He objected to the tariff of 1816, even though it benefited the northern as opposed to the southern states, because he opposed subsidization of "Hot-bed Manufactures" and taxation of farmers to support "the Scum of England and Ireland, who come out to live in Ease and Idleness as Mechanics" and put to work

---

[49] Morris to David Parish, March 6, 1813, Private Correspondence, Papers of Gouverneur Morris, III, 145; Morris to David B. Ogden, April 5, 1813, *ibid.*, IV, 150–53. See also Morris to Egbert Benson, June 23, 1813, *ibid.*, 157–58.

[50] Morris to Otis, May 15, 1813, Sparks, *Morris*, III, 293; Morris to Ogden, March 1, 1814, Private Correspondence, Papers of Gouverneur Morris, IV, 179–80; Gouverneur Morris, "Report of Committee of the New York Legislature," to David B. Ogden [n.d.], Historical Society of Pennsylvania; Morris to Rufus King, January 7, 1815, and Morris to Moss Kent, January 10, 1815, Private Correspondence, Papers of Gouverneur Morris, IV, 25–26, 26–27.

"many, poor Children who can be pent up to march backward and forward, with a Spinning Jenny, till they are old enough to become Drunkards and Prostitutes."[51]

But he believed the Federalist party dead. "Gentlemen," he counseled his friends, "let us forget Party and think of our Country. The Country embraces both Parties. . . . and, if our Country be delivered, what does it signify whether those who operate her Salvation wear a federal or democratic Cloak?"[52]

On that note of reconciliation his life ended. He had long been plagued with gout in his leg. More seriously, he had suffered from a stricture in the urinary passage, possibly the result of a cure for an earlier disease. He tried to relieve the stricture by forcing a whalebone through it, an effort which resulted, said his friend King, in "lacerations and mortification." He died on November 6, 1816, at the age of sixty-four. To the last he never lost his infectious joy of life. Four months before his death he wrote that he could still feel "the Gayety of Inexperience and the Frolic of Youth."[53]

---

[51] Morris to Moss Kent, January 23, 1816, and Morris to Randolph Harrison, March 4, 1816, *ibid.*, 52–57, 67. See also Morris to Harrison, May 8, 1816, *ibid.*, 71–74.

[52] To Committee of Correspondence, August 27, 1816, *ibid.*, 75.

[53] King to Christopher Gore, November 5, 1816, King, *Life and Correspondence of Rufus King,* VI, 35; entry of July 18, 1789, GMDFR, I, 154; entry of October 7, 1790, *ibid.*, II, 14; William Dunlap, *Diary,* (1766–1839), III, 631; Morris to John Parish, July 6, 1816, Private Correspondence, Papers of Gouverneur Morris, IV, 74.

NOTE ON
GOUVERNEUR MORRIS MANUSCRIPTS

THE GOUVERNEUR MORRIS manuscript holdings in the Columbia University Libraries and the Library of Congress, together with the papers auctioned and dispersed in sale number 3019 at the Parke-Bernet Galleries in New York City on April 7, 1970, comprise the original collection left by Morris at his death and retained in the family for more than a century. The papers at Columbia, acquired in 1954, contain drafts of letters and speeches written before 1789 and much of the correspondence received for all the years.

The Morris papers in the Library of Congress, acquired in 1932 but restricted until 1949, are valuable chiefly for the comprehensive diaries and letter books which Morris began to keep after his arrival in France in 1789. There are thirteen volumes of the diary, from March 1, 1789, to October 19, 1816, with a gap from January 6, 1793, to October 11, 1794. They are detailed and frank but for the European period rarely introspective; they are sketchy and guarded for the period after his return to America in 1798. There are four volumes of private correspondence from July 31, 1789, to October 1, 1816, and seven volumes of commercial letters from January 19, 1789, to October 11, 1816; some personal letters are included in the commercial correspondence. There are two volumes of his official correspondence as United States minister to France from August 8, 1792, to January 2, 1795, and a letter book of communications to United States consuls and agents in France from June 22, 1792, to September 2, 1794. Sparks's three-volume work (1832) contains the fullest, but still incomplete, publication of the correspondence, with sections of the diary; it is usually reliable although sometimes prudishly and pietistically edited with alterations of grammar and punctuation. Anne Cary Morris' *Diary and Letters of Gouverneur Morris* (1888) contains fairly accurate, but selected and occasionally truncated, items, some of which are not found in Sparks. Beatrix Cary Davenport, in her *Diary of the French Revolution by Gouverneur Morris* (1939), faithfully printed and sprightly edited the diary and selections from the correspondence from 1789 to 1793. I have cited the original manuscripts when available, except for the Davenport *Diary*, which is convenient for the reader who may wish to consult it. Also in the Library of Congress collection are a notebook of law entries, containing legal formulae and rules from 1771 to 1772, and a fragmentary law register of cases handled by Morris from April 9, 1772, to September 15, 1775.

The papers sold in 1970 contain commercial and legal documents, letters on the French Revolution and Constitution, an exchange of correspondence with Peter Van Schaack, and letters on family affairs. The papers are catalogued in lots in Parke-Bernet Galleries, Inc., *Americana . . ., Including Selections from the Papers of Gouverneur Morris*, pages 1–31, with some errors of notation. A small portion of the collection was purchased by manuscript libraries. A group of commercial letters from Charles John Michael de Wolf (an Antwerp banker), 1790–1809, was purchased by the New-York Historical Society. Morris' "Waste Book," or personal account book, 1791–1808, was purchased by the Library of Congress. A small group of legal papers, in which Morris and John Jay appear as opposing counsel, was purchased by Columbia University.

A few of the documents printed or cited by Jared Sparks in his *Life of Gouverneur Morris* are missing. These may still remain in family hands or may have been removed by Sparks. He had been permitted to borrow the entire collection, but when he returned it, Morris' widow and son complained that he had left it disorganized and had retained some items. Although he vehemently denied the charge, there is at least one letter in the Historical Society of Pennsylvania which he gave to the Baltimore collector Robert Gilmor.[1]

Many Morris letters have survived in the collections of the recipients. Among the most important are the Correspondence of Richard Henry and Arthur Lee in the American Philosophical Society; the John Jay Papers in the Columbia University Libraries; the Livingston Papers in the Massachusetts Historical Society; the Manuscripts of

[1] Jared Sparks to M. Meredith, January 30, 1837, Library of Congress; G. Morris to [?], July 25, 1838, Morris (G) 1838, Miscellaneous, New York Public Library; Marquis de Chastellux to Gouverneur Morris, January 16, 1787, with notation that the manuscript was given by Jared Sparks to R. Gilmor, Etting Papers, European Authors, Historical Society of Pennsylvania.

Joseph Reed, Richard Harison Papers, and Robert R. Livingston Papers in the New-York Historical Society; the Robert R. Livingston Papers (Bancroft Transcripts) and William Smith Papers in the New York Public Library; uncollected manuscripts in the New York State Library at Albany; the Papers of George Washington and the Alexander Hamilton Papers in the Library of Congress; the (Robert) Morris Papers in the Rutgers University Library; and the Nathanael Greene Papers in the William L. Clements Library of the University of Michigan.

MANUSCRIPTS

American Philosophical Society
Correspondence of Richard Henry and Arthur Lee
Indenture between John Fitch & stock company formed to finance the building of the steamboat, Feb. 9, 1787

Bronx County Courthouse, Bronx, New York
Certified Copies of Westchester County Mortgages
Map of Land in Morrisania in the Town and County of Westchester Belonging to the Honorable Gouverneur Morris

Columbia University Libraries Special Collections
Gouverneur Morris Collection
John Jay Papers
John Jay Papers (microfilm)
Samuel Johnson Correspondence

Connecticut Historical Society
Jeremiah Wadsworth Papers

Gouverneur Morris Manuscripts
Sold and dispersed at Parke-Bernet Galleries auction in New York City, April 7, 1970

Harvard College Library
Jared Sparks Manuscripts

Henry E. Huntington Library
Robert Morris Papers

Historical Society of Pennsylvania
Dreer Collection, Letters of Members of the Old Congress and Letters of English Statesmen
Etting Papers, European Authors

General Wayne Papers
Hollingsworth Manuscripts Correspondence
James Wilson Papers
Potts Papers
Society Collection
Records of the Bank of North America

Library Company of Philadelphia
Cartoon, "Zion Besieg'd & Attack'd" (1787)

Library of Congress
Affaires Étrangères, Mémoires et Documents, États-Unis, II
Alexander Hamilton Papers
Gouverneur Morris to Charles Croxall, Oct. 18, 1784
Jeremiah Wadsworth Papers (photostats)
Letters to Jeremiah Evarts (photostats)
Papers of Charles Thomson
Papers of Gouverneur Morris
Papers of George Washington
Robert Morris Diary in the Office of Finance
Robert R. Livingston Papers, 1765–1776
Thomas Jefferson Papers
USR 1778

Massachusetts Historical Society
Henry Knox Papers
Livingston Papers
Ridley Papers

Museum of the City of New York, Print Department
Mrs. Gouverneur Morris Papers

New York City Hall of Records, Office of the County Clerk
In re Morris, Richard, Chancery, Nov. 18, 1786
Minute Book of the Supreme Court of Judicature, Apr. 18, 1769–
    May 2, 1772

National Archives
Papers of the Continental Congress

New York City Hall of Records, Surrogate's Office
Will of Lewis Morris, Liber 23
Will of Sarah Morris, Liber 23

New-York Historical Society
Constable Rucker & Co. Accounts, 1786–1800
Duane Papers
Horatio Gates Papers
Manuscripts of Joseph Reed
Miscellaneous Manuscripts M
Richard Harison Papers
Robert R. Livingston Papers
William Constable & Co. Articles of Co-partnership

New York Public Library
Constable-Pierrepont Papers
  William Constable Letter Book, 1782–1790
Gouverneur Morris, Miscellaneous
Robert Morris Papers, 1785–1795
Robert R. Livingston Papers (Bancroft Transcripts)
Schuyler Letter Book, Nov. 19, 1776–Jul. 1, 1778
Thomas A. Emmet Collection
William Smith Papers

New York State Court of Appeals, Albany
Staats Long Morris, Mary Lawrence and Richard Morris v. *Sarah Morris*, Dec. 1785, Packet 68
Morris et al. v. *Morris et al.*, April 15, 1786, Packet 71

New York State Library, Albany
Gouverneur Morris to Robert Morris, May 22 and July 7, 1781

Philadelphia City Hall
Prothonotary's Office
  Sheriff's Deed Book B

Pierpont Morgan Library
Signers of the Declaration of Independence

Rutgers University Library
(Robert) Morris Papers

University of Pennsylvania Library Rare Book Room
Minutes of the Trustees of the College, Academy and Charitable Schools, Vol. I, 1749–1769

Westchester County Office Building, White Plains,
New York, Division of Land Records
Record of Mortgage D

William L. Clements Library, University of Michigan
Nathanael Greene Papers
Yale University Library
Franklin Collection

NEWSPAPERS

Freeman's Journal, 1781.
New-York Herald, 1812.
New York Journal, 1768.
Pennsylvania Evening Post, 1779.
Pennsylvania Gazette, 1778–83.
Pennsylvania Packet, 1778–80.

PUBLISHED AUTOBIOGRAPHIES, DIARIES, COLLEGE RECORDS, CORRESPONDENCE, AND GOVERNMENT DOCUMENTS

Adams, John. *Diary and Autobiography of John Adams*. Ed. by L. H. Butterfield, 3 vols. Cambridge, Harvard University Press, Belknap Press, 1961.

Annals of the Congress of the United States: The Debates and Proceedings in the Congress of the United States; . . . Compiled from Authentic Materials, by Joseph Gales, Sr., Vols. VI, VII. Washington, Gales & Seaton, 1851.

Archives of the State of New Jersey. 1st series. 42 vols. Various publishers, 1880–1949.

Armstrong, Margaret, *Five Generations: Life and Letters of an American Family, 1750–1900*. New York & London, Harper & Brothers, 1930.

Barbé-Marbois, François, Marquis de. *Our Revolutionary Forefathers: The Letters of François, Marquis de Barbé-Marbois During His Residence in the United States as Secretary of the French Legation, 1779–1785*. Tr. and ed. by Eugene P. Chase. New York, Duffield & Co., 1929.

Biddle, Charles. *Autobiography of Charles Biddle, Vice-President of the Supreme Executive Council of Pennsylvania, 1745–1821*. Philadelphia, E. Claxton & Co., 1883.

Boogher, William F., ed. *Miscellaneous Americana, a Collection of*

History, Biography, and Genealogy. Philadelphia, Dando Printing & Publishing Co., 1883, 1889, 1895.

Bourne, Edward G., ed. *The Federalist.* 2 vols. Washington & London, M. Walter Dunne, 1901.

Broglie, Prince de. "Narrative of the Prince de Broglie [1782], Translated from an Unpublished MS, Part II" tr. by E. W. Balch, *Magazine of American History, with Notes and Queries,* Vol. I (March, 1877), 231–35.

Burnett, Edmund C., ed. *Letters of Members of the Continental Congress.* 8 vols. Washington, Carnegie Institute of Washington, 1921–36.

Chastellux, Marquis de. *Travels in North America in the Years 1780, 1781 and 1782.* Tr. and ed. by Howard G. Rice, Jr. 2 vols. Chapel Hill, University of North Carolina Press, 1963.

Clinton, George. *Public Papers of George Clinton.* Ed. by Hugh Hastings and J. A. Holden. 10 vols. Albany, James B. Lyon, 1909–14.

Cochran, General John. "Reminiscences and Anecdotes," *The American Historical Register and Monthly Gazette of the Patriotic-Hereditary Societies of the United States of America,* Vol. I (January, 1895), 432–39.

Committee of [Continental] Congress, *Observations on the American Revolution.* Philadelphia, Styner & Cist, 1779.

"Correspondence Relating to the Morris Family," *Proceedings of the New Jersey Historical Society,* New Series, Vol. VII (January, 1922), 41–48.

Dawson, Henry B., ed. *New York City during the American Revolution, Being a Collection of Original Papers.* New York, privately printed, 1861.

Dunlap, William. *Diary of William Dunlap (1766–1839).* 3 vols. New York, New-York Historical Society, 1930.

"The Duane Letters," *Southern Association Publications,* Vol. VII (1904), 246–65.

Everett, Edward, "Eighteen Hundred Fourteen," *Old and New,* Vol. VII (January, 1873), 49–51.

Farrand, Max, ed. *The Records of the Federal Convention of 1787.* 4 vols. New Haven, Yale University Press, 1937.

Force, Peter, ed. *American Archives.* 9 vols. Washington, M. St. Clair Clarke & Peter Force, 1837–53.

Ford, Worthington C., and Gaillard Hunt, eds. *Journals of the Con-*

tinental Congress, 1774–1789. 34 vols. Washington, Government Printing Office, 1904–37.

Francis, John W. "Letter to Henry B. Dawson, November 17, 1860," *The Historical Magazine,* 2d Series, Vol. III (April, 1868), 193–98.

Franks, David. *The New-York Directory.* New York, Shepard Kollock, 1786.

Gérard, Conrad Alexandre. *Despatches and Instructions of Conrad Alexandre Gérard, 1778–1780.* Ed. by John J. Meng. Baltimore, Johns Hopkins Press, 1939.

Graydon, Alexander. *Memoirs of his Own Time, with Reminiscences of the Men and Events of the Revolution, by Alexander Graydon.* Ed. by John S. Littell. Philadelphia, Lindsay & Blakiston, 1846.

Hamilton, Alexander. *The Papers of Alexander Hamilton.* Ed. by Harold C. Syrett and Jacob E. Cooke. New York, Columbia University Press, 1961–.

Hamilton, James A. *Reminiscences of James A. Hamilton; or, Men and Events, at Home and Abroad, during Three Quarters of a Century.* New York, Charles Scribner & Co., 1869.

Hiltzheimer, Jacob. "Extracts from the Diary of Jacob Hiltzheimer of Philadelphia, 1768–1798," *Pennsylvania Magazine of History and Biography,* Vol. XVI (January, 1892), 93–102.

Historical Manuscripts Commission. *Report on American Manuscripts in the Royal Institution of Great Britain.* 4 vols. London, Mackie & Co. and Anthony Bros., 1904–1909.

———. *Report on the Manuscripts of J. B. Fortescue, Esq., Preserved at Dropmore.* 3 vols. London, Eyre and Spottiswoode, 1892–99.

A *History of Columbia University, 1754–1904, Published in Commemoration of the One Hundred and Fiftieth Anniversary of the Founding of King's College.* New York, Columbia University Press, 1904.

Hough, Charles Merrill, ed. *Reports of Cases in the Vice Admiralty of the Province of New York and in the Court of Admiralty of the State of New York, 1715–1788.* New Haven, Yale University Press, 1925.

Illustrated Catalogue of Important Revolutionary Letters: The Unpublished Correspondence of Robert R. Livingston, First Chancellor of New York, to Be Sold Without Reserve or Restriction by Order of the Owner, James R. Keene . . . January 25th, 1918. New York, American Art Association, 1918.

Ingersoll, Charles J. *Recollections, Historical, Political, Biographical, and Social.* 2 vols. Philadelphia, J. B. Lippincott & Co., 1861.

"Items of History of York, Penna., during the Revolution," *Pennsylvania Magazine of History and Biography,* Vol. XLIV, No. 4, (1920), 315–17.

Jay, John. *The Correspondence and Public Papers of John Jay.* Ed. by Henry P. Johnston. 4 vols. New York and London, G. P. Putnam's Sons, 1890–93.

Jefferson, Thomas. *The Writings of Thomas Jefferson.* Ed. by Paul Leicester Ford. 12 vols. New York and London, G. P. Putnam's Sons, 1904–1905.

Jones, Thomas. *History of New York During the Revolutionary War, by Thomas Jones.* Ed. by Edward F. de Lancey. 2 vols. New York, New-York Historical Society, 1879.

Lafayette, Marquis de. *Mémoires, Correspondence et Manuscrits du Général Lafayette.* Ed. by H. Fournier Aîné. 3 vols. Leipzig, Brockhaus & Avenarius, 1838.

McAnear, Beverly, ed. "An American in London, 1733–1736 [the diary of Robert Hunter Morris]," *Pennsylvania Magazine of History and Biography,* Vol. LXIV (April, 1940), 164–217.

Madison, James. *The Papers of James Madison.* Ed. by Henry D. Gilpin. 3 vols. Washington, Longtree & O'Sullivan, 1840.

Mereness, Newton D., ed. *Travels in the American Colonies.* New York, Macmillan Co., 1916.

Minutes of a Conspiracy Against the Liberties of America. Philadelphia, John Campbell, 1865.

Minutes of the Governors of the College of the Province of New York in the City of New York in America, 1755–1768, and of the Corporation of King's College in the City of New York, 1768–1770. Photolithographic reproduction. New York, 1932.

Moffatt, R. Burnham. *Pierrepont Genealogies.* New York, [L. Middleditch Co.], 1913.

Morris, Gouverneur. *A Diary of the French Revolution by Gouverneur Morris.* Ed. by Beatrix C. Davenport. 2 vols. Boston, Houghton Mifflin Co., 1939.

———. *The Diary and Letters of Gouverneur Morris.* Ed. by Anne Cary Morris. 2 vols. New York, Charles Scribner's Sons, 1888.

———. "A Discourse Delivered Before the New-York Historical Society . . . , 6th December, 1812," New-York Historical Society *Collections*, Vol. II (1814), 117–48.

——. *An Oration, Delivered on the 19th day of May, 1812, in Honor of the Memory of George Clinton, Late Vice-President of the U.S.* New York, Hardcastle & Van Pelt, 1812.

Morris, Lewis. "Letter to John Boon [Bowne], Barbados, August 8, 1665," *Historical Magazine*, Vol. I (February, 1872), 6.

[New York State]. *Calendar of N.Y. Colonial Manuscripts Indorsed Land Papers, in the Office of Secretary of State of New York, 1643–1803.* Albany, Weed, Parsons & Co., 1864.

[——]. *Journals of the Provincial Congress, Provincial Convention, Committee of Safety, and Council of Safety, 1775–1777,* 2 vols. Albany, Thurlow Weed, 1842.

[——]. *Names of Persons for Whom Marriage Licenses Were Issued by the Secretary of the Province of New York Previous to 1784.* Albany, Weed, Parsons & Co., 1860.

Niles, H., ed. *Principles and Acts of the Revolution in America . . . .* Baltimore, William Ogden Niles, 1822.

O'Callaghan, Edmund B., ed. *Documents Relative to the Colonial History of the State of New York.* 15 vols. New York, Weed, Parsons & Co., 1853–87.

Palmerston, Viscount. *The Despatches of Earl Gower, English Ambassador at Paris from June 1790 to August 1792, to which Are Added the Despatches of Mr. Lindsay and Mr. Monroe, and the Diary of Viscount Palmerston in France During July and August 1791.* Ed. by Oscar Browning. Cambridge, The University Press, 1885.

Pennsylvania Archives. 1st and 3rd Series. 30 vols.

Radziwill, Princess [Ekaterina], tr. *They Knew the Washingtons: Letters from a French Soldier with Lafayette and from His Family in Virginia.* Indianapolis, Bobbs-Merrill Co., 1926.

Read, Elizabeth. "The Chews of Pennsylvania," *Magazine of American History*, Vol. IV (March, 1880), 190–204.

Roberts, Richard A., ed. *Calendar of Home Office Papers of the Reign of George III, 1773–1775, Preserved in the Public Record Office.* 4 vols. London, Her Majesty's Stationery Office, 1899.

Robison, Jeannie F.-J., and Henrietta C. Bartlett, eds. *Genealogical Records: Manuscript Entries of Births, Deaths and Marriages, Taken from Family Bibles, 1581–1917*. New York, Colonial Dames of the State of New York, 1917.

Rutherfurd, Livingston. *Family Records and Events Compiled Principally from the Original Manuscripts in the Rutherfurd Collection.* New York, De Vinne Press, 1894.

Ryden, George H., ed. *Letters to and from Caesar Rodney, 1756–1784.* Philadelphia, University of Pennsylvania Press, 1933.

Seymann, Jerrold. *Colonial Charters, Patents, Grants to the Communities Comprising the City of New York.* Albany, [J. B. Lyon], 1939.

Smith, William. *Historical Memoirs from 16 March 1763 to 9 July 1776 of William Smith.* Ed. by William H. W. Sabine. New York, [Colburn & Tegg], 1956.

———. *The History of the Late Province of New York from its Discovery to the Appointment of Governor Colden in 1762.* 2 vols. New York, New-York Historical Society, 1830.

Stiles, Ezra. *Extracts from the Itineraries and Other Miscellanies of Ezra Stiles, D.D., LL.D., 1755–1794, with a Selection from His Correspondence.* Ed. by Franklin B. Dexter. New Haven, Yale University Press, 1916.

———. *The Literary Diary of Ezra Stiles.* Ed. by Franklin B. Dexter. 3 vols. New York, Charles Scribner's Sons, 1901.

Tansill, Charles C., ed. *Documents Illustrative of the Formation of the Union of the American States* (69th Cong., 1st Sess., H.R. Doc. 398). Washington, Government Printing Office, 1927.

Thorpe, Francis N., ed. *Benjamin Franklin and the University of Pennsylvania.* Bureau of Education *Circular of Information* No. 2, 1892. Washington, Government Printing Office, 1893.

Van Hogendorp, Graaf Gijsbert Karel. *Brieven en Gedenkschriften van Gijsbert Karel van Hogendorp, uitgegeven door zijn jongsten, thans eenigen Zoon.* Ed. by F. Van Hogendorp. 2 vols. The Hague, Martinus Nijhoff, 1866.

Washington, George. *The Diaries of George Washington, 1748–1799.* Ed. by John C. Fitzpatrick. 4 vols. New York, Hougton Mifflin Co., 1925.

———. *Washington After the Revolution, 1784–1799.* Ed. by William S. Baker. Philadelphia, J. B. Lippincott Co., 1898.

———. *The Writings of George Washington from the Original Manuscript Sources, 1745–1799.* Ed. by John C. Fitzpatrick. 39 vols. Washington, Government Printing Office, 1931–44.

Webb, Samuel Blachley. *Correspondence and Journals of Samuel Blachley Webb.* Ed. by Worthington C. Ford. 3 vols. New York, Wickersham Press, 1893.

Webster, Noah. *New York Directory for 1786* . . . . Facsimile reprint. New York, Trow City Directory Co., 1886.

White, Francis. *Philadelphia Directory.* Philadelphia, Young, Stewart, & McCulloch, 1785.

Wilkins, Isaac. *My Services and Losses in Aid of the King's Cause During the American Revolution.* Brooklyn, Historical Printing Club, 1890.

BIOGRAPHIES, MONOGRAPHS, SPECIAL STUDIES, GENERAL HISTORIES, AND ARTICLES

Akerly, Lucy D. *The Morris Manor.* New York, [1917].

Alexander, Edward P. *A Revolutionary Conservative: James Duane of New York.* New York, Columbia University Press, 1938.

Alexander, James. *A Brief Narrative of the Case and Trial of John Peter Zenger, Printer of the New York Weekly Journal, by James Alexander.* Ed. by Stanley N. Katz. Cambridge, Harvard University Press, 1963.

Bailyn, Bernard. *The Ideological Origins of the American Revolution.* Cambridge, Harvard University Press, Belknap Press, 1967.

Bancroft, George. *History of the United States of America from the Discovery of the Continent.* 6 vols. New York, D. Appleton & Co., 1888.

Barry, Richard H. *Mr. Rutledge of South Carolina.* New York, Duell, Sloan and Pearce, 1942.

Beard, Charles A. *An Economic Interpretation of the Constitution.* New York, Macmillan Co., 1960; 1st ed., 1913.

Becker, Carl L. *The History of Political Parties in the Province of New York, 1760–1776,* in *University of Wisconsin Bulletin,* Vol. II, No. 1, (1909), 1–290.

Bemis, Samuel Flagg. "Canada and the Peace Settlement of 1783," *Canadian Historical Review,* Vol. XIV, (June, 1933), 265–84.

———. *The Diplomacy of the American Revolution.* Bloomington, Indiana University Press, 1957. 1st ed., New York, D. Appleton-Century Company, 1935.

———. *Jay's Treaty: A Study in Commerce and Diplomacy.* New Haven and London, Yale University Press, 1962; 1st ed., 1923.

Bjork, Gordon C. "The Weaning of the American Economy, 1775–1815," *Journal of Economic History*, Vol. XXIV (December, 1964), 541–66.

Bolton, Robert. *The History of the Several Towns, Manors, and Patents of the County of Westchester; with Numerous Genealogies of County Families, by Robert Bolton.* Ed. by C. W. Bolton. 2 vols. 3d ed. New York, Jno. J. Cass, 1905.

Bowen, Francis. *Life of Baron Steuben.* Vol. IX in Jared Sparks, ed., *The Library of American Biography.* Boston, Hilliard, Gray & Co., 1838.

Bowman, Albert Hall. "The Struggle for Neutrality: A History of the Diplomatic Relations Between the United States and France, 1790–1801." Unpublished Ph.D. Dissertation, Columbia University, 1954.

Boyd, Julian P. *Number 7: Alexander Hamilton's Secret Attempts to Control American Foreign Policy, with Supporting Documents.* Princeton, Princeton University Press, 1964.

Boyer, Charles S. *Early Forges and Furnaces in New Jersey.* Philadelphia, Reynal & Hitchcock, 1931.

Bridenbaugh, Carl. *Cities in Revolt: Urban Life in America, 1746–1778.* New York, Alfred A. Knopf, 1955.

———, and Jessica Bridenbaugh. *Rebels and Gentlemen: Philadelphia in the Age of Franklin.* New York, Reynal & Hitchcock, 1942.

Brown, Robert E. *Charles Beard and the Constitution: A Critical Analysis of "An Economic Interpretation of the Constitution."* Princeton, Princeton University Press, 1956.

Brown, Weldon A. *Empire or Independence: A Study in the Failure of Reconciliation, 1774–1783.* Baton Rouge, Louisiana State University Press, 1941.

Bruce, William Cabell. *John Randolph of Roanoke, 1773–1833.* 2 vols. New York and London, G. P. Putnam's Sons, 1922.

Brunhouse, Robert L. *The Counter-Revolution in Pennsylvania, 1776–1790.* Harrisburg, Pennsylvania Historical Commission, 1942.

Buchanan, Roberdeau. *Genealogy of the McKean Family of Pennsylvania, with a Biography of the Hon. Thomas McKean.* Lancaster, Inquirer Printing Co., 1890.

Burnett, Edmund C. *The Continental Congress.* New York, Macmillan Co., 1942.

Burt, A. L. *The United States, Great Britain, and British North America, from the Revolution to the Establishment of Peace After the*

War of 1812. New York, Russell & Russell, 1961; 1st ed., New Haven, Yale University Press, 1940.

Campbell, William W. *The Life and Writings of De Witt Clinton.* New York, Baker & Scribner, 1849.

Cheyney, Edward P. *History of the University of Pennsylvania, 1740–1940.* Philadelphia, University of Pennsylvania Press, 1940.

Coe, Samuel Gwynn. *The Mission of William Carmichael to Spain.* Baltimore, Johns Hopkins Press, 1928.

"Constitutional Convention, 1787," *Historical Magazine,* Vol. V (January, 1861), 18.

Corwin, Edward S. *French Policy and the American Alliance of 1778.* Hamden, Archon Books, 1962; 1st ed., Princeton University Press, 1916.

Cunningham, Noble E., Jr. *The Jeffersonian Republicans in Power: Party Operations, 1801–1809.* Chapel Hill, University of North Carolina Press, 1963.

Dangerfield, George. *Chancellor Robert R. Livingston of New York, 1746–1813.* New York, Harcourt, Brace & Company, 1960.

Davis, Joseph Stancliffe. *Essays in the Earlier History of American Corporations.* 2 vols. New York, Russell & Russell, 1965; 1st ed., Harvard University Press, 1917.

Davis, William A. "William Constable, New York Merchant and Land Speculator, 1772–1803." Unpublished Ph.D. Dissertation, Harvard University, 1955.

Delafield, Julia. *Biographies of Francis Lewis and Morgan Lewis.* 2 vols. New York, Anson, D. F. Randolph & Co., 1877.

Dexter, Franklin B., ed. *Biographical Sketches of the Graduates of Yale College.* 6 vols. New York, Henry Holt & Co., 1885–1912.

Dillon, Dorothy R. *The New York Triumvirate: A Study of the Legal and Political Careers of William Livingston, John Morin Scott, William Smith, Jr.* New York, Columbia University Press, 1949.

Dunlap, William. *History of the New Netherlands, Province of New York, and State of New York.* 2 vols. New York, Carter & Thorp, 1839–40.

Du Simitière, Pierre Eugène. *Thirteen Portraits of American Legislators, Patriots, and Soldiers . . . Drawn from the Life by Du Simitière and engraved by B. Reading.* London, W. Richardson, 1783.

Einstein, Lewis. *Divided Loyalties: Americans in England During the*

War of Independence. Boston and New York, Houghton Mifflin Co., 1933.

Ernst, Robert. *Rufus King: American Federalist*. Chapel Hill, University of North Carolina Press, 1968.

Farrand, Max. *Framing of the Constitution*. New Haven, Yale University Press, 1913.

Ferguson, E. James. *The Power of the Purse: A History of American Public Finance, 1776–1790*. Chapel Hill, University of North Carolina Press, 1961.

Fischer, David Hackett. *The Revolution of American Conservatism: The Federalist Party in the Era of Jeffersonian Democracy*. New York, Harper & Row, 1965.

Fishlow, Albert. "Discussion," *Journal of Economic History*, Vol. XXIV (December, 1964), 540–66.

[Flick, Alexander C., ed.] *The American Revolution in New York: Its Political, Social and Economic Significance*. Albany, University of the State of New York, 1926.

——. ed. *History of the State of New York*. 10 vols. New York, Columbia University Press, 1933–37.

Forsyth, Mary E. "The Burning of Kingston," *Journal of American History*, Vol. VII (July, 1913), 1137–47.

Fox, Dixon Ryan. *The Decline of Aristocracy in the Politics of New York, 1801–1840*. Ed. by Robert V. Remini. New York, Evanston, and London, Harper & Row, 1965; 1st ed., Columbia University Press, 1919.

Freeman, Douglas S. *George Washington, a Biography*. 6 vols. New York, Charles Scribner's Sons, 1948–54.

George, Mary Dorothy. *Catalogue of Political and Personal Satires Preserved in the Department of Prints and Drawings in the British Museum, 1771–1783*. London, British Museum, 1935.

Gerlach, Don R. *Philip Schuyler and the American Revolution in New York, 1733–1777*. Lincoln, University of Nebraska Press, 1964.

Goodspeed's Catalogue 271. Boston, Goodspeed's Bookshop, Inc., 1936.

Gottschalk, Louis. *Lafayette Joins the American Army*. Chicago, University of Chicago Press, 1937.

Green, Rufus S. "City, Village and Township Histories. Morristown," *1739, History of Morris County, New Jersey, with Illustrations, and*

Biographical Sketches of Prominent Citizens and Pioneers. New York, W. W. Munsell & Co., 1882.

Greene, Evarts B., and Virginia D. Harrington. *American Population Before the Federal Census of 1790.* New York, Columbia University Press, 1935.

Hamlin, Paul. *Legal Education in Colonial New York.* New York, New York University Law Quarterly Review, 1939.

Hammond, Bray. *Banks and Politics in America from the Revolution to the Civil War.* Princeton University Press, 1957.

Hammond, Jabez D. *The History of Political Parties in the State of New-York, from the Ratification of the Federal Constitution to December, 1840.* 2 vols. Syracuse, Hall, Mills & Co., 1852.

Harrington, Virginia D. *The New York Merchant on the Eve of the Revolution.* New York, Columbia University Press, 1935.

Harrison, Lowell H. *John Breckinridge: Jeffersonian Republican.* Louisville, Filson Club, 1969.

Hatch, Louis C. *The Administration of the American Revolutionary Army.* New York, Longmans, Green & Co., 1904.

Henderson, Herbert James, Jr. "Congressional Factionalism and the Attempt to Recall Benjamin Franklin," *William and Mary Quarterly,* Vol. XXVII (April, 1970), 246–67.

———. "Political Factions in the Continental Congress, 1774–1783." Unpublished Ph.D. Dissertation, Columbia University, 1962.

Higgins, Ruth L. *Expansion in New York, with Especial Reference to the Eighteenth Century,* Ohio State University *Studies, Contributions in History and Political Science,* No. 14, (1931).

Hofstadter, Richard. *The American Political Tradition and the Men Who Made It.* New York, Alfred A. Knopf, 1948.

Hough, Franklin B. *A History of St. Lawrence and Franklin Counties, New York, from the Earliest Period to the Present Day.* Albany, Little & Co., 1853.

Hufeland, Otto. *Westchester County During the American Revolution, 1775–1783.* White Plains, Westchester County Historical Society, 1926.

Jay, William. *The Life of John Jay, with Selections from His Correspondence and Miscellaneous Papers.* 2 vols. New York, J. & J. Harper, 1833.

Jenkins, Stephen. *The Story of the Bronx, from the Purchase Made by the Dutch from the Indians in 1639 to the Present Day.* New York & London, Knickerbocker Press, 1912.

Jensen, Merrill. *The New Nation: A History of the United States During the Confederation, 1781–1789.* New York, Alfred A. Knopf, 1950.

Johnson, E. A. J. *Predecessors of Adam Smith: The Growth of British Economic Thought.* New York, A. M. Kelley, 1960; 1st ed., Prentice-Hall, 1937.

Johnson, Monroe. "The Gouverneur Genealogy," *New York Genealogical and Biographical Record,* Vol. LXX (January, 1939), 134–38.

Johnson, Victor L. *The Administration of the American Commissariat During the Revolutionary War.* Philadelphia, University of Pennsylvania Press, 1941.

King, Charles R. *The Life and Correspondence of Rufus King, Comprising His Letters, Private and Official, His Public Documents and Speeches.* 6 vols. New York, G. P. Putnam's Sons, 1894–1900.

Knollenberg, Bernhard. *Washington and the Revolution, a Reappraisal: Gates, Conway, and the Continental Congress.* New York, Macmillan Co., 1940.

Kohn, Richard H. "The Inside History of the Newburgh Conspiracy: America and the Coup d'État," *William and Mary Quarterly,* Vol. XXVII (April, 1970), 187–220.

Krieger, Leonard. *The Politics of Discretion: Pufendorf and the Acceptance of Natural Law.* Chicago and London, University of Chicago Press, 1965.

Labaree, Leonard Woods. *Conservatism in Early American History.* New York, New York University Press, 1948.

Lamb, Martha J. *History of the City of New York, Its Origin, Rise, and Progress.* 3 vols. New York and Chicago, A. S. Barnes & Co., 1877–[96].

Lefebvre, Georges. *The French Revolution from Its Origins to 1793.* Tr. by Elizabeth Moss Evanson. New York and London, Columbia University Press, 1962.

Lefferts, Elizabeth M. *Descendents of Lewis Morris of Morrisania.* New York, T. A. Wright, [1907].

Lemay, J. A. Leo. *Ebenezar Kinnersley, Franklin's Friend.* Philadelphia, University of Pennsylvania Press, 1964.

Levy, Leonard W. *Legacy of Suppression: Freedom of Speech and Press in Early American History.* Cambridge, Harvard University Press, 1960.

Lincoln, Charles Z. *The Constitutional History of New York* . . . .
5 vols. Rochester, Lawyers Cooperative Publishing Co., 1906.

Livingston, Edwin B. *The Livingstons of Livingston Manor* . . . .
New York, Knickerbocker Press, 1910.

Lossing, Benson J. "Washington's Life Guard," *Historical Magazine,*
Vol. II (May, 1858), 129–34.

Lovejoy, Arthur O. *Reflections on Human Nature.* Baltimore, Johns
Hopkins Press, 1961.

McAnear, Beverly. "American Imprints Concerning King's College,"
Papers of the Bibliographical Society of America, Vol. XLIV (Fourth
Quarter, 1950), 325–41.

McDonald, Forrest. *We the People: The Economic Origins of the
Constitution.* Chicago, University of Chicago Press, 1958.

———. *E Pluribus Unum: The Formation of the American Republic,
1776–1790.* Boston, Houghton Mifflin Company, 1965.

Main, Jackson Turner. *The Antifederalists: Critics of the Constitution,
1781–1788.* Chapel Hill, University of North Carolina Press, 1961.

Manning, William Ray. "The Nootka Sound Controversy," American
Historical Association *Annual Report* for 1904, 279–478.

Maricourt, Baron André de. *Madame de Souza et sa Famille: Les
Marigny, Les Flahaut, August de Morny (1761–1836).* Paris, Émile-
paul Frères, 1913.

Mason, Bernard. *The Road to Independence: The Revolutionary
Movement in New York, 1773–1777.* Lexington, University of Kentucky Press, 1966.

Miller, Nathan. *The Enterprise of a Free People: Aspects of Economic
Development in New York State During the Canal Period, 1792–
1838.* Ithaca, Cornell University Press, 1962.

Mitchell, Broadus. *Alexander Hamilton.* 2 vols. New York, Macmillan
Co., 1957–62.

Monaghan, Frank. *John Jay.* New York, Bobbs–Merrill Company,
1935.

Montgomery, Thomas H. *A History of the University of Pennsylvania,
from Its Foundation to A.D. 1770.* Philadelphia, George W. Jacobs
& Co., 1900.

Montross, Lynn. *The Reluctant Rebels: The Story of the Continental
Congress, 1774–1789.* New York, Harper & Brothers, 1950.

Morgan, Edmund S. "The Puritan Ethic and the American Revolution," *William and Mary Quarterly*, Vol. XXIV (January, 1967), 26–33.

———, and Helen M. Morgan. *The Stamp Act Crisis: Prologue to Revolution*. Chapel Hill, University of North Carolina Press, 1953.

Morison, Samuel E., and Henry S. Commager. *The Growth of the American Republic*. 2 vols. New York, Oxford University Press, 1950.

Morris, Anne C. "Gouverneur Morris," *New York Genealogical and Biographical Record*, Vol. XX (January, 1889), 23–24.

Morris, Richard B. "The Confederation Period and the American Historian," *William and Mary Quarterly*, Vol. XIII (April, 1956), 139–56.

———. *The Peacemakers: The Great Powers and American Independence*. New York, Harper & Row, 1965.

———, ed. *The Era of the American Revolution*. New York, Columbia University Press, 1939.

Nettels, Curtis P. *The Emergence of a National Economy, 1775–1815*. New York, Holt, Rinehart and Winston, 1962.

Nussbaum, Frederick L. "The French Colonial Arrêt of 1784," *South Atlantic Quarterly*, Vol. XXVII (January, 1928), 62–78.

Palmer, R. R. *The Age of the Democratic Revolution: A Political History of Europe and America, 1760–1800*. Princeton, Princeton University Press, 1959.

Parke-Bernet Galleries, Inc. *Americana: Printed Books, Manuscripts & Autograph Letters, Including Selections from the Papers of Gouverneur Morris . . ., Public Auction, Tuesday, April 7, at 2 p.m*. New York, Parke-Bernet Galleries, Inc., 1970.

Peterson, A. Everett. *Landmarks of New York: A Historical Guide to the Metropolis*. New York, City History Club, 1923.

Pickering, O. *Life of Timothy Pickering*. 4 vols. Boston, Little, Brown and Company, 1867–73.

Pirenne, H. *Histoire de Belgique*. 6 vols. Brussels, Maurice Lamertin, 1900–26.

Potts, William J. "Du Simitière, Artist, Antiquary, and Projector of the First American Museum, with some Extracts from His Notebook," *Pennsylvania Magazine of History and Biography*, Vol. XIII, No. 3 (1889), 341–75.

[Purple, E. R.] "Morris—Gouverneur," *New York Genealogical and Biographical Record*, Vol. IX (January, 1878), 94.

Rawle, William Brooke. "Laurel Hill and Some Colonial Dames Who

Once Lived There," *Pennsylvania Magazine of History and Biography*, Vol. XXXV, No. 4 (1911), 385–414.

Read, William T. *Life and Correspondence of George Read, Signer of the Declaration of Independence*. Philadelphia, J. B. Lippincott & Co., 1870.

Redlich, Fritz. *The Molding of American Banking: Men and Ideas, 1781–1784*. 2 vols. New York, Hafner, 1951.

Reed, William B. *Life and Correspondence of Joseph Reed*. 2 vols. Philadelphia, Lindsay & Blakiston, 1847.

Renwick, James. *Life of Dewitt Clinton*, New York, Harper & Brothers, 1840.

Roche, John F. *Joseph Reed: A Moderate in the American Revolution*. New York, Columbia University Press, 1957.

Roosevelt, Theodore. *Gouverneur Morris* in John T. Morse, Jr., ed., *American Statesmen*. Boston and New York, Houghton Mifflin Co., 1888.

Sabine, George H. *A History of Political Theory*. New York, Henry Holt & Co., 1937.

Sabine, Lorenzo. *The American Loyalists; or, Biographical Sketches of Adherents to the British Crown in the War of the Revolution*. Boston, Charles C. Little & James Brown, 1847.

Scharf, J. T., ed. *History of Westchester County, New York, Including Morrisania, Kings Bridge, and West Farms, Which Have Been Annexed to New York City*. 2 vols. Philadelphia, L. E. Preston & Co., 1886.

Schlesinger, Arthur M. *Prelude to Independence: The Newspaper War on Britain, 1764–1776*. New York, Alfred A. Knopf, 1958.

Schneider, Herbert, and Carol Schneider. *Samuel Johnson, President of King's College: His Career and Writings*. 4 vols. New York, Columbia University Press, 1929.

Sedgwick, Theodore, Jr. *A Memoir of the Life of William Livingston*. New York, J. & J. Harper, 1833.

Shaw, Ronald E. *Erie Water West: A History of the Erie Canal, 1792–1854*. Lexington, University of Kentucky Press, 1966.

Sparks, Jared. *The Life of Gouverneur Morris, with Selections from His Correspondence and Miscellaneous Papers*. 3 vols. Boston, Gray & Bowen, 1832.

Sprague, William B., ed. *Annals of the American Pulpit*. 9 vols. New York, Robert Carter & Bros., 1857–69.

Steuart, Sir James. *An Inquiry into the Principles of Political Oeconomy*. Ed. by Andrew S. Skinner. 2 vols. Chicago, University of Chicago Press, 1966.

Stinchcombe, William C. *The American Revolution and the French Alliance*. Syracuse, Syracuse University Press, 1969.

Sullivan, Kathryn. *Maryland and France, 1774–1789*. Philadelphia, University of Pennsylvania Press, 1936.

Swiggett, Howard. *The Extraordinary Mr. Morris*. Garden City, Doubleday & Co., 1952.

Tansill, Charles Callan. *The United States and Santo Domingo, 1798–1783: A Chapter in Caribbean Diplomacy*. Baltimore, The Johns Hopkins Press, 1938.

Thach, Charles C., Jr. *The Creation of the Presidency, 1775–1789: A Study in Constitutional History*. Baltimore, Johns Hopkins Press, 1922.

Thomas, Milton H. "The King's College Building, with Some Notes on Its Later Tenants," *New-York Historical Society Quarterly*, Vol. XXXIX (January, 1955), 23–60.

Turnbull, Archibald D. *John Stevens: An American Record*. New York & London, Century Co., 1928.

Turner, Lynn W. *William Plumer of New Hampshire, 1759–1850*. Chapel Hill, University of North Carolina Press, 1962.

Upton, L. F. S. *The Loyal Whig: William Smith of New York & Quebec*. Toronto, University of Toronto Press, 1969.

Van Buren, Martin. *Inquiry into the Origin and Cause of Political Parties in the United States*. New York, Hurd & Houghton, 1867.

Van Schaack, Henry C. *The Life of Peter Van Schaack*. New York, D. Appleton & Co., 1842.

——. *Memoirs of the Life of Henry Van Schaack*. Chicago, A. C. McClurg & Co., 1892.

Ver Steeg, Clarence L. *Robert Morris, Revolutionary Financier, with an Analysis of His Earlier Career*. Philadelphia, University of Pennsylvania Press, 1954.

Walther, Daniel. *Gouverneur Morris, Témoin de Deux Revolutions*, L'Université de Geneve, Faculté des Lettres, These No. 64. Lausanne, Impremerie Mérinat-Brive, 1932.

Warren, Charles. *A History of the American Bar*. Boston, Little, Brown & Co., 1911.

———. *The Making of the Constitution*. Boston, Little, Brown & Co., 1928.

Wharton, T. I. "A Memoir of William Rawle, LL.D.," Historical Society of Pennsylvania *Memoirs*, Vol. IV, Part 1 (1840), 33–91.

Wheeler, William Ogden, comp., and Lawrence Van Alstyne, and Charles Burr Ogden, eds. *The Ogden Family in America, Elizabethtown Branch, and their English Ancestry*. Philadelphia, J. B. Lippincott, 1907.

Whitaker, Arthur Preston. *The Mississippi Question, 1795–1803: A Study in Trade, Politics, and Diplomacy*. Gloucester, Peter Smith, 1962; 1st ed., American Historical Association, 1934.

Whitehead, William A. *East Jersey Under the Proprietary Governments* .... Newark, Martin R. Dennis, 1875.

Wilson, James G., ed. *The Memorial History of the City of New-York, from Its First Settlement to the Year 1892*. 4 vols. New York, New-York History Company, 1892–93.

Wood, Gordon S. *The Creation of the American Republic, 1776–1789*. Chapel Hill, University of North Carolina Press, 1969.

Young, Alfred F. *The Democratic Republicans of New York: The Origins, 1763–1797*. Chapel Hill, University of North Carolina Press, 1967.

Young, Eleanor. *Forgotten Patriot: Robert Morris*. New York, Macmillan Co., 1950.

Index

Academy of Philadelphia: *see* College, Academy, and Charitable School of Philadelphia

Adams, Samuel: as member of Continental Congress committee on British negotiations, 104; as member of Continental Congress committee on reception of French minister, 108

Albany, N.Y.: danger of capture of, by Burgoyne, 84; Gouverneur Morris and legal case in, 228

Alexandria, Va.: 171

Allen, Ethan: and Green Mountain Boys, 135; and dispute with New York State over Vermont, 135; promotion of, blocked by Gouverneur Morris, 136

"American, An": letter from, in *Pennsylvania Gazette*, 105; letters from, in *Pennsylvania Packet*, 110–11, 126, 138–39, 155–56; as pseudonym of Gouverneur Morris, 123; letter from, in *New York Herald*, 238

American Revolution: young men's movement in, 46; work of activists during, 48

"Antinationalists" and national debt: 156

Antwerp, Belgium: 121; *see also* Belgium

Aristocracy: Gouverneur Morris on, 44, 190; George Mason on, 195; *see also* nobility

Armstrong, John: 160

Army, British: dispute of, with American officers over currency exchange rate, 90, 91, 125; occupation of Philadelphia by, 107–108; *see also* Associated Loyalists, British Board of Directors of

Army, Continental: organization of, 46; appointment of Washington as head of, 46; dispatch of troops of, to New York City, 46, 57; "New York Line" of, 56–57, 61; Gouverneur Morris' application for commission in, 56–57; Gouverneur Morris' mission from, for reinforcements for Schuyler, 83–84; and replacement of Schuyler by Gates, 83; hardships of, 89, 149; reorganization of, 89, 94–95; commissary department of, 94–95; Quartermaster Department of, 94–95; and Gouverneur Morris' fight for half-pay pensions for, 99–100; seven-year pensions for, 100; contracting system for, 152; as public creditor, 157; petition of officers of, to Congress, 157–59; mutiny of Pennsylvania Line of, 160–61; five-year pensions for, 161; *see also* "Newburgh Addresses"

Army, subordination of, to civilian authority: 98–99

Army, standing: 99

Arnold, Benedict: Pennsylvania court case against, 126; Gouverneur Morris and, 126, 147; letter to, 147

Arrêt: *see* France

Articles of Confederation: 110, 178; Gouverneur Morris' proposal for acceptance of, 132; revision of, in Constitutional Convention, 183, 184; *see also* Confederation

Ashfield, Catherine Morris (Mrs. Vincent Pearse Ashfield): marriage of, 39; death of, 127

Ashfield, Redford: 12

Ashfield, Vincent Pearse: marriage of, 39; loyalism of, 47, 56; imprisonment of, 47; departure of, for England, 47; on Gouverneur Morris, 56; letter from, 56

Asia (ship): 52–53